INSIGHT GUIDES

Created and Directed by Hans Höfer

BuenosAiRes

Edited by Kathleen Wheaton
Editorial Director: Brian Bell

Houghton Mifflin

APA PUBLICATIONS

ABOUT THIS BOOK

Wheaton

Pittman

Perrottet

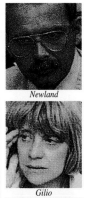

Newland

Gilio

Welna

Boroughs

An article in *National Geographic Traveler* once advised: "Look up names in the Buenos Aires phone book, and you think you're in Italy. Look at the architecture, and you're sure you're in Paris. Bite into a steak, and you think you're in heaven. Try to cross town in a cab at five in the afternoon, and you know you're in purgatory." This neatly encapsulated the magic and mystery of Buenos Aires – magic and mystery which are thoroughly analyzed in this book.

Such a destination, with its contradictions and panoramas, is perfectly suited to the approach taken by the 190-title *Insight Guides* series, created in 1970 by Hans Hofer, founder of Apa Publications and still the company's driving force. Each book encourages the reader to celebrate the essence of the place rather than try to tailor it to their expectations and is edited in the belief that, without insight into a people's character and culture, travel can narrow the mind rather than broaden it.

Insight Guide: Buenos Aires is carefully structured: the first section covers the nation's history, and then analyzes its culture in a series of magazine-style essays. The main Places section provides a run-down on the things worth seeing and doing. Finally, a listings section contains useful addresses, telephone numbers and opening times.

The project editor for the original edition of this book was **Kathleen Wheaton**, a native of California who had previously edited the award-winning *Insight Guide: Spain*. Her task was to assemble a team of writers and photographers who could bring Buenos Aires stunningly to life.

One of the most prolific contributors was **Patricia Pittman**. Born in Wash-ington, DC, Pittman went to Argentina with a Ford Foundation-funded human rights project after graduating from Yale University. She works from her home in suburban Buenos Aires as a freelance writer and consultant.

Most of the history section was written by Australian journalist, **Tony Perrottet**. Enchanted by stories from relatives who had worked as wool classers in Patagonia, he embarked on an 18-month trek across South America after graduating from Sydney University. Now resident in New York, Perrottet has edited a number of *Insight Guides*, ranging from *Iceland* to *Ecuador*, *Cuba* to *Peru*.

Former *Buenos Aires Herald* editor **Dan Newland** has a first-hand perspective on the city's turbulent past, having lived in Argentina since 1973. Newland has contributed to national newspapers in Britain as well as to *Newsweek* and *Business Week*.

Uruguayan journalist **María Esther Gilio** is well-known throughout the Spanish-speaking world for her incisive interviews, many of which are anthologized in such books as *Protagonistas Sobrevivientes* and *Emergentes*.

David Welna, a correspondent for America's National Public Radio, went to Argentina in 1981, shortly before the Malvinas/Falklands War. Born in Minnesota, he received a degree in Latin American studies from Carleton College and has traveled extensively in Latin America, spending a year in Brazil on a Watson Fellowship.

Michigan-born journalist **Don Boroughs** had a particular interest in Argentina since he played the role of Che Guevara in the musical *Evita*. He traveled through 19 of Argentina's 24 provinces, and finally made his home in the barrio of Palermo, where he wrote for the United Nations publication *Mazingira* and *The Progressive*.

Joseph Hooper spent a month in

Byrne

Weil

chic Barrio Norte, visiting the cafés, museums, and the cemetery while preparing a chapter on that neighborhood. Born in Baltimore, Hooper was arts editor for the *Palo Alto Weekly*. He has traveled extensively in South America and has written travel pieces and other articles for many magazines.

Freelancer **Louise Byrne** has contributed to a range of travel publications and to *Half the Earth*, a feminist travel guide.

Five Buenos Aires-based writers brought their particular expertise for special features to this book. *Buenos Aires Herald* sports-writer **Eric Weil** was born in England and has been a journalist in Argentina since 1951.

Reuters correspondent **Rex Gowar** was born in Argentina to British parents and studied literature at Essex University in England. He returned to Argentina in 1978, where he has written on sport for many publications.

Judith Evans is a correspondent for the *Wall Street Journal*, and has also contributed to the *New York Times*. In addition, she lectures on the tango and architecture.

Helga Thomson applied considerable knowledge to the chapter on Argentine painting and printmaking. Of German-Argentine descent, she studied printmaking in Buenos Aires, Paris and Washington, DC, and has won several awards for her work.

No guidebook to Buenos Aires would be complete without the epicurean touch of food writer **Dereck Foster**. Argentine-born Foster is food and wine editor for the *Buenos Aires Herald* and owner-editor of the gastronomic magazine *Aromas y Sabores*.

Hooper

The original photography for *Insight Guide: Buenos Aires* is the result of the tireless work of two outstanding Argentine photographers. **Fiora Bemporad** is best known for her penetrating portraits of famous Argentines from Borges to Alfonsín. A *porteña* with Italian roots, Bemporad has won numerous prizes for her photography and has been extensively exhibited in Argentina and Italy.

The inimitable vision of Buenos Aires-based photographer **Eduardo Gil** can be seen on the cover and throughout the book. Gil worked as a commercial airline pilot and studied meteorology and sociology before dedicating himself full-time to photography. His work has appeared in most South American *Insight Guides*.

Other contributing photographers include **Miguel Doura**, **Jorge Schulte** and **Alex Ocampo**.

Special thanks must also go to *Ediciones de la Flor* editor **Daniel Divinsky** for his kind advice and encouragement, and to **Bernardino Rivadavia**, whose unique perspective on the city gave the editor many new insights. **Jose María Peña** of the Museum of Buenos Aires and historian **Felix Luna** also freely contributed some of their vast knowledge of the city's rich history.

This latest edition of the book comes with many changes in content – and in the life and times of Buenos Aires.

The renewed visual content is largely due to the aforementioned Eduardo Gil, and all the heavy work on bringing old text bang up to date was done by US-born multimedia and television producer **Rachel Raney**, who divides her time between Buenos Aires and San Francisco. Rachel spent patient days exploring those parts of the city she never thought she'd need to know. She also extensively re-worked the practical information in the Travel Tips section.

Raney

The update was supervised from Insight's London office by **Andrew Eames**, and proof-read and indexed by **Pam Barrett**.

CONTENTS

TRAVEL TIPS

The air of Buenos Aires – this is the air that captivated the Spaniards, and every day I'm more convinced that they baptized her "The City of Good Airs" because they were seduced by her perfume and her illusion.
— Ramón Gómez de la Serna

By the time you enter Buenos Aires on Avenida 9 de Julio, you'll have heard that you are riding along the world's widest street, headed towards the world's widest river, the Rio de la Plata. A huge obelisk looms in the middle of the avenue, and on either side are heavy-limbed subtropical trees and Parisian-style office buildings, some with balconies where employees are looking out at the traffic. The damp air smells of diesel, grilled meat and caramelized sugar.

By this time, you'll also have heard that Buenos Aires resembles a European capital. At first glance, the comparisons are evident: there are tidy plazas with Rodin statues, sidewalk cafés, prêt-à-porter windows where beautiful women gaze at the clothes and their own reflections. You are in the heart of South America, but you can drink tap water and eat raw salads, and buy almost any new magazine or exquisite cosmetic.

Buenos Aires is an old-fashioned city; her charms and quirks refer mostly to the 19th century. Here, you will want to stroll along boulevards, dawdle over several courses at lunch, poke into bookstores, have tea and cakes at five, go to the opera, spend Sunday at the races or walk in the graveyard.

Buenos Aires or *la gran aldea* (the big village), is a city with a population of 4 million where the telephone and the post office are such doubtful mechanisms that business is conducted and bills are paid in person; where an unknown shopkeeper will say, as you fumble for the right number of

centavos, "Bring it tomorrow;" where part of the ritual of shopping involves having your purchase painstakingly wrapped in colored paper, even if it's only toothpaste.

Everyone stands on ceremony. Say "*perdón*" to a fiercely-dressed punk and he will politely step aside. Ask a passer-by for directions and he will not only answer you at length but probably give you his name card.

European dreaming: Throughout her convulsive and sometimes bloody history, Bue-

nos Aires has kept her eyes fixed lovingly on Europe. The sweeping Avenida de Mayo is a tribute to Madrid's Gran Via; the Colón Opera House faithfully emulates La Scala; swanky Barrio Norte is a shrine to the Right Bank. At the turn of the century, rich Argentines went to Europe to school and to shop. It wasn't unheard of for these families to take a cow along with them – so the children would not have to drink strange milk – and they brought back clothing, furniture, and art.

The opulent municipality meanwhile imported statues for public intersections, cob-

Preceding pages: statuesque doorway; satirical singing group Gambas al Ajillo; Basilica of Nuestra Señora del Pilar, Barrio Norte; old schooner; Colon Opera House; guards; waiters and stuffed cows. **Left**, reflection of clock tower. **Right**, a mask vendor posing with his wares.

blestones (there are very few stones in the pampas), and occasionally whole buildings, such as the hallucinatory waterworks (Obras Sanitarias, 1950 Córdoba) which was shipped over tile by tile from England and France.

This reverence for the Old World reveals itself in small ways as well as in grand gestures. There are scores of humble cantinas named after villages of Galicia or Calabria, where old men in berets play card games they learned a long time ago. "I'm not really Argentine, I'm Spanish (or Italian, or Polish or Irish)," someone might say. "I still have my passport. I only came here 30 years ago, to work." "Are you going back, then?"

street, through the sycamores. Don't you feel as though you're in the South of France?"

Obligingly, you look, stand, and imagine as instructed. Different cities and moods fade in and out cinematically. Gradually, a common thread begins to emerge: everything looks as though a local builder had been handed a drawing and told, "Please, recreate this." Buenos Aires doesn't look like Europe; it looks like pictures of Europe – like a Spain or Italy a homesick immigrant might see in a dream.

Homesickness and history: Why are *porteños* so homesick? It's a question they like to consider. In the late 19th century, when most

"Ah, no, why would I do that?"

People in Buenos Aires might keep citizenships or bank accounts in other places, but unless there is an urgent political or economic reason, they don't often move back home. They call themselves *porteños* (the people of the port), and they love the city for reasons which strike visitors as peculiar. The *porteño* who gives you a tour of his favorite neighborhood is apt to point out an English-style train station, with its scalloped roof and wrought-iron railing, a Spanish cupola, an Italian balustrade covered with moss. "Now, stand here and look up this

of the immigrants came, Buenos Aires appeared to hold out the same kinds of golden promises as New York, as well as a graceful, Latin way of life.

In the 20th century, dictatorships and economic woes caused many of those promises to fail; add to that, some say, the nostalgic Southern European temperament, and you get a city in a permanent state of longing. In the 1930s one Spanish immigrant wrote, "Most disconcerting of all... is that one cannot swear to one's beloved to look at the same star during the nights of separation. Even the moon is useless, because the moon she sees has not arrived here yet." During World War II, the Spanish journalist Ramón Gómez described Buenos Aires as a balcony on the world: "Sitting on divans in tranquil houses...we can see when the news is false, when history is mistaken, when the great man dies." *Porteños* might boast that the great dangers of the nuclear age don't touch them, but they are intensely eager for news from abroad. Morning newscasters often hold up instant facsimiles of the *New York Times* and *Le Monde* to the television cameras.

This air of remoteness, however sophisticated, gives Buenos Aires an identity that is more American than European. Buenos Aires made mogul in *Citizen Kane*. As in San Francisco, in Buenos Aires the golden age was so recent that history has an intimate feeling. Museums seem more like dusty attics, and are full of family treasures – spurs, pistols, letters – whose significance is obscure to outsiders. In the Fernandez Blanco Museum, which houses colonial silver, you can overhear a well-dressed woman murmur, "Look, isn't that just like the *mate* we have at home?"

In the National Historical Museum, a gaily-painted colonial hacienda on the edge of Lezama Park, visitors wander through rooms full of portraits of handsome military men.

is also closer in spirit to San Francisco – another muddy Spanish port town which became suddenly magically wealthy – than to Barcelona or Milan. For all their formality, *porteños* share with their North American cousins a certain expansiveness, a willingness to confess their salaries and emotional lives to a stranger on a bus. Looking at some of the oversized villas sprinkled here and there in Barrio Norte, you're reminded not so much of an Italian noble as of the self-

Left, polo game at Palermo field. **Above**, retired gentlemen relax on a park bench.

As you exit, you will have learned that most of the streets of Buenos Aires were named after soldiers, but the historical narrative remains mysterious.

This is less the fault of museum directors than it is the result of the *porteño* attitude towards the past, which tends to be a personal, involate set of beliefs. Borges describes this near-religious approach in his poem, *The Mythological Founding of Buenos Aires*: "To me it is a fairy tale that Buenos Aires was founded. It seems as eternal as water and air."

In Buenos Aires, history and politics have

long tended to be synonymous. A conversation about a president in office a century ago will be no less emotionally charged than a discussion of Peronism or the recent military government. Not that you shouldn't ask questions; simply be prepared for a passionate reply. In general, *porteños* want very much to tell their side, like feuding family members trying to engage the sympathies of a house-guest.

Sightseeing: The figure who still arouses the most fervent controversy is Eva Perón. In Argentina, she is worshipped as a saint and reviled as a prostitute. Abroad, she is probably the Argentine who is best known to the

ing beside the brass plaque bearing her name, and a bouquet of carnations. If the porter at the cemetery entrance happens not to approve of Peronist politics, he will merely say to enquirers, like a haughty butler, that she is not here, and he doesn't know where she is.

In the park outside, teenaged boys take clusters of pure-bred dogs for walks, and little girls wearing impractical, gauzy dresses clamber over the roots of a giant rubber tree. The setting is slightly macabre, attractive and sensual.

All around the cemetery are the city's most elegant shops and cafés. As an antidote to an afternoon of boutiques and cream pastries

world, thanks not least to the Tim Rice and Andrew Lloyd Webber musical; tourist board officials wryly concede that her grave in Recoleta Cemetery is the monument visitors to the city most often ask to see.

On Sundays, the cemetery is a promenade for well-born mourners, who go in and out of the baroque pantheons with flowers, like any Sunday caller, and with difficulty restrain their children from laughing and swinging on the quaint wrought-iron gates. The presence of populist Evita does not sit well with many aristocrats whose ancestors lie nearby, but there is usually an admirer or two stand-

you could spend the evening in a raucous Italian cantina in the *barrio* of La Boca, where diners get up between family-style courses and dance around the tables.

Also popular with *porteños* is a night out at the theater, and with so much to choose from it can be overwhelming. From the big name productions on Avenida Corrientes to an intimate show in a basement theater in Monserrat or an avant garde performance in one of the many cultural centers, Buenos Aires is never without options.

No matter where you go, the sense of being part of a scenario is always present. The city thrives on spectacles, whether it's an impromptu tango show on a sunny back street, a gala opera opening at the Colón, or a political march with drums and songs and flapping banners.

Whatever the occasion, the spectators are also actors in the drama; at polo matches they are as glamorous, slender and nervous as the horses on the field; at soccer games and political rallies they are young and furious with loyalty; at the racetrack they are elderly and dandified, full of hope and melancholy.

For *porteños*, half the enjoyment of any outing is the opportunity to join a crowd, to observe and to be observed. Even a meal in

in jazz clubs and walked in parks, bought Italian shoes or an antique box, seen *La Bohème* and an old Bergman film, you might find you crave horizons.

You set out for an estancia in the countryside, or the beach at Mar del Plata, cross the river to visit charming Colonia, travel to the tropical Iguaz Falls, or even the sweeping plains of Patagonia. When you come back, either by river ferry or across the pampas, there is nothing to obstruct your line of vision, and Buenos Aires rises up out of the low river banks.

Probably no other city is so welcoming late at night. The restaurants are jammed at

a restaurant is a chance for people to feast their eyes on one another. In the words of contemporary novelist Luisa Valenzuela: "When you walk in, everyone turns around to look, not at who you are but what you are wearing." For a curious visitor, this love of show is greatly satisfying: so much of Buenos Aires willingly meets the eye.

After you have been in the city for a while – after you have eaten leisurely suppers, sat

Far left, a political rally is fortified by hamburgers, and left, a pretty *porteña*. Above, classical musicians at a concert-demonstration.

one in the morning, there are street musicians playing to crowds along Calle Florida, and whole families are eating ice-cream beside illuminated fountains. At such times, it seems impossible that *porteños* almost universally claim to be melancholic.

With its seductively sweet climate, stage-set prettiness and dedication to refined pleasures, Buenos Aires might be regarded as a kind of urban paradise, and *porteños* as the fortunate characters of fairy tales. But the borders of the city are the edges of their stage, and all around are endless water and endless pampas.

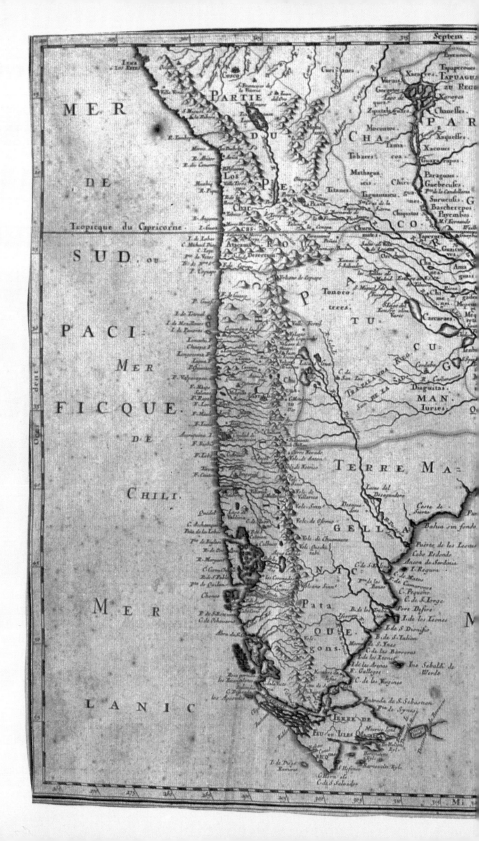

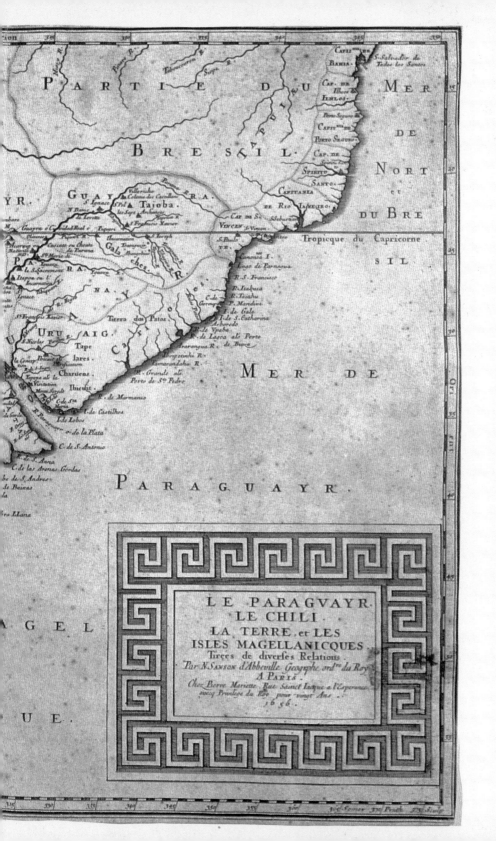

Few of the world's great cities have had so inauspicious a start as Buenos Aires. A series of accidents, mistakes and defeats followed one another as the Spanish explored and tried to settle the Rio de la Plata region. Wild dreams of gold and silver in the early years contrasted sadly with the reality of Buenos Aires as a lonely outpost stagnating at the fringe of the Empire.

The ill-fated explorers: To Juan Diaz de Solis, the first European to lay eyes on the Rio de la Plata, the muddy estuary was a certain passage to the riches of the East and the fabled kingdoms of Orphir and Tarsis. A Portuguese explorer working for the Spanish crown, the enthusiastic de Solis made a landing on the east bank in 1516 but unfortunately took only six men with him.

He quickly encountered a hostile band of Querandí Indians, one of the many wild nomadic tribes that had roamed the region's plains for centuries. De Solis and his hapless crewmen were set upon, killed, and – if the chronicler is to be believed – devoured while the rest of the crew watched helplessly from the boats.

Ten years later, the more cautious but no less imaginative explorer Sebastian Cabot made his way upstream. It was Cabot who optimistically gave the name "river of silver" to the muddy waters after he reached modern-day Paraguay and secured some metal trinkets from the Guaraní Indians.

Convinced that he was on the track of "the Kingdom of the White Caesars," Cabot hurried back to Spain. But to secure the discovery, he left guards in a roughly pallisaded fort called Sancti Spiritus. The region's first permanent settlement was promptly attacked by Indians, its buildings burned and its inhabitants slaughtered.

A false start at Buenos Aires: Cabot's few trinkets easily convinced the Spanish king that vast wealth must be hoarded somewhere near the Rio de la Plata. He commissioned the aristocrat Don Pedro de Mendoza to find it, sending him off with what would be the largest expedition ever to leave for the New World: 1,600 soldiers, three times more than Cortés needed to conquer Mexico, set sail in 14 ships.

In 1536 de Mendoza arrived in South America to make the first attempt at settling Buenos Aires. In a solemn ceremony at what is today the *barrio* of La Boca, he gave it the grandiose title *Puerto Nuestro Señora Santa Maria de Buen Aire* – a reference not to pure antipodean airs but a patron saint then fashionable with European navigators.

But while conquistadors and missionaries were busily pillaging great and opulent Indian empires in Peru, Mexico and Central America, de Mendoza's expedition found not a piece of gold. The Indians of the pampas were elusive and hostile. Forcing them to find food for the settlement quickly provoked war. Within 18 months, starvation, disease and Indian raids had already killed two-thirds of the population.

A Bavarian foot soldier, Ulrich Schmidl, who gave the first written account of Buenos Aires, observed: "The situation was so terrible… that it wasn't enough to just eat rats or mice, reptiles or insects. We had to eat our shoes and leather and everything else."

Schmidl records that three Spaniards stole a horse and later admitted under torture that they had eaten it. The robbers were hung in the main square. The next morning, it was found that other *porteños* had hacked the flesh from the robbers' thighs and taken them home to devour.

Not long after, Indians attacked the settlement with flaming arrows, forcing de Mendoza to take refuge on board the moored ships. Admitting that his mission had been a spectacular failure, de Mendoza moved the entire outpost to Asunción, where there were plentiful vegetables, wild game and more cooperative Guaraní women.

Unfortunately, de Mendoza contracted syphilis and died on his way back to Spain,

Preceding pages: 17th-century map. **Left,** cartoonist Oski satirizes conflict between Spanish explorers and Indians at the city's founding.

Meanwhile his second-in-command had marched off into the Paraguayan Chaco in search of treasure, but ill-fate probably befell him too, for he was never to be heard from again.

Juan de Garay's successful attempt: It was not until 40 years later that settlers tried again with Buenos Aires. This time the conquistador Juan de Garay moved down from Asunción with 66 men and an unknown number of women. Known more for his pragmatism than his intellect, de Garay succeeded where de Mendoza had failed: at what is today the Plaza de Mayo, he chose the first *cabildo* or town council, and planted a

Yrigoyen was traded for a horse and a guitar.

Life was certainly not easy at the new settlement and many gave up and returned to Asunción. The missionaries constantly complained that there was no way to stop animals wandering into their makeshift chapel, while the rest of the settlers were more concerned by the occasional Indian raid. De Garay lost his reputation for pragmatism when he took a summer siesta by the river bank and was surprised by Indians and killed.

The backwater of the empire: For its first 100 years, Buenos Aires was little more than a collection of shacks lost in a lonely swamp. It remained on the outskirts of the Spanish

"tree of justice". Then, de Garay proceeded to draw up a classic Spanish grid plan for Buenos Aires on a piece of cow hide.

With food supplies coming from Asunción, the settlers left the Indians alone and went ahead with the business of building a town. Everyone received a plot of land, and rights to capture the horses which de Mendoza had left behind to grow wild and breed on the pampas. The only single woman, a widow named Ana Diaz, received the entire area which is now at the intersection of Florida and Avenida Corrientes, while the block now on the corner of Bolívar and Hipolito

Empire in the New World, which had as its center Lima and the mines of Upper Peru. For the Spaniards, the region had little to offer: all the quests for silver came to nothing and the native Querandí could not be pressganged into agricultural pursuits; they continued roaming and hunting in the pampas and harassing intruding Europeans.

Buenos Aires was far less important than other inland towns such as Córdoba and Tucumán. It was the last link in a chain of

Above, gruesome portrayal of a cannibalistic ending to the first attempt to found Buenos Aires.

settlements which stretched to Peru, supplying the mines with food, mules and clothes.

The great problem that bedeviled Buenos Aires for the first 200 years of its existence was the prohibition of free trade into or out of its port. The Spanish Crown insisted that it did not have the seapower to protect merchants crossing the Atlantic from enemies and pirates.

This meant that most goods to Buenos Aires from Europe first went via the Caribbean to Panama, then overland to the Pacific, by boat to Lima, and finally were transported by ox-cart the thousands of miles to the Rio de la Plata.

Porteños complained that woolen clothes cost 10 times more in Buenos Aires than in Spain thanks to this trading arrangement. A horse-shoe actually cost more than a horse. There were acute shortages of every manufactured good, from soap and cooking oil to nails and weaponry.

The response to this illogical situation was to turn to smuggling with the Portuguese in order to survive. Even so, Buenos Aires in the 17th century enjoyed only a tenuous existence. At its 100th anniversary in 1680, the town had only 5,000 inhabitants and had just built its first brick house.

One early traveler to Buenos Aires reported that it was a fairly wretched place, with mostly adobe huts and a population of "poor devils without a shirt to their backs and their toes sticking through their shoes." Anybody who could afford European clothes wore them only on special occasions to avoid wearing them out.

Colonial society was dominated by those born in Spain and the white *criollos*, or Spaniards born in the New World. In the country towns these people were rigidly separated from *mestizos*, people of mixed blood who were the artisans and laborers. Buenos Aires was somewhat more egalitarian, since Juan de Garay had started the settlement with nearly all *mestizos* and very few Spanish women had made the arduous journey to the Rio de la Plata. Spanish artisans found themselves mixing easily with *mestizo* workers.

The Church continued to play an important role in providing education and organizing the religious fiestas that would bring *porteños* together. The Spanish daily routine and pastimes were imported: morning Mass, afternoon siestas, evening promenades, cockfights, games of billiards and bull-fights. The educated *criollos* would gather in one another's houses to discuss the latest European philosophies or poetry.

Meanwhile Indian tribes often cut the trade routes to Peru and left Buenos Aires isolated from the Empire. A more organized culture of Araucanian Indians was pressing up from Southern Chile, mastering the wild horses of the pampas and regularly knocking down the Spanish forts.

A smuggling capital: As the 18th century approached, Buenos Aires began to develop its illegal trading until it became one of the great commercial centers of South America – without the Spanish Crown's approval.

Porteños developed a skill for avoiding rules and regulations that would continue to the present day. Spain tried dozens of schemes in an effort to control the secret trading – at one stage even banning the use of money – but were powerless against the *porteños'* wily schemes.

The annual "permission ship" granted by the crown to bring goods was restocked by smugglers in its mooring for weeks. Foreign boats would declare themselves "in distress" with false leaks and pull into Buenos Aires for "refitting" while dropping merchandise by night. Poorly paid town officials would "confiscate" illegal goods only to resell them to their original owners at mock auctions. The founding of Colonia del Sacramento by the Portuguese in 1680 provided a permanent smuggling outlet.

Buenos Aires also became a slave market: a compound to sell black slaves was set up at the present site of Retiro station. *Porteños* blamed the slaves' unhygienic conditions for various epidemics running through the town, but they accepted them in the name of profit. Freed blacks, given the lowest social status in the town, made up at least a quarter of the population by the 19th century.

But the real fortunes were to be made in cattle hides – Rio de la Plata leather equipped soldiers in endless European wars. Cattle-hunts or *vaquerías* occurred less and less frequently as *estancias* (cattle ranches) were set up. Huge tracts of land were set aside for a small number of Spanish families, whose names would recur again and again as the power-brokers of Argentina.

Mule-breeding was less glamorous but only slightly less profitable. By the 1750s Buenos Aires boasted an elite who walked the streets in the finest French silks and even had two-story brick houses.

La gente perdida: From the earliest days of Buenos Aires, individuals had fled to the country and mixed with the Indians. Fleeing criminals, escaped slaves and deserting militia-men lived at the fringes of society and were known as *la gente perdida:* the lost

The wandering, vagrant population had always irritated the *porteño* officials, who tried to licence the gauchos, tie them to the new estancias, and forbid them from using knives – all without success. One English traveler in the period wrote in despair: "Vain is the endeavor to explain to him the luxuries and blessings of a more civilized life!"

Saga of the Jesuit missions: The Jesuit presence in what is now the north of Argentina and south of Paraguay has become well known with Roland Joffé's 1986 Academy-Award winning movie *The Mission*, starring Robert De Niro and Jeremy Irons. The plot revolved around the threat posed to the Jesu-

people. They developed their own harsh, nomadic lifestyle on the pampas, following and killing cattle herds for fresh meat and hides (which they traded for *yerba mate* or alcohol). The men developed their own style: special knives or *facónes*, distinctive bagged trousers, Spanish hats and woven Indian shawls. Now called gauchos (cowboys), they were known for gambling, horsemanship and knife fighting.

The women, called *chinas*, played a subsidiary role in this macho lifestyle, raising children in small huts which were indistinguishable from those of the Indians.

its South American missions by the territorial conflicts between Spain and Portugal.

In 1609 the Buenos Aires *cabildo* supported the Jesuits in setting up Indian missions to protect Spanish holdings. Free from taxes, the missions brought Guaraní Indians together in societies which organized every moment of daily life. By 1700, more than 50,000 Guaraní Indians were growing crops, rearing sheep and making musical instruments in conditions far better than those of other plantations.

The missions suffered early losses from raids by slave traders. However, the Jesuits learned from their mistakes and organized a standing army of Indians which eventually developed into the largest, most efficient military machine in the Rio de la Plata region. And its position remained unchallenged for 100 years.

When in 1750 the Spanish gave the missions to Portugal, the Indians rebelled and defended themselves. Only in 1768 when the Jesuits were expelled from the Spanish Empire was the system's weakness revealed: the paternalistic structure collapsed without the priests, leaving the Guaraní totally unprepared for change. Most fled into the jungle and the missions became overgrown ruins.

Spain appeases the *porteños*: The Spanish Crown eventually had to admit that smuggling in Buenos Aires was out of control and that corruption and inefficiency were rampant in the city.

In 1776, Spain made Buenos Aires the capital of a new vice-royalty of the Rio de la Plata which stretched from modern-day Bolivia to Paraguay and Uruguay. Trade was opened up and administrative reforms made.

Left, a Pauke print depicts the prominent role of the Jesuits in colonial Buenos Aires. **Above**, 1806 artilleryman.

The man sent to be the first viceroy was the Spanish general Pedro de Cevallos, a religious fanatic hated by his own men for his ruthlessness. Considered the last of the conquistadors, he managed to capture Colonia del Sacramento from the Portuguese at a time when Spain was being soundly defeated everywhere else in the world.

De Cevallos puffed the pride of *porteños* by telling them that Buenos Aires was Spain's "most important bastion in America, whose development we must encourage by every means possible, for here we will win or lose South America."

With the growth of trade bringing unseen prosperity, Buenos Aires began to improve its image. The streets were paved and lit, a hospital and orphanage were built, theaters were opened and Spanish professionals began to migrate to the new capital. By the end of the 18th century, Buenos Aires had eight churches and a main cathedral.

But visitors were still not overly impressed by the improvements. Another English traveler at the time remarked dryly: "The city of Buenos Aires, observed from the outer anchorage, has an imposing appearance. The public buildings and cupolas of the various churches give it a certain air of grandeur which vanishes as soon as we draw near."

Buenos Aires remained notorious for its terrible sanitation. Most of the population depended for their drinking water on vendors who filled their leather vats with the same river water used for bathing and sewage. Disease was rife and visitors reported that the streets were full of lepers, and rats the size of rabbits.

But all of Spain's reforms finally backfired. The boost in *porteño* self-confidence provided by the new wealth only served to encourage the idea of ending all ties with Spain, while the new administrators sent by the Crown were only seen as meddlers by the local *criollos*.

When in 1796 war with Britain finally cut Atlantic trade routes, leaving piles of goods to rot in the warehouses of Buenos Aires, *porteños* decided that connections with Spain were undesirable.

The Crown's authority would never be fully restored in Buenos Aires again.

The street names of Buenos Aires constitute a roll-call of heroes from its struggle for independence and the civil wars that followed. Although *porteños* seized power to improve their commercial prosperity, the provincial towns refused to cooperate. It was not until 70 years later that Argentina would settle down as a political unit with Buenos Aires in control.

The British take over: The *porteños'* eventual separation from Spain was partly due to longstanding resentment against the Crown and partly due to outside influences beyond Spanish control: the examples of the French and American revolutions, Enlightenment ideas of popular participation in government and, above all, the misguided plans of Englishman Sir Home Popham.

Popham was commanding a British naval force on its way back from South Africa in June 1806, when he decided, completely without orders, to capture Buenos Aires. Like all good Britons of the time, he felt that if foreigners would not trade with the British willingly, they should be forced to do so. Popham landed his Scottish highlanders, backed by gunboats, to take the city. The Spanish viceroy promptly scurried for cover in Córdoba, for which he would never be forgiven by the *porteños*.

Proclaiming the Rio de la Plata region to be a "New Arcadia" for British merchants, Popham sent home boats full of war booty. The takings, which were emblazoned with the word TREASURE in gold, were paraded through the streets of London.

Its appetite whetted, the British government sent massive reinforcements to Buenos Aires. But before they could arrive, the *porteños* had already tired of the British, rebelled and easily captured the whole occupying force. The British colors were hung in the church of Santo Domingo, where they

Preceding pages: room of nationalist Juan Manuel de Rosas in the Fernandez Blanco Museum. *Left,* a gaucho soldier in Rosas' army. *Right,* Monvoisin painting shows *porteña* mourning Civil War dead.

can still be found today. Captured officers spent their time fishing and horse-riding in the *estancias* of the provinces, and *porteños* hastily organized a popular militia using captured weapons.

The new British commander, General George Whitelocke, found himself in Montevideo with no fewer than 70 boats full of merchant goods which were supposed to be sold to *porteños*. A weak and indecisive leader, Whitelocke decided that his prede-

cessors had been defeated by a Spanish conspiracy rather than a popular uprising. He ordered his troops to land and retake Buenos Aires, but the *porteños* were ready. The British were caught in the narrow streets of the city as patriots showered them from the rooftops with "musketry, hand grenades, stink pots, brickbats and all sorts of combustibles."

Four hundred British soldiers were killed in the chaotic confrontation, as many were wounded, and over 2,000 captured. The enemy fell back to Montevideo and Whitelocke was recalled to London for court-martial. Days of celebration followed the victory in Buenos Aires: a new confidence had been achieved by the *porteños* for defeating a powerful invader without the slightest help from Spain. The viceroy returned from his hiding-place in the provinces but his prestige had been shattered. A Portuguese spy in the city at the time noted that "Buenos Aires is, in fact, a republic already."

The independence movement: The ejected British also left behind the memory of their cheap manufactured goods and had given the *criollo* merchants their first taste of unrestricted trade. These merchants led the push for local autonomy, organizing the militia under their own control so that the independ-

The climax came on May 25, when the viceroy and the cabildo watched the assembling militiamen in the Plaza de Mayo and admitted that they no longer controlled Buenos Aires. They surrendered their power to a *junta criolla* which declared that it would rule in the name of the Spanish Crown. It was only on July 9, 1816 that full independence was announced for the whole Rio de la Plata region in the provincial town of Tucumán, which is why Argentines celebrate two national independence days.

Before that date, however, Buenos Aires saw a bewildering number of experiments at the new experience of self-government rang-

ence movement would never become a truly popular revolt.

Napoleon's invasion of Spain provided *porteños* with the opportunity they had been awaiting. In May 1810, news arrived in Buenos Aires that the interim government of Seville had fallen and that there was now no direct link with the Spanish Crown. For four tense days, the leading *porteño* citizenry pressured the viceroy to hand over his authority, while the muddy streets of Buenos Aires became crowded with merchants, soldiers, *estancieros* and bureaucrats debating the best course for the future.

ing from new juntas to triumvirates, congresses and directorates.

Despite this, Buenos Aires remained the only South American capital that the Spanish never managed to recover and *porteños* carried their struggle to other countries. The campaign was led by the only historical figure to have kept the universal respect of Argentines: General José de San Martín. This polite and reserved veteran of the Spanish war against Napoleon returned to his home country after hearing of the events of May 25. Realizing that the newly-declared Republic could never be safe while its neighbors were Spanish-dominated, San Martín spent years preparing for a massive expedition to Chile.

The crossing of the Andes was timed with precision, not only liberating Santiago but later freeing Lima, the Spanish capital in South America. San Martín, who was becoming increasingly depressed about the constant bickering and growing chaos back in Buenos Aires, tried to convince the other great liberator of the continent, Simón Bolívar, that a new monarchy was the only solution. After Bolívar refused to back the idea, San Martín gave up and went to France, where he died, lonely and disillusioned.

The civil wars begin: No sooner had the *porteños* declared the vice-royalty of the Rio de la Plata to be independent than the whole of Upper Peru, Uruguay and Paraguay announced that they wanted to be separate from Buenos Aires. Soon, the various provincial towns that now make up Argentina were declaring their own autonomy.

The inhabitants of the interior were understandably not as thrilled by the idea of Buenos Aires' leadership as the *porteños* themselves. The *criollo* merchants saw vast profits in opening up the whole country to free trade, indifferent to the fact that this would destroy the provincial economies.

During these years, *porteños* accepted aid from wherever they could get it. The Irishman William Brown had deserted the British Navy and arrived in Buenos Aires to eventually lead a naval squadron which broke a blockade. The Frenchman Jean-Jacques d'Auxion, who commanded *porteño* troops, was said to have been one of Napoleon's own generals who had fled to South America after the Waterloo fiasco.

Left, *mataderos* **or slaughter houses flanked the city and were the source of its wealth. Right, 1831 Pellegrini painting of the Cabildo.**

Porteños were also hurrying to trade with their old enemies, the British. They knew that woolen ponchos, modeled on Tucumán's products, could be bought from Manchester factories at a fraction of the Tucumán price, while Sheffield knives would easily outsell those from Jujuy.

The division between Buenos Aires and the interior is often described as a struggle between Unitarists and Federalists: the Unitarists wanted to keep a strong central government in Buenos Aires and the Federalists wanted to preserve local autonomy. But the wheeling and dealing in the many complex civil wars that followed often made the distinction meaningless.

From the confusion after independence emerged the figure of the *caudillo*, the local strongman, usually a landowner from a traditional family who took control of each of the provinces. They fought with Buenos Aires and among themselves, developing a habit of chopping off their defeated enemies' heads and hanging them in their main plazas.

Buenos Aires tried to win over the *caudillos* by offering a new constitution, but instead, they marched on the city with their gaucho armies and captured it, forcing *porteños*, at least for the time being, to accept federalism.

Buenos Aires under Rivadavia: A brief respite from the civil wars during the 1820s allowed *porteños* to take stock of their newfound freedom. Under their Anglophile governor Bernardino Rivadavia, it appeared that very little had changed.

Travelers were still astounded by the number of accidents caused by racing horse-and-buggies in the city streets. They noted the number of children hanging around smoking tobacco in the plazas and were shocked by wild black dances at night in San Telmo. One English writer observed that Buenos Aires now had five cafés – one of which he thought superior to anything in London but not up to Parisian standards – while the port area was crowded with bars and brothels.

Young single foreigners arrived from the poorer parts of Europe to find work, with many Irish and Basques accepting the lonely and rough life of shepherding in the country. Another English traveler noted that an Irishman digging ditches on an *estancia* could earn enough in three weeks to buy 1,500 sheep, while his homeland offered nothing but starvation.

In the same year as independence, landowners became richer with the introduction of the *saladero*: a crude factory which processed every last part of cattle and horses amid an overwhelming stench of blood and gore. Hides, salted meat, hair and melted hooves left in the many schooners that passed by Buenos Aires.

Rivadavia tried to make some more profound changes but only succeeded in provoking further civil war. He first upset the large landowners by proposing to create a democracy of small landowners such as that existing in the United States. He then enraged the Church with his anti-clerical measures, creating a university free from religious control and setting up a public library which boasted the works of the most radical French thinkers.

The people of the interior rose up against Buenos Aires yet again under the banner "Religion or Death." More turmoil followed, with years of war, assassination, alliances and back-stabbings until the most infamous of all *caudillos* appeared on the scene: Juan Manuel de Rosas.

The restorer of the laws: Rosas still arouses debate among *porteños*. He is denounced by some as a cruel and bloody tyrant while praised by others as a nationalist hero.

The "Caligula of the River Plate" came from a wealthy ranching family of Buenos Aires province. He handled himself with equal ease among the urbane *porteños* and the gauchos of the pampas, where he had slept under the stars in his youth and learned to tell the weather by chewing blades of grass. Rosas had already led militia troops against Buenos Aires in the name of Federalism, but the chaos of the civil wars was so destructive that *porteños* decided to call on this *caudillo* to protect them.

From the moment of assuming governorship in 1829 until his expulsion 23 years later, Rosas ruled Buenos Aires as if it were his own private *estancia*. He silenced his critics through censorship, intimidation and exile – sending to Montevideo the intellectuals who later became known as "the Generation of '37."

As the *caudillo* of Buenos Aires province, Rosas soon became *de facto* ruler of Argentina by defeating various provincial leaders. When he left the governorship for a short break to kill Indians instead, *porteños* invited him back with virtually unlimited dictatorial powers.

Pictures of Rosas were hung over church altars: "Rosas the Restorer of the Laws" next to "Christ the Redeemer." Many schools were closed, radical books banned and the *Carnaval* suppressed. Bureaucrats who did not unquestioningly do their master's bidding could expect a nocturnal visit from the secret police, called the *mazorca*, who slit their victims' throats.

Rosas' residence in what is now Palermo Park was known as *el Versailles criollo* for its sumptuous mansion, sculptures, park and zoo. His city residence in Monserrat was famous for its giant telescope.

The dictator paid constant lip-service to Federalism, going so far as to force all *porteños* to wear a ribbon of the Federalist color – red. Even the fashionable ladies of the aristocracy did not feel they could disregard this directive, while Rosas' wife appeared which allowed Buenos Aires province to prosper while dooming many of the provincial industries to destruction.

Under Rosas' rule, *porteños* increasingly had to tolerate more wars against *caudillos*, as well as various blockades of the Rio de la Plata by the British and the French, to break the protective tariff. Rosas started a 12-year siege of Montevideo, which *porteños* jokingly called "the Troy of the River Plate," but when the British took the Malvinas/Falkland Islands in 1833, he managed only a stern note of protest to London.

The cost of maintaining Rosas' army and wars was soon interfering in the happy pursuit

peared in scarlet satins and his gauchos in scarlet ponchos. All legal documents began: "Long live the Federation and Death to the Unitarist Savages."

Yet it was Rosas more than anyone else who guaranteed the end of Federalism and the supremacy of Buenos Aires. He crushed uprisings by other *caudillos*, and ensured *porteño* control of revenues from trade. He also introduced a system of protective tariffs

Above, an early 19th-century Bacle print spoofs the exaggerated *peinetones* or combs which were fashionable at that time.

of profit by *porteño* merchants, which turned his own supporters against him. When one of Rosas' former commanders, Justo José de Urquiza, turned against him and marched on Buenos Aires, many *porteños* rebelled.

Rosas was defeated and his supporters massacred. Buenos Aires was sacked by looters, forcing foreign boats to put marines ashore to protect their merchandise.

The ageing dictator himself fled on a British ship to Southampton, where he spent the next 25 years wasting his considerable fortune trying to recreate the conditions of his old *estancia* on a plot of English soil.

Life after Rosas: Forty years of independence and chaos had still not profoundly changed life in Buenos Aires or provincial society. But the Rosas years had shown how the city could be a political capital of the Rio de la Plata. In the decades that followed, economic growth and the unification of Argentina went hand in hand.

The provinces had once again defeated Buenos Aires, but they could not control it. Exhausted by wars, everybody at last agreed to a new constitution. In 1862, Bartolome Mitre became the first President of La Republica Argentina. The theory of Federalism was maintained, with the national govern-

tion or ambition. They secured the brightest minds coming from Europe. Meanwhile the "Generation of '37" returned from exile in Montevideo to fill the city's cafés and supply Argentina with statesmen, writers and historians who would paint the Rosas years in lurid colors.

The most influential of these was Domingo Sarmiento. He had followed the final campaign against Rosas with a printing press on an ox-cart to send out propaganda condemning him as a tyrant. Sarmiento divided the world into "civilization" – represented by all things European – and the barbarous: *caudillos*, gauchos and Indians.

ment ruling from Buenos Aires as the guests of the provincial rulers.

An economic boom followed, based on sheep farming and agriculture. Argentina accepted its neocolonial role of selling raw materials to industrial countries and buying back manufactured goods. Steamships with regular schedules helped trade and brought Buenos Aires closer to Europe, while the expansion of railroads backed by British investors tied the provinces even more securely to their only port.

Porteños now culled from the interior anyone with even the slightest talent, imagina-

The old *caudillo* with his motley cavalry bands no longer fitted in with Argentina's new style of politics. The country's leaders would increasingly dress in collar and tie, eager to appear highly cultured and urbane.

The gauchos who still roamed the pampas and made up *caudillo* armies were seen as a threat to Sarmiento's great dream for the country. Rosas had already tried to control them, but now codes were introduced to regulate their movements, dress, drinking habits and diet. Thousands were pressed into military service as punishment for not possessing a passport they could not even read.

President Mitre led wars to exterminate the gauchos, advised by Sarmiento that they were "biped animals of the most perverse stripe" whose carcasses were only good to fertilize the earth.

Soon, the gaucho was virtually extinct as a social grouping, leaving only an idealized literary memory.

In the great literary work of the 1870s, *The Gaucho Martín Fierro*, José Hernandez would lament: "And listen to the story told by a gaucho who's hunted by the law, who's been a hardworking father and a loving husband – yet in spite of all that, taken to be a criminal."

Buenos Aires at federation: It was not until 1886 that the final step towards nationhood was made when Buenos Aires was separated from its province and declared the capital of Argentina. Poised before the great expansion of the 1880s, the city was still known as *la gran aldea* – the big village. Most of its buildings were still colonial-style, built around courtyards, sparsely furnished and unheated. Streets were mostly unpaved and the port's facilities still inadequate.

Although Buenos Aires had banks, factories, tramways, a gasworks and a telegraph station, many of the *porteños*' habits had not changed since pre-independence days. They

Meanwhile, the Araucanian Indians continued to threaten estancias. One raid as late as 1876 broke through the defensive forts to reach within 250 km (155 miles) of Buenos Aires. After this, General Julio Roca embarked upon the "conquest of the wilderness" with the simple expedient of killing any Indian who stood in his path and herding the rest into reservations. For his efforts, *porteños* made him President.

Left, a *pulpería* or combination saloon/general store. **Above left**, first President Bernardino Rivadavia. **Above right**, President Roca.

still took long siestas after huge lunches of roasted meat with a little alcohol, drank *mate*, went to Mass, and kept strong family ties.

But compared to the provinces, the city was a cosmopolitan center. The monotonous pace of the conservative interior was only enlivened by the occasional cockfight or game of billiards. In Buenos Aires, the immigrants were arriving and with them came new ideas, and a new wave of restaurants, cafés, hotels, brothels and even some foreign-language newspapers.

Yet the changes had just begun. Buenos Aires was on the verge of its Golden Age.

The close of the 19th century saw Buenos Aires change from a dusty, colonial town to the "Paris of South America," a center of commerce and culture claiming to be unmatched in the hemisphere. Development of the pampas brought unimagined wealth and waves of immigrants from Europe. However, it was not long before the end of the Argentine dream was in sight.

The "great leap forward": An agricultural revolution on the vast pampas beyond Buenos Aires proved to be more important in shaping the future of Argentina than all the civil wars and conflicts of the 1800s. Booms occurred first with wheat-growing, followed by sheep-raising and finally with beef cattle.

Expansion into the fertile plains went on unchecked for the next 40 years, making the pampas the richest area in Latin America and the Argentine *estanciero* (rancher) a near-mythical figure of wealth in his day, to stand alongside the Brazilian rubber lord and the Texan oil baron.

The most dramatic change was made in the production of beef. In the mid-19th century, only a fraction of the meat on slaughtered cattle was used; most of it rotted in the open air and was picked at by wandering gauchos. Meanwhile in Europe, beef was selling at outrageous prices and considered a luxury on the finest dinner tables. With slow shipping and no refrigeration to speak of, the problem was to get the meat across the Atlantic before it went bad.

It was in 1876 that an experimental shipment of frozen beef first arrived in Buenos Aires from France. The elated *estancieros* threw a grand banquet for the Frenchmen. Their enthusiasm was only slightly dulled by the discovery that technical imperfections had left the meat unchewable after the three-month voyage. But within years Argentine beef was crossing the Atlantic in large quantities to be sliced on European tables.

Preceding pages: gaucho woos his pretty *novia*. Left, Turkish immigrant with hookah. Right, dockside warehouse.

Bigger and faster steam ships began transporting live cattle until Argentine stock was found to be ridden with foot and mouth disease. A new Chicago-based technique was soon developed to chill rather than freeze meat, increasing both the beef's quality and the *estancieros'* massive profits. Cultivation of the pampas skyrocketed to keep up with the new demands. Railways were laid across the country by British companies, to move produce as quickly as possible towards Bue-

nos Aires and other coastal ports. Argentina was soon outstripping its rivals, Canada and Australia, in agricultural advances, and some observers predicted that it would overtake the United States.

The immigrants arrive: Laborers were needed to keep the boom going, and these were made available through immigration. Before 1880, there was only a trickle of foreign workers into Argentina. Overnight they became a flood, the greatest influx of immigrants in relation to population patterns in history.

The majority of immigrants were peasants from northern Italy, with the next largest group coming from Spain. Nearly all paid their own way across the Atlantic on a third-class passage, spending weeks crammed below decks in a constant battle against seasickness and food poisoning.

Most arrived penniless, secure only in the knowledge that two weeks' work in Argentina would cover the cost of the fare. News of easy riches spread quickly.

The newcomers' first taste of Buenos Aires was usually five days' free lodging at the dreaded Immigrants' Hotel, a horse barn which was eventually upgraded in the style of a concrete prison. Anyone who was able picked up a cheap hotel room, contacted

richest *porteños*, who avoided the 40,400-hectare (100,000-acre) limit on purchases by using false names.

Immigrants were instead offered two-year tenancy leases in the pampas, moving on when they expired. The landowners provided the seed and tools, the immigrants the brawn. Their existence as tenants was harsh and lonely; the nearest town was often 50 km (30 miles) away. Staying for such a short time, farmers rarely bothered to construct anything more permanent than a hut of straw and thatch with sheepskin for a door.

Their only social contact would be the local store, usually at the distant railway

relatives or drifted around the waterfront.

By the turn of the century, the system was refined so that laborers were off their boats and into Retiro station on the same day, where a train would whisk them directly to the pampas.

But unlike in North America, the immigrants were not able to buy their own small plots of land. The Argentine *estancieros* refused to break up their huge tracts of territory, easily ignoring the laws that had been passed to control concentration of property. Even the plains opened up by Roca's Conquest of the Desert were snapped up by the

station, which was a development of the gauchos' *pulpería*: some idle conversation could be had over cheap red wine, meat and dry biscuits. The farmer lived without roads through the countryside, let alone churches, doctors or schools.

Not surprisingly, the vast majority of immigrants ended up staying in Buenos Aires and other coastal ports, making seasonal forays into the pampas only at harvest time. They worked in the meat-packing plants, railways and service industries that were needed to channel the produce to the outside world. Those who did well formed a new, prosperous middle class in the city, where they became the shopkeepers, bank clerks, teachers, minor officials and small factory-owners of the 20th century.

It was the *estanciero* who amassed vast fortunes from the boom, living in the capital with holiday houses in Tigre and Mar del Plata. The phrase "rich as an Argentine" fell into common usage in France as the *porteño* playboy began to cut a notorious figure in the salons of Paris (the women had to wait some decades before escaping needlework and cooking classes).

The wealthy *estancieros* became leaders of a tight-knit group of some 200 families, bankers, politicians and businessmen. Educated in Europe, cosmopolitan and aloof, they set about shaping the city of Buenos Aires to their ideals.

There was, of course, a flip side to the picture, as described by W. H. Hudson – the lives of the imported laborers. Hudson describes the scene at his beach. "It was the spot where the washerwomen were allowed to wash all the dirty linen of Buenos Aires in public. All over the ground the women, mostly Negresses, were seen on their knees, beside the pools among the rocks, furiously scrubbing and pounding away at their work...they were exceedingly vociferous and their loud gabble, mixed with yells and shrieks of laughter, reminded me of the hubbub made by a great concourse of gulls, ibises, godwits, geese and other noisy waterfowl on some marshy lake."

The transformation of Buenos Aires: *Porteños* greeted the centennial of independence in 1910 with boundless optimism, convinced that the future was assured by beef, wheat and sheep. "We are living the most glorious day," announced one writer ecstatically, "bet-

European immigrants gather in the bleak dining-hall of the Immigrants' Hotel.

ter than the trumpeted century of Pericles, better even than the Renaissance." Buenos Aires was now the largest city in Latin America and second only to New York on the American continent. *Porteños* made sure that the benefits of the pampas revolution stayed in the capital, thereby changing the face of the city.

Buenos Aires shed its Hispanic colonial atmosphere to become an expression of *porteño* admiration for all things French. The Plaza de Mayo, which had been full of garbage and market stalls, was cleared and a lawn was laid. The Casa Rosada was completed. De Garay's 16th-century street plan was finally cast aside and streets widened into grand avenues, to be lined with Parisian cafés, jacarandas and footpaths made of Swedish marble.

Palermo Park was remodeled along the lines of the Bois de Boulogne in Paris, while the Avenida 9 de Julio was planned in imitation of the Champs-Élysées. The British architects of Retiro and Constitution railway stations managed to resist the fashion and instead took their inspiration from models in London and Liverpool.

Horse-drawn carts gave way to electric trams in the chaotic streets. Travelers who had once complained about *porteño* horsemanship now found automobile drivers in the city no more considerate and decidedly more dangerous. A subway line was opened only 10 years after New York's. Meanwhile, engineers scoured the world for a grade of asphalt which would not melt in the summer sun and would provide comfortable coach rides for well-to-do young ladies.

The modern-day contours of Buenos Aires were defined: Florida became a shopping area; Corrientes a focus for cabaret and dance; north of the Plaza de Mayo was the banking center; and the waterfront was the red-light district. Beyond these were the *barrios*, where most people lived and worked. Each *barrio* had its own bar, shops, and priests.

As Buenos Aires became more sophistacted the gulf widened with the "interior": most pampa towns remained colonial backwaters where nobody of talent or importance would consider staying. One English traveler of the time, aghast at the dusty main squares and the dirt roads, wrote: "If a man ever wishes to know what it is to have an inclination to commit suicide, let him pass a week in a camptown in the Argentine."

The rise of the Radicals: Despite the changes occurring over the turn of the century, political power remained in the hands of the few old *estanciero* and business families referred to simply as "the oligarchy." A nominal democratic system was arranged so that the oligarchs could choose presidents and congressmen from their own ranks, while corruption in the courts and bureaucracy bent the system to their needs.

A protest movement against the oligarchs' grip grew in the 1880s with the Unión Cívica, pulling together students, university professors and scattered groups from the *criollo* middle class. After a failed attempt at revolution in 1890, this was transformed into the Unión Cívica Radical, forerunner of today's political party of the same name. The Radicals' influence extended under the leadership of Hipolito Yrigoyen, a figure still revered by party members: a shy and introverted man, Yrigoyen was a poor speaker and dictatorial in his methods, but a brilliant organizer. He undertook the tedious shuffling and manouvering for support that made the Radicals a powerful force.

Yrigoyen's demand was wonderfully simple: free elections. Once it was obvious that the only thing "radical" about the middle-class protest movement was its name, the oligarchs decided on a strategic retreat to protect their interests.

A democratic poll was held in 1916 with universal male suffrage (women had to wait until the regime of Perón for the vote). Yrigoyen won the presidential race by only one ballot in the electoral college. He was drawn through the streets of Buenos Aires by throngs of young supporters, hailing what they hoped would be a new age of reform.

But the Radicals proved from the very beginning they had little interest in changing the old order. Although the university system was updated, most other reforms were either blocked in Congress or failed through party division.

Argentina stood still. Anarchist cells were formed in Buenos Aires, leading strikes which the Radicals were eager to crush. *La Semana Trágica* (Tragic Week) of 1919 followed a general strike, with right-wing vigilante groups storming the slums of the capital in search of "Bolsheviks." Three years later, Yrigoyen allowed the Army to break a shepherds' strike in Patagonia and carry out mass executions.

Between the wars: Buenos Aires in the 1920s became the cultural mecca of Latin America. The Teatro Colón put the city on par with Berlin and Milan for opera and ballet. A dozen newspapers thrived. Art galleries opened along Florida. Writers flocked to the city from across the Hispanic world, lured by the reputation of literary magazines such as *Martín Fierro* and the works of poet Leopoldo Lugones, novelist Manuel Gálvez and the young Jorge Luis Borges.

As a freer age was ushered in, women walking alone on the streets were no longer denounced as whores or insane. Bohemians gathered in the Café Tortoni to imitate the latest rage from Paris, from nude follies to "cocaine mania."

Even tango emerged from the dark bars of La Boca once it became fashionable in France, reaching new heights with the work of singer and movie heart-throb Carlos Gardel (*see the*

the Wall Street Crash the next year. He did nothing to soften the impact of the world depression and let corruption run out of control. The Radicals appeared completely unable to deal with the situation.

Meanwhile the Argentine army had spent the 1920s practising the goosesteps taught by German instructors and admiring Mussolini's Italy from afar. Increasingly critical of democracy, on September 6, 1930 they made what would be the first of many interventions: General José Uriburu strolled unopposed with his troops into the Casa Rosada and took over the government.

Two years later Uriburu passed control to

Tango chapter, pages 161–64).

Yet, despite the heady enthusiasm and wild parties of small *porteño* cliques, the cracks were already showing in the great edifice of Argentine prosperity. The country was still contentedly supplying raw materials to Europe and developing little industry, making no allowance for changes in the world economy. A nearly senile Yrigoyen was re-elected president in 1928, only to face

Above, the revolution of September 6, 1930, in which President Hipolito Yrigoyen was overthrown by General José Uriburu.

a series of conservative presidents, who led Argentina through *la década infame* ("the infamous decade"). Firmly back in power, the oligarchy continued to run the country as if it were still the 1890s.

As the "infamous decade" of the 1930s progressed, the middle class became increasingly restive. But the great wellspring of discontent would be the workers, many of whom were the children of immigrants. Crammed into one-room family houses, working long hours for unprotected wages, they still had no political voice.

Into this void stepped Juan Domingo Perón.

PERÓN TO THE PRESENT

The two most significant events in Argentina's past half-century of history have been the rise to power of Juan Domingo Perón in the mid-1940s and the return to real representative democracy in 1983.

Perón was the most influential personality in Argentina's history to date, and one of the best loved and most hated leaders in contemporary political history.

Perón is remembered by his detractors as a cruel and ruthless dictator who modeled his regime on that of Italy's Benito Mussolini and Germany's Adolf Hitler, and who plundered the wealth and well-being of the nation. He is seen by his admirers, meanwhile, as the great benefactor of the unsung worker, the man who made all Argentines equal, created a national industry and ended the feudal exploitation of the laborer by the landed gentry.

Perhaps, as is usually the case with remarkable figures in history, a little of both views is true. But one thing is certain – no Argentine, even today, more than a decade after the leader's death, is indifferent to the name of Juan Domingo Perón.

Born in the little town of Lobos about 100 km (60 miles) southwest of Buenos Aires in 1895, Perón joined the Army when he was 16 years old. He attended officers' training and, after receiving his commission, made rapid progress through the ranks. He stood over six feet tall and possessed the kind of daring and flintiness which made him the target of admiration and envy in the cadre and the ranks. He was a champion swordsman, an efficient boxer and a good skier. But he also did well in the classroom, especially in history and political science.

Perón was indeed influenced in his early political career by the Italian dictator Benito Mussolini. In the 1930s, he served as Argentina's military attaché in Rome, seeing with his own eyes the rapid inroads made in Europe by Mussolini's and Adolf Hitler's nationalism.

During World War II, as during World War I, Argentina remained nominally neutral, although in practice the country was split and at severe odds over the issues raised by the struggle against the Nazis. Neutrality was basically a matter of economics. In both world wars, Argentina was a universal supplier of food and leather.

In 1938, at the start of the conflict, the Conservative Coalition government of Roberto Ortiz came to office. Ortiz's administration followed the relative stability of six years under the Progressive Conservative government of Agustín Justo. But the new government quickly proved itself unequal to the task of preserving that stability in the face of growing controversy over the issues of World War II.

Less than four years later, in 1942, Ortiz fell ill, resigned and died shortly thereafter. He was replaced in office by his Vice-President, Ramón Castillo, who was slated to serve out the rest of Ortiz's term until 1944. But he didn't last a year.

Perón's rise to power: In June of 1943, Generals Arturo Rawson, P.P. Ramírez and Edelmiro Farrell mustered troops at the Campo de Mayo Army base outside Buenos Aires and marched to the center of the city where they took over the Government House and ousted Castillo.

Perón was, from the beginning of the uprising, one of the chief aides to the new ruling junta. Efficient, opportune and highly politicized, he accepted greater and greater responsibilities from the three generals, garrison types who knew next to nothing about politics and "people power," whose strength was that they had all the weapons.

Early on in the regime Perón was named labor secretary, and it was here that he began to gather his power base among the country's largely unprotected and non-unionized workers. He began working on draft legislation to benefit workers, particularly lower-class laborers, expanding his sphere of influence

Preceding pages: Juan Perón and Evita at a gala opera. **Left**, Eva Perón was a good orator and clever politician.

into the social welfare secretariat as well. Finding Colonel Perón ever willing and able to accept greater responsibility, the generals, in 1944, also named him minister of war – in time for him to foresee the outcome of World War II and break the regime's neutrality and rather obvious friendship with the Axis and declare its sudden loyalty to the Allies.

By 1945, Perón had also become vice-president of the nation. Now without doubt the real power figure in the military government, Perón pushed through measures to further endear him to the workers.

All through this period, a personality cult was growing around what workers saw as

of the tracks. But they persevered and soon he was the real power behind the regime and she was at his side. Together, they could make the country do their bidding.

Their chance to prove this came in 1945. Perón's gathering of worker support was beginning to worry influential sectors of society, which put pressure on the military regime to do something about it. The fear among the wealthy was that Perón might eventually lead the workers in a move toward a communist state. The last straw came when he began laying the groundwork for the formation of an umbrella union organization, which was aimed at "Peronizing" labor

their own caudillo, and now that cult was rapidly extending to his beautiful young actress mistress, María Eva (better known as "Evita") Duarte.

It was logical that this should happen. Buenos Aires society was a class-conscious place where the rule of thumb was that you had to be from "a good family" and often one of *the* families in order to get anywhere. Perón and Evita were living proof that this wasn't necessarily true, and that you only had to be smarter, bolder and bigger than the rest to get to the top. He was a smalltown boy and she was a poor girl from the wrong side

as a whole, called the General Confederation of Labor (CGT).

The regime stripped him of his official posts and packed him off to the Martín García military prison on an island in the middle of the River Plate near Buenos Aires. But the generals had not reckoned on the charisma and consumate political strength of Evita, who quickly rallied the workers of Buenos Aires, and solicited the help of sectors of the Army loyal to Perón.

Perón had been in jail for less than a fortnight before being released. He made a triumphant return to Buenos Aires on October 17, 1945 (the date is still celebrated by Peronists as the anniversary of the founding of Peronism), and spoke from the balcony of Government House to some 300,000 people gathered in Plaza de Mayo below. The speech, in which he promised to become President and lead the nation to strength and social justice, was also broadcast nationwide on radio. Several days later, Perón married Evita, to the delight of followers who were becoming ever more swept up in the fairytale glamor of the life of Juan Perón.

The discredited generals called elections for February of the following year. After a brief campaign – in which the liberal oppo-

Peronism, however, called the policy "distributionism," since, they claimed, it distributed the reserves and assets of the nation among the workers, thus gradually impoverishing the state.

Whatever it was, it reshaped society in Buenos Aires. Justicialism showered Perón's most fervent followers, laborers known in Perónist lingo as *los descamisados* (the shirtless ones), with social benefits, housing and jobs in the public sector. All workers benefited from guarantees against dismissal and received blanket wage-rises and institutionalized fringe benefits.

On the business front, Perón controlled

sition claimed it had been repressed by the Federal Police and Peronist strong-arm squads – Perón was voted into office with 56 percent of the popular vote.

"Justicialism": His domestic policy was dubbed Justicialism, because the idea behind it was to give social justice to long-oppressed workers. (The Peronists of today are known as Justicialists and their movement as the Justicialist Party.) The opponents of

Left and **above**, thousands of supporters show their loyalty to the Peróns, appearing on the balcony of the Casa Rosada.

prices and foreign trade and carried out an ambitious nationalization program, bringing the formerly British-owned railways under state control and taking over other foreign interests in public utilities and other areas of industry.

When it came to foreign relations, Perón may very well have been the inventor of a political philosophy which has become known in the world today as the "non-aligned" stance – and of which, despite decades of political upheaval and change, Argentina is still a major exponent. Perón, however, called it the Third Position: a neutral stance which belonged to neither the much-feared communism of the time, nor the incipient capitalism.

The fairytale Evita: In a purely personal sense, Perón put Argentina on the map. In the post-war days, both in Argentina and other countries, people weary of the seriousness and realism of war-time days, were looking for Cinderella-like success stories. Juan and Evita Perón became celebrities in the US and Europe. They were a kind of Latin American royalty, seen as the romantically intriguing rulers of a distant land.

Indeed, although he was an elected leader, Perón ruled with confidence in the backing

of the majority and with the iron hand of a military leader. Evita, for her part, thrived on the kind of worldwide royal social status she was gaining and put her power to work to change the lives of workers in the only way she knew how: by granting their wishes one by one like a fairy godmother.

The waiting-room of her office in what is today the palatial headquarters of the Buenos Aires city council was as big as a good-sized ballroom. (Under subsequent governments the room was actually used as a ball-room reception hall for large diplomatic gatherings.) She held audience for the public, per-

son by person, in her plush, high-ceilinged study with its tall French doors. Her waiting-room was generally thronged with people who wanted favors from Peronism or answers to their dreams of a job, a pension, or a home. And many humble workers walked away with the answer to their dreams clearly in sight.

It has been said that Evita was the real power behind Perón. This is, without a doubt, an oversimplification. But it is nonetheless obvious that Evita's charisma and her considerable control over the labor movement gave strong support to Perón's own powerful personality and authority, and increased his following within the armed forces. It was thanks fundamentally to a monumentally crowd-pleasing campaign which was carried out by Evita in 1951 that Perón was re-elected by an even wider margin than the one he had managed in 1946.

It is little wonder, then, that it came as a real blow to Perón and Justicialism when Evita died the following year of uterine cancer, at the age of 33. The shock and sorrow of millions of workers dramtically shrouded Buenos Aires. A grief-stricken Perón had Evita's body specially embalmed so that it would remain intact indefinitely (although her memory was to be perpetuated more effectively though less respectfully in the 1970s by the Tim Rice and Andrew Lloyd Webber musical *Evita*).

With Evita gone and new problems of state – worsening terms of trade, growing inflation, dwindling reserves – to occupy Perón, the General Confederation of Labor began to take wings of its own, even while remaining loyal to the leader. This once again began to spark fears, among rich landholders and other business interests which had already been stung by Perón's social and domestic economic policies, of an eventual turn toward communism. These sectors had the ear of conservative sectors of the army linked to the regime Perón deposed in 1946.

The situation came to a head with a military rebellion that began in June 1955. A naval battery in the River Plate supported by airforce fighter planes blasted and strafed the main square of the city, setting Government House on fire and tearing up the facades of government buildings nearby. Under air and naval support, a detachment of marines sought to take over Government House, but failed in the attempt.

After that attack, in which scores of people, including many innocent bystanders, were killed or injured, Perón was on his way out of government, and out of the country. In mid-September of that same year, he was forced to flee the country aboard a Paraguayan gunboat provided by his friend General Alfredo Stroessner who had just come to power in the neighboring country.

Exile and chaos: Perón went off to exile, first in Paraguay and finally in Madrid. The the name of Perón in public was forbidden. Playing or singing *La Marcha Perónista*, the Peronist anthem, was banned.

But Peronism, despite being banned from two elections in the shaky years from 1955 to 1973, remained a dominant factor in Argentine politics – it was largely responsible for the fact that not a single military or civilian government in those 18 years managed to consolidate the popular power necessary to rule effectively.

Throughout this period of chaos and confusion in which generals played musical chairs with political power, the country's youth were becoming ever more alienated

Argentine leader would spend the next 18 years watering the roses in his sumptuous Spanish villa, holding interviews and working on his political writings. He would find another wife – in 1961 he married cabaret dancer María Estela Martínez (better known by her stage name, "Isabelita") whom he met in Panama in 1956. But he was also planning his return to Argentina.

Back in Buenos Aires, official anti-Peronism became a psychosis. Writing or saying

Left, Evita. **Above**, Perón's widow, Isabel, with advisors during her brief term as *La Presidenta*.

and frustrated. Argentina thus became the perfect breeding ground for guerrilla movements and political terrorism. In the face of growing civil strife and open opposition to military rule, the way was paved for new democratic elections.

And this time they were indeed democratic, since they did not forbid the participation of any party, not even the Peronist one. More than 20 parties, from the extreme right to the extreme left, ran in the 1973 elections, but the main positions were Radicalism and Peronism.

The intervening years had split Peronism

to such an extent that one could find philosophies in Peronist ranks from the most staunch rightists to the most radicalized leftists: Practically the only thing these Peronists had in common was Perón.

While the party was not banned from the polls, Perón himself was. But it was made clear in the Justicialist campaign that Perón was on his way back to power in Argentina. It was left-wing Peronist Héctor Cámpora who was running for president, but the campaign slogan affirmed that a vote for Cámpora was a vote for Perón.

Cámpora won the election with 48.7 percent of the popular vote. Lanusse handed the

field as a gun battle broke out between opposing factions in which over 100 people were killed or wounded.

The following month, Cámpora resigned after just 49 days in office. He was provisionally replaced by Lower House congressional chairman Raúl Lastiri, who called extraordinary elections for September to legitimize the return of Perón. In those polls Perón captured 7.4 million of the 12 million votes cast and by October 15, 1973, he was starting his third presidency, with "Isabelita" as his vice-president.

By now, the once seemingly indestructible Perón was 78 and on his last legs. His doctor

presidency over to him on May 25 – a national holiday marking the start of Argentina's 1810 revolution against Spanish rule. On June 20, 1973 (Flag Day), less than a month after Cámpora's inauguration, Perón returned to Argentina, 18 years after his hasty departure.

But his triumphant return was marred by the deep split between left and right-wing Peronists who turned out to meet him at the Ezeiza International airport. Push led to shove in the crowd of leftists and rightists who awaited their leader and Perón's plane, in the end, had to be re-routed to another landing

had warned him that the pressures of the presidency and the humid, bone-chilling winters of Buenos Aires could kill him. The doctor was proved correct less than a year later, when Perón died of pneumonia in the rainy Buenos Aires winter month of July.

Mourning workers ground the nation to a complete halt, and hundreds of thousands of tearful Argentines queued in the cold and rain in order to file past the coffin in the rotunda of Congress where the President's body lay in state.

A shaken, and basically politically inept, Isabelita Perón assumed the presidency of a country as violence broke out between the right and left factions.

As the violence increased, Isabelita's feeble grip on government began to slip to an ever greater degree. In the end, she had even lost the backing of Perón's own CGT labor movement. In 1975, a strained and nervous Isabel Perón was sent out of the country for a rest and was temporarily replaced by Senate President Italo Luder, who signed a decree declaring a state of siege and ordering the armed forces to annihilate armed left-wing subversions.

But this was not enough to save the Peronist government. Battered by general strikes, nearly 800 percent annual inflation, a paralyzed economy and increasing civil strife, the government was totally discredited and removed from office in a bloodless military coup on March 24, 1976.

Dark days: The revolt itself was bloodless, but what followed was the darkest period in Argentine history, known as "the dirty war." Armed with the order of the deposed Peronist government to "annihilate subversion," the new military regime set about doing just that. Once real armed leftist subversion had been crushed, however, the regime began to use the repressive machinery it had set up to eliminate any resistance to military rule.

In the period from the mid to late 1970s, at least 8,900 people "disappeared;" a large proportion of them in and around Buenos Aires. Hundreds more languished at clandestine detention centers or in regular jails, held under the state of siege decree.

But the National Reorganization Process, as the regime became known, tempered its fearsome policy of "national security" with an ambitious program of economic recovery that promoted foreign investment and offered encouragement for private enterprise.

This careful balance between harsh authoritarian rule and liberal economics was kept under the political leadership of General Jorge Rafael Videla and Economy Minister José Martínez de Hoz in the first three years of the regime. But when Videla was

Left, silhouettes of the "disappeared" victims of the dirty war. Right, jubilant supporter of Raúl Alfonsín cheers his election in 1983.

replaced, as planned, after this first period, by Army Commander Roberto Viola and his own economic team, the balance which had saved the regime from a storm of condemnation went haywire.

Projects produced by Videla's team fell apart, inflation began to reheat and the value of Argentine currency began to crumble. Unwell and politically unprepared, Viola lost the confidence of his peers, and was replaced by General Leopoldo Galtieri.

But it was too late for Galtieri to rescue the National Reorganization Process. The bottom had fallen out of the economy, industry was stalled, projects for which enormous

international loans had been granted were paralyzed and creditors began wondering about Argentina's ability to pay back the loans. Inflation was checked by severe austerity measures which in turn sent the unemployment figures soaring.

Return of democracy: To stem the tide of protest against him, Galtieri sought an issue on which he could base a consensus on which to continue to rule. And he found one: the islands known to Argentines as the Malvinas and to the British as the Falklands, which lay just a few hundred miles off the southern coast of Argentina.

On April 2, 1982, the country awoke to the news that the nation's armed forces had reclaimed the islands in a military operation in which not a single British subject had been killed or injured. By noon, Plaza de Mayo was brimming with tens of thousands of wellwishers, waving flags and carrying signs reading, "The Malvinas are Argentine." It would have been difficult to guess that just the week before, in this same square, anti-government rioters had been shouting insults at Galtieri and battling with the police.

But Galtieri's glory was short-lived. He had misjudged the resolution of British prime minister Margaret Thatcher, and the subse-

political declaration, thus making way for the democratic elections in which Raúl Alfonsín came to office.

Human rights trials: The strides taken by the Alfonsín administration toward the stabilization and democratization of Argentina were impressive. For a start, for the first time in Argentine history former military rulers were brought to trial. The trials of nine former junta members were based on evidence collected by the National Commission on Missing People (CONADEP) which Alfonsín formed immediately on taking office. Five former military rulers were sentenced to terms ranging from 12 years to life for their

quent war between Argentina and Britain lasted only 10 weeks and ended in a humiliating defeat for Argentina and the loss of thousands of lives, British and Argentine. The announcement of the surrender brought another night of anti-government street violence in which rioters fought police in an unsuccessful attempt to break down the doors of government house in the apparent hope of laying hands on Galtieri.

Utterly discredited, Galtieri was forced to resign and was replaced by General Reynaldo Bignone, backed by a military junta which promised and delivered an immediate

parts in crimes against humanity from the mid to late 1970s.

While the human rights trials brought international recognition to Alfonsín's government, locking the generals away did not end conflicts between the military and civilians. Humiliated and discredited, the armed forces continued to pressure Alfonsín to put a stop to further prosecutions. In April 1987, a barracks revolt led by Colonel Aldo Rico threatened to put an end to Argentina's fledgling democracy. Hundreds of thousands of Argentines poured into the Plaza de Mayo in a dramatic show of solidarity with their elected leaders. The military backed down, but not, it was later learned, without concessions. Alfonsín agreed to halt all further prosecution under a "due obedience" law – which excused many officers who'd committed atrocities during the regime, under the argument that they were only following their superiors' orders.

Added to Alfonsín's authority problems with the military was the shambles of the economy he'd inherited from them, which included a $40 billion foreign debt. Attempts to cut the government's deficit spending were met with sharp resistance in Congress, and public mutiny: there were 13 general

country after the elections, with inflation out of control at 200 percent a month, and with food riots intensifying, Alfonsín judged it best to resign and hand over the presidential sash to Menem several months before his term was technically over.

Recognized around Argentina for his giant, grey-streaked sideburns, Menem was a "man of the people" who had worked as a truck driver and laborer before entering the union movement and becoming Governor of rural La Rioja province. Before his push for the presidency, he could be found yelling his support for soccer teams in Buenos Aires, driving a rally car in the provinces, or at

strikes during his five-year administration. In abundant Argentina, where even the humblest laborer was used to having steak for lunch, food prices skyrocketed. In consequence riots broke out and grocery stores were sacked as inflation climbed to over 100 percent a month.

The 1989 presidential elections saw the defeat of Alfonsín's Radical party, and a new era of Peronism ushered in under Carlos Saul Menem. Faced with a nearly ungovernable

Left, Radical party members championed human rights. **Above**, Menem was first elected in 1989.

nightclubs with local TV stars. During his campaign he promised to engineer a return to the palmy days of General Perón. Once he took office, however, he shocked his followers by stocking his cabinet with corporate executives and arranging to sell off the huge state-run companies originally nationalized by Perón. Menem's economic medicine has met with some successes and many setbacks, but it reflects a growing trend among developing nations – a turning away from economic dependence on the state and an embracing of free enterprise.

Unarguably, drastic measures were needed.

Even so, Menem's policies proved a surprise both to his critics and to his supporters: announcing that "the fiesta is over," he abandoned one Peronist sacred vow after another to begin the severest period of austerity that Argentina has seen.

Bloated, state-owned companies like the national airline, Aerolineas Argentinas, and the telephone company ENTEL were privatized and massive layoffs ordered. Government subsidies and controls over the economy were sacrificed on the altar of the free market. Despite protests by Menem's former Peronist supporters, the reforms went through, cementing a new friendly relationship with the United States – with Menem going so far as to offer Argentine troops to serve in the Gulf War of 1991. The following year he offered to take in East European immigrants, settling them in remote areas such as the Patagonian pampas.

In relations with the military, Menem shocked human rights activists by pardoning the former junta leaders who had been convicted for their "dirty war" crimes, undoing what many had seen as the greatest achievement of the Alfonsín years. Choosing a date between Christmas and New Year to minimize international attention, Menem ignored nearly a million demonstrators in Buenos Aires to sign the generals' release.

Looking to the future: After a long period of crisis, Menem's policies brought inflation to a virtual halt. In 1992, the austral was replaced by yet another new currency called the peso, pegged to the US dollar. This "Convertibility Plan" stabilized the economy, and free-spending upper middle-class Argentines began reappearing in the hotels of Miami and the shops of New York.

But all was not as rosy as the government would like to pretend. The one peso to one dollar exchange rate skyrocketed the cost of living, making Argentina one of the most expensive countries in Latin America. And as a result, Argentine products began to carry high price tags, making a rather large dent in manufacturing and export industries. In 1995, the unemployment rate rose to 20–25 percent, an all time record for the country.

In terms of solutions, the government is considering a second round of privatizations, including banks and other large businesses in the provinces. Menem has also requested special executive powers to carry out extensive reforms regarding public administration, greatly tightening the belt around the domestic budget. Also in the works is a plan to recuperate the investment and capital that fled the country in 1995 due to the "tequila effect", which shook Latin America after the Mexican peso crisis.

There are still many doubts about Argentina's future. Although Menem's financial rescue-job was widely praised around the world, many economists believe there is still a long way to go before the country's economy will be out of trouble. What's more, Menem's administration has been marked by corruption scandals. He himself tends to rule by decree, illustrated by his successful 1994 campaign to change a constitutional article limiting the president to one six-year term. After his overwhelming victory in 1994, he will hold office until 1999, and there is already talk of reforming the constitution once again, allowing him yet a third term in power.

Social problems have scarcely lessened either. Women in Argentina are still largely excluded from public life, and the imbalances remain not only between Buenos Aires and "the interior" but also between the glittering and international wealth of the capital's northern suburbs and the misery of the nearby urban slums.

Yet despite the chaos, civilian rule has become firmly established in Argentina. In 1995, for the first time since democracy was reinstituted, the military officially recognized the illegal repression, torture and murder that took place during the dirty war. While the Argentines continue to criticize the government and one another with astonishing vigor, they remain for the present united on one point: democracy, for all its shortcomings, is preferable to the straitjacket of military rule. As long as both major parties remain deeply involved in this process of change, most observers feel that this is a propitious time for the building of a long-lasting and stable democratic system.

Right, a pro-democracy rally of the 1980s.

FAMOUS QUOTES ABOUT BUENOS AIRES

"They set up a few tremulous ranches along the coast and fell asleep homesick."
—Jorge Luis Borges, describing the 16th-century founding of Buenos Aires in his poem *Fundación mitíca de Buenos Aires.*

"A cigar factory perfumed the desert like a rose. The afternoon sank into yesterdays, the men shared an illustrious past. Only one thing was missing: the sidewalk across the street."
—Jorge Luis Borges

"My beloved Buenos Aires
when I see you next
there will be no more pain or forgotten times.
The lamp on the street where I was born, was the sentinel
of my promises of love, under the still light I saw her,
my shining darling, like the sun.
Destiny desires that I see you again, port city,
the only one for me."
— *Mi Buenos Aires Querido*, tango written by Alfredo Le Pera and made famous by Carlos Gardel.

"The city of Buenos Aires is large and I should think one of the most regular in the world."
—Charles Darwin, recording his impression of Buenos Aires in the 1830s.

"A vast prison, a plethoric body which suffocates you and stops you from walking, extending your arms or breathing, because if you do, the pavement disappears from under your feet and taking in a breath, you might swallow a motorcar."
—Domingo F. Sarmiento, describing the narrow streets of Buenos Aires which existed before the broad elegant Avenida de Mayo was built.

"Everyone seems to have money, and to like spending it, and to like letting everybody else know that it is being spent."
—James Bryce (North American traveler) describing the high society he found when he visited the city in the early 20th century.

"Juan's bar, talking in cafés...the smells...the neighborhoods, Corrientes by night, Corrientes by day, the cinemas, pizza, salami, beef, mate, the girls on Santa Fé, the girls on Florida, the girls, the magazines I like, the radio programs I like, the parts of town I like, the politics, the struggles, the demonstrations, the artists, the football, the horseraces...there are so many things I'm going to have to take with me!"
—Cartoon character "Loco Chavez" thinking of everything in Buenos Aires he will miss if he goes abroad.

"In our country, forgetfulness runs quicker than history, in a way that one can publish an episode from ten years ago, perfectly secure in not upsetting the living nor cloud the memory of the dead."
—Adolfo Bioy Casares, contemporary writer, in a speech from La Obra (*"The Play"*)

DESCRIPTIONS OF ARGENTINA: 1800–1920

Today's traveler to Argentina follows in the wake of a tremendously diverse group of characters which has probed and prodded the country for its secrets, climbed every mountain, witnessed the major events in its history and invariably compared the customs and mores of her people, so similar yet so different from themselves.

While Magellan and Darwin are the most familiar names, a surprising number of others have felt compelled to publish their travel diaries. Perhaps these visitors were encouraged to share their experiences because many in Europe and the United States were curious to know what it was really like in the distant reaches of Patagonia and Tierra del Fuego and among the wild gauchos of the windy pampas.

The reader of travel literature, especially of the 18th- and 19th-century variety, discovers many of the wonders of Argentina that no longer exist. These fabulous tales do need to be approached somewhat cautiously because many of the western travelers did not speak the language nor necessarily understand the events unfolding before them. Nonetheless, these accounts do provide the color and flavor that is sometimes missing from published scientific diaries. Additionally, their perspectives are noteworthy in providing a more complete picture of the Argentines and their country.

As one might expect, the early traveler faced a broad spectrum of perils that, in the case of Argentina, included robbery, Indian attacks, diseases such as yellow fever and syphilis, lack of food and shelter, and painful modes of transportation.

The dangers, though, seemed to be far outweighed by the joys the voyager experienced. Unexpected hospitality in the most out of the way places, chance encounters along the road, the sight of Tehuelche natives and gauchos displaying their equestrian skills, and the exhilaration of visiting places few had seen before were some of the high points the foreigner might come across.

The city of good airs: The 19th-century traveler would often commence his or her itinerary in Buenos Aires. Charles Darwin, in 1833, described the city as "large and I should think one of the most regular in the world. Every street is at right angles to the one it crosses, and the parallel ones being equidistant, the houses are collected into solid squares of equal dimensions, which are called quadras."

Writing 10 years after Darwin, Colonel J. Anthony King commented that, "The market place of Buenos Ayres is made the center of all public rejoicings, public executions, and popular gatherings. It is in the market place that Rosas [the 19th-century dictator] hung up the bodies of many of his victims, sometimes decorating them in mockery, with ribbons of the Unitarian colour (blue), and even attaching to the corpses labels, on which were inscribed the revolting words, 'Beef with the hide.'"

J.P. and W.P. Robertson wrote a series of letters from South America which they published in 1843. What first impressed them were the methods of transportation in the city. "Nothing strikes one more on a first arrival in Buenos Aires than the carts and carters. The former are vehicles with large wooden axles, and most enormous wheels, so high that the spokes are about eight feet [2 meters] in diameter, towering above both horses and driver; he rides one of these animals… The first sight you have of these clumsy vehicles is on your landing. They drive off like so many bathing-machines to your hotel, a dozen carters, just like a dozen porters here, struggling in rude contention for the preference in carrying ashore passengers and their luggage."

By the turn of the century, Buenos Aires had become the noisiest and brashest city in Latin America, as wealth poured into the country and chilled beef was exported to Europe.

Thomas Turner, who lived in Argentina from 1885 to 1890, was greatly amused by some of his compatriots who brought to the capital their preconceptions, expecting to find a wild and uncivilized place. They arrived "so thoroughly imbued with these silly notions that the outfits they have brought with them would have been better suited to

Left, morning tea in an upper-class salon.

the necessities of the Australian bush or the Canadian backwoods than to the requirements of the life they were likely to experience in Argentina. Where they should have brought dress suits and dancing shoes, they came provided with a whole defensive arsenal and a supply of coarse apparel."

G.L. Morrill, an American minister who wrote about Buenos Aires in his *To Hell and Back: My Trip to South America* (1914), had this to say about the cosmopolitan nature of the Argentine capital: "An afternoon walk shows the city very much like Paris in its architecture, fashionable stores, cafés and sidewalks filled with little tables where males and females flirt and gossip. There are news-

best travelogues on Latin America, was well aware of and prepared for the violence he knew he would face.

Head wrote that, "In crossing the pampas it is absolutely necessary to be armed, as there are many robbers or saltadors, particularly in the desolate province of Santa Fe. The object of these people is of course money, and I therefore always rode so badly dressed, and so well armed that although I once passed through them with no one but a child as a postilion, they thought it not worth their while to attack me. I always carried two brace of detonating pistols in a belt, and a short detonating double-barreled gun in my hand. I made it a rule never to be an instant

paper kiosks and flower girls selling violets on the corners. The side streets are crowded with cars and carts and the main avenues with taxis which rest in the center or rush up and down either side. At nights it is a big white way with electric lights blazing a trail to the light-hearted cafés and theatres."

Perils: Dangers on the road were certainly plentiful for both traveler and native alike. Francis Bond Head, an English mining engineer who spent two tempestuous but enjoyable years, 1825–26, in the Argentine outback, and whose book *Rough Notes Taken During Some Rapid Journeys Across the Pampas and Among the Andes* is one of the

without my arms, and to cock both barrels of my gun whenever I met any gauchos."

Darwin, the mild-mannered scientist, concurred with Head when he wrote that, "A traveler has no protection besides his firearms and the constant habit of carrying them, is the main check to a more frequent occurrence of robbery."

Head, aptly named "Galloping Head," describes the dangers Indians posed. "A person riding can use no precaution, but must just run the gauntlet, and take his chance, which, if calculated, is a good one. If he fall in with them, he may be tortured and killed, but it is very improbable that he should happen to find them on the road; however, they are so cunning, and ride so quick, and the country is so uninhabited, that it is impossible to gain any information."

Along with the violence one might have encountered in the wild-west style atmosphere, there were natural hazards to be overcome along the way. Darwin soon experienced the trials of the terrain. "Changing horses for the last time, we again began wading through the mud. My animal fell, and I was well soused in black mire – a very disagreeable accident, when one does not possess a change of clothes."

Darwin also noted that the wild animals of the pampas could prove problematic. "It is

with in Buenos Aires in 1918. "Before leaving for Buenos Aires everybody in New York told me that the Plaza Hotel was the only hotel in Buenos Aires, and that of course I would make it my headquarters during my sojourn there. But my information had been given me by men, and neither they nor I expected to find that the Plaza did not take women unaccompanied by their husbands or supposed husbands. Not even sisters accompanied by their brothers, or wives whose husbands have to travel, or widows, are made welcome. Much less respectable maiden ladies!"

Tehuelche and Puelche: The native Americans were of constant interest to the traveler

very difficult to drive animals across the plains; for if in the night a puma, or even a fox, approaches, nothing can prevent the horses dispersing in every direction; and a storm will have the same effect. A short time since, an officer left Buenos Aires with five hundred horses, and when he arrived at the army he had under twenty."

A woman traveling alone faced another sort of problem. The American Katherine S. Drier described what she had to contend

Left, rampant Spaniards on the hunt in Puerto Deseado, 1586. **Above**, boleadora-wielding pampean Indians.

of the 1800s, although by the 1870s they were becoming rarer and rarer as the campaigns to conclude the "Indian problem" reached their peak. One intrepid individual, the Jesuit Thomas Falkner, spent almost 20 years living among the Puelche and Tehuelche tribes of southern Argentina, from the 1730s until the religious order was expelled from the country. His account, *A Description of Patagonia*, was used as a guide by Darwin a century later.

Meeting an Indian could be a highpoint of a journey, as Lady Florence Dixie related in her *Across Patagonia* (1881). "We had not gone far when we saw a rider coming slowly towards us, and in a few minutes we found ourselves in the presence of a real Patagonia Indian. We reined in our horses when he got close to us, to have a good look at him, and he doing the same, for a few minutes we stared at him to our hearts' content, receiving in return as minute and careful a scrutiny from him."

Of the Indians themselves, many travelers remarked on their positive characteristics, especially of the doomed Tehuelche. Julius Beerbohm, who wrote *Wanderings in Patagonia or Life Among the Ostrich-Hunters* (1879), had much to say about the original inhabitants of Argentina.

"The Tehuelches are on the whole rather was to be able to spend time with the native South American. "His profession is war, his food simple, and his body is in that state of health and vigor that he can rise naked from the plain on which he has slept, and proudly look upon his image which the white frost has marked out upon the grass without inconvenience. What can we 'men in buckran' say to this?"

Country life: The gauchos (Argentine cowboys) were often perceived as being as wild as the Indians, and just as interesting. Additionally, the gauchos and others living in the countryside were noted for their hospitality. Colonel King writes that, "whether in health or sickness, the traveler is always welcome

good-looking than otherwise, and the usual expression of their faces is bright and friendly. Their foreheads are rather low but not receding, their noses aquiline, their mouths large and coarse, but their teeth are extremely regular and dazzlingly white… in general intelligence, gentleness of temper, chastity of conduct, and conscientious behavior in their social and domestic relations, they are immeasurably superior not only to the other South American indigenous tribes, but also, all their disadvantages being taken into consideration, to the general run of civilized white men."

One of Galloping Head's fondest wishes to their houses and boards, and they would as soon as think of charging for a cup of water, as for a meal of victual or a night's lodging."

Darwin, too, was greatly struck by their manners. "The gauchos, or countrymen, are very superior to those who reside in the towns. The gaucho is invariably most obliging, polite, and hospitable. I did not meet with even one instance of rudeness or inhospitality." And once, when Darwin inquired whether there was enough food for him to have a meal, he was told, "We have meat for the dogs in our country, and therefore do not grudge it to a Christian."

But traveling in the countryside was generally not a very comfortable affair. Galloping Head presents a none too appealing description of his night's accommodations. "We arrived an hour after sunset – fortified post – scrambling in the dark for the kitchen – cook unwilling – correo (the courier) gave us his dinner – huts of wild-looking people – three women and girls almost naked ('They be so wild as the donkey,' said one of the Cornish party, smiling; he then very gravely added, 'and there be one thing, sir, that I do observe, which is, that the farther we do go, the wilder things do get!') – our hut – old man immovable – Maria or Mariquita's figure – little mongrel boy – three or four other persons. Roof supported in the center by

and cut open two puppies and bind them on each side of a broken limb. Little hairless dogs are in great request to sleep at the feet of invalids."

Many travelers were impressed by the skills the gauchos demonstrated as they worked their horses, threw *bolas* to fell cassowaries – the South American ostrich – or lassoed cattle. Darwin mentioned a sight to which he was witness. "In the course of the day I was amused by the dexterity with which a gaucho forced a restive horse to swim a river. He stripped off his clothes, and jumping on its back rode into the river till it was out of its depth; then slipping off over the crupper, he caught hold of the tail, and as

crooked poles – holes in roof and walls – walls of mud, cracked and rent… Floor, the earth – eight hungry peons, by moonlight standing with their knives in their hands over a sheep they were going to kill, and looking on their prey like relentless tigers."

In the country, far from doctors and hospitals, the people often relied on an assortment of folk medicine. Darwin was appalled at the remedies and only felt able to mention the following: "One of the least nasty is to kill

Left, Indian settlement by the Sierra de la Ventana. **Above**, Darwin's research vessel, the *HMS Beagle*.

often as the horse turned around, the man frightened it back by splashing water in its face. As soon as the horse touched bottom on the other side, the man pulled himself on, and was firmly seated, bridle in hand, before the horse gained the bank. A naked man on a naked horse is a fine spectacle; I had no idea how well the two animals suited each other. The tail of a horse is a very useful appendage."

Earth and sky: The size of the country and the rough paths made the traveler's trip a very long one, indeed. E.E. Vidal, an early 19th-century traveler, quotes the unnamed author of *Letters from Paraguay,* who describes his trip from Buenos Aires to Mendoza, at the foot of the Andes, as taking 22 days in a large cart drawn by oxen. "We set off every afternoon about two, and sometimes three hours before sunset, and did not halt till about an hour after sunrise."

Having a sufficient supply of water was one of the obstacles the writer faced in his journey. "We were obliged to halt in a spot, where even the grass seemed to have been burned to the very roots, and nothing was presented to the eye but barrenness and desolation...We had but one small jar of water left, our thirst seemed to increase every moment."

Nature intervened as a thunderstorm struck the camp. "'Look at the oxen; they smell water.' We all eagerly turned to the poor panting animals, and saw them stretch their heads to the west, and snuff the air, as if they would be certain of obtaining drink could they but raise themselves into the atmosphere. At that moment not a cloud was to be seen, nor a breath of air felt; but in a few minutes the cattle began to move about as if mad, or possessed by some invisible spirit, snuffing the air with most violent eagerness, and gathering closer and closer to each other; and before we could form any rational conjecture as to what could occasion their simultaneous motion, the most tremendous storm of thunder, lightning, and rain I ever witnessed in my life came on. The rain fell in perpendicular streams, as if all the fountains of heaven had suddenly broken loose."

Many travelers commented on the seemingly endless flat pampas. W.J. Holland, an American scientist on an expedition to Argentina in 1912, described the scene from his train compartment. "I have crossed the prairies of Minnesota and the Dakotas, of Kansas and Nebraska, of Manitoba and Alberta; I have traveled over the steppes of Russia; but in none of them have I seen such absolutely level lands as those which lie between Rosario and Irigoyen. The horizon is that of the ocean; an upturned clod attracts attention; a hut looks like a house; a tree looms up like a hill."

Food and politics: The customs of the Argentines, whether of city folk, gauchos, or Indians, have always been cause for comment. Thomas Turner, describing one well-known and wealthy family at supper in the 1880s had this to say: "Of the domestic habits of the Argentines, their manners at table, *en famille*, it is impossible to give an attractive description. Their manners at table are ultra-Bohemian. They read the papers, shout vehemently at each other, sprawl their limbs under and over the table, half swallow their knives, spit with true Yankee freedom on the carpeted floor, gesticulate and bend across the table in the heat of argument, smoke cigarettes between the courses, and even while a course of which some of them do not partake is serving – a soothing habit which stimulates expectoration and provokes discussion – use the same knife and fork for every course – fish, entree, or joint, in a word, the studied deportment of the street is, in the house, exchanged for the coarse manners of the tap-room."

Turner was also shocked at the way politics dominated discussions, something that still is prevalent. "Although forbidden subjects are discussed by both sexes with zest and freedom, the staple topic of conversation is politics. Everybody talks politics... Even children talk politics, and discuss the merits of this, that or other statesmen with parrot-like freedom of opinion and soundness of judgment."

Many of the travelers' accounts are tinged with racism and the deep-seated assumption that the writers' own cultures were nearly always superior to that of the Argentines. Comments abound such as, "Most of the corruption which exists in public life is due to the participation of foreigners therein; Italians chiefly," or "the Argentine is not old enough yet to have developed the sense of humor," or, "I was becoming accustomed to the polite airs of this town that prints literature mad with Yankeephobia to snarl and bite all over SA against North America whose Monroe Doctrine, money, mentality and morality have been Argentina's help in the past and is her only hope in the future." These attitudes can be found in many first-hand descriptions of Argentina.

At the same time, the wanderers and explorers have passed on the country's lore, which might otherwise have been lost to us in the passing years. Their tales are sometimes unintentionally amusing to today's reader but they are almost always fascinating and illuminating.

Right, a 19th-century gentleman farmer.

Once you've met them, they will stand out in any crowd – their Italian-accented Spanish, their flair for style, their striking intensity. These are *los porteños*, the inhabitants of Buenos Aires, so-named for their proximity to the port on the Rio de la Plata. Any description of them is invariably colored with ambiguous adjectives: sophisticated, self-important, skeptical, stylish, verbose, clever, and (always) melancholic.

A hardware storekeeper in downtown Buenos Aires once tried conveying to me how idiosyncratic his fellow *porteños* really were. "The entire world's peoples," he explained, "can be divided into four areas: East, West, Japan, and Argentina." Surely he meant Buenos Aires in that last category, since it is the *porteños*, not the 20-odd million Argentines who do not live in this city, who have earned such peculiar renown.

Just who is *el porteño*? A popular joke has it that he is a Spaniard who talks like an Italian, dresses like a Frenchman, and thinks he is British. Indeed, it often seems that in this southernmost country of the world, Europe is more a state of mind for the *porteño* than a place on the map. "Buenos Aires," writes Argentine Eduardo Crawley, "playacts at being a city that really belongs in the northern hemisphere, and, although it somehow drifted down to the South Atlantic, it is still attached to the parental body by an imaginary umbilical cord."

Such other-worldly attitudes are by no means a recent fad. In his 19th-century tome exalting the "civilization" of Buenos Aires versus the "barbarism" of the backlands, the educator and former Argentine President, Domingo Sarmiento, wrote that Europeans visiting Buenos Aires fancied themselves to be in the salons of Paris: "Nothing was wanting; not even the insolence of the Parisian elegant, which was well imitated by the same class of young men in Buenos Aires."

Style is everything: Putting on airs seems to suit *porteños*. In a city where theater thrives (they say you can go to the theater every night for a month and never see the same performance twice) and where the lurid tango is still danced punctiliously, if not universally, illusions become very much a part of reality. What meets the eye is crucial: *porteños* relish seeing and being seen. They choose carefully what they wear and when they wear it. They carry themselves like dancers, some erectly, others with proud weariness. In vain Buenos Aires, one must always be prepared for the scrutiny of others' eyes and reflecting surfaces.

This obsession with appearances is perhaps part of the *porteños'* unrelenting quest for respectability. Intellectual achievement is highly esteemed and flouted. It is a rare well-educated *porteño* who does not remind others of his or her academic background with a title reflecting his degrees. Lawyers and PhDs (and countless others with more questionable credentials) are "Doctor," college graduates are *Licenciado*, and engineers and architects wear their professions like badges before their names.

Nothing establishes more immediately one's public respectability than the automobile. Possession of this status symbol earns the *porteño* respect for it consecrates him as a fully-fledged member of the middle class, the station in society that epitomizes the notion of respectability.

If the *porteño* also owns some land, so much the better. In this elegant cow town flanked by slaughterhouses, nobody gets more respect than someone whose wealth is derived from the land. But getting dirt under the fingernails is not the landed gentry's method. They hire others to perform that kind of work so they may devote themselves more fully to the pleasures of the great city.

Residents regard Buenos Aires with a kind of ingrained reverence, as if living there were a privilege akin to belonging to an exclusive social club. That privilege is not

Preceding pages: discussing the price of beef at the traditional August Cattle Show; a new generation of middle-class city-dweller. Left, tango singer attracts crowds in San Telmo.

without its strictures. Up until the government returned to civilian rule in 1983, men who wore shorts on the streets were arrested for indecency. Eating in the parks is still frowned upon. You are unlikely to find a *porteño* visibly drunk in public. Nor will you see litter accumulate for long on the streets.

This sense of order fits snugly with the ritualistic ways of the *porteños*. Buenos Aires is a city that moves in rhythms. More so, perhaps, than other cities. *Porteños* are a homogeneous group with defined tastes, and few venture to stray from the established norms. They know what they like and they like what they know.

weekends, as if their biological clocks were all running several hours slow.

This fascination with the city's night and its indoor diversions parallels the *porteños'* fascination with their own dark sides and secrets. Perhaps no other city in the world has such a brooding, introspective populace. For all the glories of life in "the pearl of the River Plate," *porteños* are afflicted with a chronic sense of malaise. They spend a great deal of time on the analyst's couch; there are three times more psychiatrists and psychologists per capita in Buenos Aires than there are in New York State. Though loath to admit it, *porteños* take a certain relish in

Look on the dark side of life: What *porteños* seem to like most is the night. The *porteño* is like a cat: he prefers to sleep when the sun shines and prowl when darkness wraps the city. The hour has then arrived for the seduction of the bright lights and box offices of Lavalle and Corrientes. *Una salida,* or an evening out, can begin with either food or entertainment, provided it starts late and ends at dawn. *Porteños* sometimes brace themselves for such carousing with a late afternoon nap, but more often they defy sleep with sheer hedonistic willpower. You will find them thronging the streets at 3am on

life's complications. It's that much more grist for the verbal mills that grind away over coffee or a bottle of wine. While it is debatable whether the human condition really is more poignant in Buenos Aires than elsewhere, *porteños'* capacity for talking about the sorry hand that life has dealt them is unrivalled.

You can see the *porteño* passion for talking most vividly in the street debates that form spontaneously on pedestrian malls like Florida and Lavalle. Red-faced, rapidly gesticulating interlocutors argue over who's responsible for the mess they're in, but the exchanges rarely come to blows. Talking, even when it sounds more like shouting, is considered dignified. Street fighting is regarded as behavior befitting only barbaric louts (unless, of course, a woman's honor is being defended).

Three topics dominate *porteño* conversation: money, games and sex. *"La guita,"* which means money in the local argot, never seems to stretch as far as do *porteños'* consumer appetites, particularly during inflation's frequent gusts into the triple-digit range. There's a sense that money eludes any personal control. Nearly everyone dreams of winning one of the many local and national lotteries. Many of these games of chance are

sion for a graphic illustration of the selling power of sex. Or listen to passers-by. Attractive women are frequent targets of declarations of love (some exquisitely poetic, others vulgar) from passing men. Historian James Scobie describes the gaucho ideal of virility as finding its *porteño* expression in the strutting, precise steps of the tango, a perfect showcase for the macho's "aggressive parade of masculinity."

Most *porteños* these days are sexually active before finishing high school, although less conspicuously so than in northern latitudes. Private accomodations are not always available for love affairs, so *porteños* fre-

connected to sports, and they fuel already abundant discussions about soccer clubs and *"los burros,"* as *porteños* affectionately call the horse races.

Sex and family: What stirs *porteños'* passions even more deeply than soccer and money is the topic that even when not on their tongues is still usually on their minds: sex. The manifestations of this preoccupation are ubiquitous. Watch the ads on television.

Left, the sidewalk cafés around Recoleta Cemetery attract the elite. Above, all dressed up for a Sunday in the park.

quently resort to the city's officially regulated trysting establishments. These *albergues transitorios*, or temporary hostels, are as dignified as a *porteño's* public demeanor; from the outside, they look like funeral parlors. Known informally as *"telos,"* they do a brisk business during lunch hours and on weekends.

Despite liberal pre-marital sexual attitudes, the family remains a sacrosanct institution among *porteños*. Families tend to be small and cohesive, often with three generations under the same roof. Children are expected to live at home until marriage. High costs for

THE JEWISH COMMUNITY

L atin America's largest concentration of Jews, by a significant margin, is to be found in Buenos Aires. After all, as Argentina's best-loved writer Jorge Luis Borges said, "What exists here is a ludicrous form of nationalism. Our entire country is imported. Everyone here is really from somewhere else."

Most estimates put the size of the city's Jewish population at about 250,000, making this the world's fourth largest Jewish collective as well as Argentina's third largest ethnic group, after Spaniards and Italians.

For historical reasons Jews in Buenos Aires are

commonly referred to as "los rusos" (the Russians). This rather cavalier label is a hangover from the times of the first massive Jewish immigration to Argentina a century ago, when Jews fleeing the pogroms of czarist Russia first arrived in great numbers. They came as part of an ambitious colonization scheme which was financed by a German philanthropic Jew, Baron Maurice Hirsch. In all, about 70,000 Jews settled primarily in agricultural colonies, mostly to the north of Buenos Aires in the province of Entre Rios.

They constituted the first Jewish peasantry in the southern hemisphere, and by most accounts they mixed well with the gauchos who inhabited the region. "We learned the language of the gauchos," recalls Maximo Yagupsky, one of the first Jews born in the colonies. "And then some of the gauchos learned our Yiddish, and even some of our songs and cooking."

Like most of the "Jewish gauchos," Yagupsky ended up in Buenos Aires. "If your aspiration is to advance, you go to the city – there you have civilization and culture," says Yagupsky. By the 1920s, almost all the immigrant Jews had moved away from the countryside and settled in Buenos Aires, where they established themselves with jobs as street peddlers, craftsmen, and shopkeepers, forming a large, active community, largely keeping to two neighborhoods crossed by Avenida Corrientes.

Today, as in many parts of the world, the Jews of Buenos Aires have assimilated into Argentine society. But there remain three neighborhoods where a high concentration of Jews reside – in Villa Crespo, along Corrientes between Estado de Israel and Dorrego, in Belgrano, just north of Palermo, and in Once, a largely commercial area centered around Avenida Corrientes between Callao and Pueyrredón.

Once was the first Jewish "ghetto" and today is still the hub of Jewish cultural and social life. It is a garment district, with street after street lined by fabric shops that sell both wholesale and retail, although recently a multitude of other wholesale shops have opened, many run by an influx of Korean immigrants. Nevertheless, "kosher" signs appear in the display windows of some meat markets and grocery stores, and small shops known as rotiserías offer Jewish pastries, breads, and smoked fish.

The **Taam Tov** bakery on Corrientes at Ecuador is a magnet for gourmets. Similarly, if you want to sit down and enjoy a typical kosher meal, don't miss **Sucat David** on Tucumán between Pasteur and Azcuenaga, and **El Gorro Blanco** on the corner of Pueyrredón and San Luis, which is the only place in Buenos Aires with a kosher parrilla (a typical Argentine steakhouse).

On Sarmiento between Pasteur and Uriburu is **Hebraica**, a sports, cultural, and social club of the Jewish community run by an umbrella organization of all the Jewish associations in the country.

The center hosts a variety of exhibitions, conferences, theater, cinema, and other social events. There is even a Jewish theater in Once, called **Teatro IFT**, on the street Boulogne Sur Mer at number 549, with some productions in Hebrew and Yiddish.

The two most historic synagogues in Buenos Aires are referred to not by their official names, which practically no one remembers, but instead by the street they are on. In Once is the **Templo Paso**, on Paso at Corrientes, and next to the Teatro Colón is the **Templo Libertad**, on Libertad at Córdoba. Inside the Templo Libertad is a small museum centered around the history of Jewish immigration to Argentina. ∎

setting up a new abode partially account for the reluctance to cut the umbilical cord, but perhaps more decisive is the unpleasant fact that in Buenos Aires, leaving the nest "early" (that is, unmarried) still raises scandalous questions about filial loyalty.

Ninety percent of *porteños* consider themselves Roman Catholics, and the president of Argentina is still required to be a member of the church. Yet if you look inside any of the city's churches on a Sunday morning, you will find plenty of seats. Older people, and especially older women, seem to comprise the bulk. The rest of the population is Catholic when it's time to get married or buried.

come only once a month – if the streets seem less crowded than usual, it's probably been a spell since the last pay day.

It is leisure, not labor, that defines the *porteño:* where he takes his vacation, how he spends his weekends, which movies he's seen. Well-established amusements are the rule. *Porteños* crowd like lemmings to the Atlantic beaches in summer time, battle each other in ticket lines for the symphony, and patronize restaurants that invariably offer the standard fare of beef and pasta.

Ethnic roots: For all their cultural homogeneity, *porteños* are a people with diverse ethnic origins. As Argentina's principal port,

Buenos Aires is regarded throughout Argentina as a frenzied city where people have forgotten the art of relaxing. Yet for all their activity, work remains a sore subject with most *porteños*. Surveys show that people tend to regard employment more as a means of survival than a source of personal growth and fulfillment. Many hold down several jobs simultaneously, racing from one to the next in six-hour shifts. Paychecks normally

Left, deli owner poses with fresh challah and bagels. <u>Above</u>, mother and daughter enjoy a snack in a San Telmo pub.

Buenos Aires was always the first stop for waves of European immigrants, many of whom went no farther. First came Spaniards, later Britons and Italians, then Eastern European Jews, Arabs, Irish, Welsh, and Germans. The most recent arrivals are Koreans and Argentina's neighbors from Uruguay, Chile, and Paraguay.

While the Spanish cultural heritage prevails, Italian influences abound. You'll remember listening to the soaring and dipping nuances of *porteño* Spanish. Buenos Aires also has the fourth largest Jewish community in the world, although its conspicuous presence is far less than its size. Virtually no blacks and few traces of Argentina's indigenous peoples remain in the city; dark complexions prevail but fair skin and light hair are also commonplace.

Notwithstanding their links with Europe, *porteños* are surprisingly irreverent towards the large ethnic groups from the Old World. Ethnic jokes portray Italians as humorless drudges, Spaniards as simple-minded country bumpkins, Englishmen as cunning exploiters, and Jews as culturally unadaptable. Such chauvinism is frequently the product of resentment felt towards hard-working immigrants for their upstaging work ethic.

This resentment too may account for the *porteños'* admiration for what's known locally as *"viveza criolla"* – native cunning used to swindle unsuspecting outsiders. Such con-man attitudes have prevailed not only towards foreigners: as early as the 1820s an Argentine observer wrote that "the *porteño* mentality may be summed up roughly as the inner conviction that Argentina exists for Buenos Aires."

Proud middle-class city: Latin American neighbors of Argentina take umbrage at what they regard as swaggering airs of superiority put on by *porteño* visitors. Such arrogance in Buenos Aires, however, is seldom tolerated. A waiter may not earn much more in a month than the bill he presents to a party of customers, but he expects the guests to treat him respectfully.

In a city where nearly every worker belongs to a trade union, menial jobs in general are better paid than elsewhere in Latin America. Some bus drivers even consider themselves members of the middle class, an unthinkable status for their colleagues in neighboring countries. City buses, in fact, may be one of the best places for the visitor to observe the coexistence of social classes in Buenos Aires. Women wrapped in opulent furs sit primly and unselfconsciously next to factory workers clad in dungarees. It is a sight almost inconceivable in most other large Latin American cities.

This is not to say there are no class divisions in Buenos Aires. High society has survived the spread of the middle class. The slurred nasal speech of the *gente bien*, or beautiful people, can be heard at the Colón Opera House and at polo matches as well as in the city's best private schools. These frequently belong to members of the landed gentry, descendents of the military heroes of the wars for independence who were rewarded with giant tracts of land. Their offspring are among those who can still take fabled shopping excursions abroad and who bury their dead in the exclusive crypts of Recoleta Cemetery.

At the other end of the *porteño* economic spectrum are the slum dwellers who inhabit the tenements of *barrios* such as San Telmo and Monserrat. Often they are recent arrivals to the metropolis who live in former mansions that have been divided up into *conventillos*. They are the waiters, the housecleaners, and construction workers of Buenos Aires. But this is primarily a proud city of the middle class. There is an atmosphere here of egalitarianism seldom found elsewhere in Latin America. The *porteño* relishes the city's epicurean delights as one of many rather than as part of an elite.

Left, girls having some fun while waiting for the bus in La Boca. **Right**, *porteño* families tend to be close-knit and affectionate.

Roberto Fontanarrosa, *who wrote this chapter, is the author of several collections of cartoons and short stories. His drawings appear regularly in the newspaper* Clarín. *He lives in Rosario.*

While vacationing in a coastal town in southern Brazil, I went to the local tourist office in search of information. Among the group of people clustered around the counter, I noticed an Argentine (decked out in vacation togs, a cigarette stuck to his lower lip) with a Brazilian who evidently worked there as a guide and interpreter.

Perhaps attempting to make the wait more pleasant, the Brazilian said to the tourist, "I know a bit of your country – Salta, Jujuy, and a few other places in the north. What part of Argentina are you from, sir?" "Pompeya" [a neighborhood of Buenos Aires], the *porteño* replied.

This anecdote pretty well sums up the image *porteños* have in the interior of their country. For them, the country *is* Buenos Aires. That immense, formidable city is enough; an abstract of everywhere else.

I often get the impression that the *porteño* is one type of person in Buenos Aires and another type outside. Within the city limits, he's a splendid fellow: cordial, hearty, happy to help out a passer-by. Once outside, he becomes sarcastic, biting and scornful, not above abusing his ability to push himself to the head of every queue – an ability at which one becomes daily adept while struggling to survive in a hostile city of more than 10 million inhabitants.

His sense of superiority is not without a certain logic. For the *porteño*, the vast majority of cities in the provinces (and in South America) are towns with squat buildings, few cars, and dark, dull nights.

Personally, I have nothing but affection and sympathy for a large number of those long-suffering inhabitants of Buenos Aires.

Some of my best friends live in the city, especially after the flowering of so many *porteño*-provincial romances along the Ramblas in Barcelona, during the recent Argentine diaspora.

Since I first began making trips into the city to visit publishers or solicit advice from established cartoonists (now considerably more than 20 years ago), I have always been received with hospitality and warmth. This openness says something about the city's tremendous ability to incorporate foreigners from all latitudes, whether they come there seeking wealth, fame, notoriety, or mere subsistence.

The typical inhabitant of Buenos Aires, who likely as not holds down two full-time jobs, leaves home at six in the morning and doesn't return until midnight. The provincial, on the other hand, goes home for lunch, takes a siesta, and invests the two hours that the *porteño* spends in the *colectivo* or behind the wheel of his car, chatting with friends in the corner café.

As the mongoose is the natural enemy of the cobra, so is the siesta the natural enemy of stress. Yet to utter that word in Buenos Aires is to open oneself up to jokes about yokels. I have sometimes suggested to *porteños* that we arrange to meet "at the hour of the siesta" and have been given disconcerted, condescending looks.

And in that judgemental glance, which one cannot help but elicit, lies the power which *porteños* wield and the rest of us accept: the need for approval from the Big City.

You can write marvellously in La Rioja, act to perfection in Corrientes, or sing like an angel in La Pampa, but none of it counts until you "pass" in Buenos Aires.

Perhaps that qualifying power of Buenos Aires stimulates the insecurity, respect and irritation the rest of us feel with regard to the *porteño*, the city dweller who is indifferent to the rest of the country, for whom the city is more than sufficient. The man who lives within the confines of Capital Federal – in Pompeya, perhaps.

THE PORTEÑA

The *porteña* walks the streets of Buenos Aires with the bearing of a queen. She is followed by the glances of *porteño* males who, however hurried they might be, comment on her passing in the best Italian manner. Meticulously groomed and anointed with shampoos, creams and perfumed bath salts, she always seeks to emphasize her best physical features. She tends to follow fashion but is not enslaved by it.

Chic and conservative at the same time, she usually disdains extreme styles which might make her the center of too much attention. She wears her skirts a bit shorter or longer than the prevailing whim. If brilliant colors are the mode, she'll wear a bright scarf or necklace, but will find it hard to dress completely in a way that announces her presence flamboyantly.

Caught halfway between a Roman Catholic past in which the Church imposed its regulations on love, sex and family, and a present greatly influenced by psychoanalysis, the *porteña* has overcome the old-fashioned prejudices of a few decades ago and lives more in the style of an American or European woman. Today, it's possible to say that the *porteña* is a liberated woman. She is able to make her own decisions about what work she will do and how many children she will have, or even whether she wants to be a mother at all.

Guilt, sex and melancholia: Given to introspection, she reads everything she can get her hands on about the female character, about parent–child relationships, about love. Introverted and melancholic, she has a tendency to feel guilty, especially with regard to her children.

If she works outside the house, she'll try to arrange a schedule which permits her to be there when her children get home from school. If she divorces the father of her children and finds another partner (until quite recently Argentine law did not permit divorced peo-ple to remarry), she will try to compensate her children for the pain she believes she has inflicted on them.

Her introspection, the demands she makes on herself, and her propensity for melancholy often lead her to psychoanalysis. There are very few *porteñas* who have not had some experience with psychotherapy, whether it's orthodox Freudianism, Freudian-Lacanianism, or simply brief, American-style therapy such as Gestalt.

Her behavior with regard to men is comparable to that of most Western urban women, although many Spanish and Italian men say she is not typically Latin; that she is more direct, less wily and seductive. She may embark on a sexual adventure without the requisite long flirtation, the *paseos* and romantic dinners other Latin women expect. Although she's shy about expressing emotion, and tends not to exclaim over music or landscapes, the *porteña* is capable of saying to a man, without blushing: "I'd like to make love with you."

Generally, she has a lot of women friends. Day and night, the restaurants and cafés of Buenos Aires are full of tables of women talking about films, politics and clothes, but above all, about relationships. Using a language which is proof of at least a passing contact with psychoanalysis, the *porteña* will speak of sexual frustration, somatization, repression, etc.

French women, American men: The society and culture she most admires is that of France. She likes French films, literature, and the language itself. She admires the discretion and elegance of French women, their capacity for seduction. Catherine Deneuve is perhaps the *porteña*'s ideal.

She is somewhat ambivalent about American women. She finds them attractive, and irresistible to men, but just a bit obvious. American men, on the other hand, fascinate her. She tends to see them as efficient and capable of making decisions in difficult moments, unlike her brooding male counterparts in Buenos Aires.

Left, mother and daughter admire lingerie on elegant Avenida Santa Fé.

The gaucho stands as one of the best-known cultural symbols of Argentina. This rough, tough, free-riding horseman of the pampa, a proud cousin of the North American cowboy, is maintained in Argentine culture as the perfect embodiment of *argentinidad*, the very essence of the national character. He has been elevated to the level of myth, celebrated in both song and prose, and well endowed with the virtues of strength, bravery and honor.

However, as with all elements of national history, the gaucho and his culture continue to be hotly debated topics among the Argentine people.

Some say the gaucho disappeared as an identifiable social character in the late 19th century. Others will argue that, although his world has undergone radical changes in the last few centuries, the gaucho still survives in Argentina. However, while there are still people scattered throughout the country who call themselves gauchos, their lives bear only a limited resemblance to the lives of their forebears.

Pampean orphans: Gaucho life had its beginnings on the pampa, the vast grasslands of the east-central Southern Cone some time in the 18th century. There is some dispute as to the exact location, but a favored theory gives the gauchos their origin on the so-called East Bank, in the territory that is today called Uruguay.

As to the origin of the name gaucho, there are again many theories which trace the word back to everything from Arabic and Basque, to French and Portuguese. The most likely answer, however, is that the word has joint roots in the native Indian dialects of Quechua and Araucanian, a derivation of their word for orphan. It is not hard to imagine how a word meaning orphan evolved into a term for these solitary figures, as they were neither loved nor ruled by anyone.

The first gauchos were mostly *mestizos*, of mixed Spanish and native American stock. As with the North American cowboy, some

also had varied amounts of African blood, a legacy of the slave trade.

Hides and tallow: Cattle and horses that had escaped from early Spanish settlements in the 16th century had, over the centuries, proliferated into enormous free-roaming herds, and it was this wild, unclaimed abundance that was the basis for the development of the gaucho subculture. The horses were caught and tamed, and then used to capture the cattle.

Beef at that time did not have any great commercial value; there was more meat than the tiny population of Argentina could consume, and methods to export it had not yet been developed. This surplus led to waste on a grand scale; any excess meat was simply thrown away.

The primary value of the cattle was in the hides and tallow they provided, which were non-perishable exportable items. The first gauchos made their living by selling these in exchange for tobacco, rum and *mate*; gauchos were said to be so addicted to this stimulating tea that they would rather have gone without their beef. Their existence was fairly humble, with few needs. Most did not possess much beyond a horse, a saddle, a poncho and a knife.

The work was not terribly rigorous, and early travelers' accounts of the gauchos portray them as savage and uncouth vagabonds. They were left with plenty of extra time on their hands, and much of this was spent drinking and gambling.

This unwise combination of activities often led to a third favorite pastime: the knife fight. The violent lifestyle of the gaucho was looked upon with horror and disdain by the city folk, but the animosity was mutual. The gauchos had nothing but scorn for what they saw as the fettered and refined ways of the *porteños*.

Skilled horsemanship: The primary reputation of the gaucho, however, was that of a horseman, and this was well deserved. It was said that when a gaucho was without his horse he was without legs.

Almost all his daily chores, from bathing to hunting were conducted from atop his steed. The first gauchos hunted with lassoes

Preceding pages: ornamental waistline of a gentleman gaucho. **Left**, gauchos of Salta with their stiff leather *guardamontes*.

and *boleadoras*, both of which they borrowed from Indian culture. The *boleadoras* consisted of three stones or metal balls attached to the ends of connected thongs. Thrown with phenomenal accuracy by the gauchos, this flying weapon would trip the legs of the fleeing prey.

Charles Darwin, in his descriptions of Argentine life in the 1830s, has an amusing account of his own attempt to throw the *boleadoras*. He ended up catching nothing more than himself, as one thong caught on a bush, and the other wound around his horse's legs. As one might imagine, this ineptitude was the source of much chiding and laughter from the attendant gauchos.

skills in everyday survival is the practice of *pialar*. In this challenge, a man would ride through a gauntlet of his lasso-wielding comrades, who would try to trip up the feet of his mount. The object of the exercise was for the unseated man to land on his feet with reins firmly in hand. This kind of control was often necessary on the open plain, where hidden animal burrows presented a constant danger underfoot.

As outsiders bent on enforcing order in the countryside sought to control the lives and activities of the gauchos, these competitions came under increasing restrictions. Organized and contained rodeos became the forum for the showing off of skills.

The great emphasis placed on equestrian skills inevitably led to competition. Strength, speed and courage were highly prized, and the chance to demonstrate these came often.

In one event, the *sortija*, a horseman would ride full tilt with a lance in his hand to catch a tiny ring dangling from a crossbar. Another test of both timing and daring, the *maroma*, would call for a man to drop from a corral gate as a herd of wild horses was driven out beneath him. Tremendous strength was needed to land on a horse's bare back, bring it under control and return with it to the gate.

A good illustration of how these competitions were born of the necessity to develop

Ranch hands: Profound change came to the gauchos' way of life as increasing portions of the pampa came under private ownership. Beginning in the late 18th century, large land grants were made to powerful men from Buenos Aires, often as a form of political patronage.

The gauchos, with their anarchistic ways, were seen as a hindrance to the development of the land. Increasing restrictions were put on their lives, in order to bring them to heel and to put them at the service of the new landowners.

It was not only the land which came under private ownership, but the cattle and horses that were found on them as well, making them inaccessible to the free riders.

The gauchos were suddenly put in the position of being trespassers and cattle thieves. This made their situation similar to that of the remaining tribes of Plains Indians. The shaky reputations of the gauchos grew worse. When they got into trouble in one area, they simply rode on to another, and little by little they were found further from the settled areas.

New order: With such an obvious conflict of interests, there had to be a resolution, and it was, predictably enough, in favor of the landowners. The open prairie lands were fenced off, and the disenfranchised gauchos

markets opened up, an ever-increasing amount of land was turned over to agriculture, and the gaucho work ethic ensured that the business of planting and harvesting was all done by the immigrants.

When barbed wire fencing was put up, fewer hands were needed to maintain the herds. Combined with the increase in agriculture, this led to even harder times for the gauchos and animosity grew between them and the employable newcomers. Many of the gauchos could only find temporary work on the *estancias*, and they moved from one place to another, branding cattle or shearing sheep. These itinerant laborers were paid by the day or the task.

were put to work at the service of the *estancieros*. Their skills were employed to round up, brand and maintain the herds. Wages were pitifully low.

However, the gauchos maintained their pride. They refused to do any unmounted labor, which was seen as the ultimate degradation. Chores such as ditch digging, the mending of fences and planting of trees were reserved for the immigrants who were arriving in increasing numbers from Europe. As the opportunities for exports to the European

Through the 19th century a whole new order came to rest on the pampa; the gaucho had ceased to be his own man. His new status as a hired ranch hand did not sit well with the gaucho's rebellious spirit. But the forces working against him were strong. The landowners had powerful friends in the capital, and the politicians saw the ordering of the countryside as a major priority. Argentina was finally beginning to take its place among the developing nations, and the traditional life of the gaucho could only be seen as a hindrance to that course.

Informal armies: However, while the gaucho ceased to present an independent threat,

<u>Left</u>, early gaucho, with toe-held stirrups. <u>Above</u>, roundup in Corrientes.

he still had a role to play in the new social structure of the rural areas. As the domestication of the gaucho increased, new bonds of loyalty were formed between the worker and his master.

Powerful *caudillos* were gaining control over large parts of the interior, backed up by their gauchos, who served as irregular troops in private armies. This formation of regional powers was in direct contradiction to the goals of centralized government.

Years of civil warfare followed Argentina's independence from Spain, and it was only when the Unitarians, led by José de San Martín, gained the upper hand, late in the 19th century, that the powerful Federalist

bands were finally brought under control.

Gauchos were also, at various times, put to work in the defense of the central government. These skilled horsemen were first used in the armies that routed the British invasion forces in 1806 and 1807, and by all accounts, their services were invaluable. Although they were forcibly inducted, they fought bravely and did not have the high desertion rates of other groups.

Gaucho squadrons were next used in the war of independence from Spain, and again they·displayed great valor. The last time that the gauchos fought as an organized force in the nation's army was during the Desert

Campaign of the 1880s. Ironically, the gauchos, many of whom were of mixed Indian blood, were being used this time to exterminate the Indian tribes who were seen as an obstacle to territorial expansion. The campaigns opened up vast new areas for Europeans to settle on, but gaucho songs from the period lament their compromise of honor in the endeavor.

Las chinas: The family life of the gaucho was never a very settled one. Supposedly, the women of their early camps were captives from raids on nearby settlements. This primitive theft was perhaps one of the practices that made the gauchos so unpopular with the forces of civilization. But even when women later moved voluntarily out onto the pampas, the domestic arrangements were rather informal. Church weddings were seen as inconvenient and expensive, and common law marriages were the norm.

The *chinas*, as these women were called, were rarely welcome on the *estancias* where the gauchos worked. The few that were allowed were employed as maids, wet nurses, laundresses, and cooks. They also participated in the sheep shearing. Home life for the *china* reflected the primitive conditions on the *estancias*. Shelter was usually a simple adobe hut, thatched with grass. Crude furniture was fashioned from the bones and skulls of cows. Some women managed to find independent employment as midwives and faith healers.

Snappy dressers: Although gaucho clothing was designed for comfort and practicality, the men were born dandies, and their outfits were always worn with a certain amount of flair.

The *chiripá*, a loose diaper-like cloth draped between the legs, was very suitable for riding. It was often worn with long, fringed leggings. These were later replaced by *bombachas*, pleated pants with buttoned ankles that fitted inside their boots.

Although store-bought boots with soles became popular with gauchos in later years, the first boots were homemade, fashioned from a single piece of hide, slipped from the leg of a horse. This skin was moulded to the gaucho's foot while still moist. Often the toe was left open. This had a practical function, as the early stirrups were nothing more than a knot in a hanging leather thong. The rider would grasp the knot between his first and second toes. Over time this caused the toes to be permanently curled under, and gave the gaucho an awkward gait in addition to the permanent bowlegged stance characteristic of the professional rider.

Around his waist the gaucho wore a *faja*, a woolen sash, and a *rastra*, a stiff leather belt adorned with coins – the amount varied according to the man's wealth. This leather belt provided support for the back during the long hours in the saddle. At the gaucho's back, between these two belts, was tucked the *facón*, a gaucho's most prized possession after his horse. This knife was used throughout the day for skinning, castrating, eating and self defense.

fine leather crop, was always carried in hand.

Martín Fierro: Just as the traditional gaucho way of life was fading in reality it was being preserved in art. Poetry and music had always been popular with the gauchos, and the poet was usually a revered figure within the community.

The songs, stories and poems of the *gauchesco* tradition, many of them composed in colorful dialect, often deal with the themes of love and nostalgia, but many of them are highly political in nature.

One of the masterpieces of Argentine literature is a two part epic poem, *El Gaucho Martín Fierro*. Written by José Hernandez, and published in the 1870s, the work is a

The outfit was completed with a kerchief, a hat, a set of spurs and a vest, for dress occasions. Over all this, a gaucho wore his poncho, which served as a blanket at night and a shield in a knife fight.

The gaucho saddle was a layered set of pads, braces and molded leather, on top of which sat a sheepskin that made the ride more comfortable. In the region of the pampas where high thistles grew, a set of stiff, flaired leather guards called *guardamontes* were used. The *rebenque*, a heavy braided

Left, a *sortija* competition. **Above**, a gaucho sorely tested.

strong defense of the proud and independent ways of the gaucho, and a diatribe against the forces that conspired to bring him down, from greedy landowners to corrupt policemen and conscription officials.

A second work, *Don Segundo Sombra*, by Ricardo Güiraldes, was published in 1926 and is heavily nostalgic about the lost element of the national heritage that the romantic gaucho represented.

Ironically, these poems and stories served to elevate the stature of the gaucho in the minds of the public, but not enough and not in time to save him. The free-riding gaucho passed into the realm of myth, a folk hero who was the object of sentimentality and patriotic pride in a nation searching for cultural emblems.

Gauchos, paisanos and peónes: Although the traditional historical line places the demise of the gaucho in the late 19th century, there is much that remains of the culture in Argentina today. While the reduction of labor needs in the countryside forced many gauchos into the cities to work as policemen, firemen, plumbers and carpenters, many remained on the *estancias* to work under the new established order.

Wherever cattle and sheep ranching is done in Argentina, one will find ranch hands working at the rough chores of herding and

branding. Most are settled with a regular wage, but there are still itinerants who provide services such as fence mending and sheep shearing.

While many of these men call themselves gauchos, the job of ranch hand has taken on different names in the different regions of Argentina. Some are called *paisanos*, others are called *peónes*.

These cowboys are still found on the *estancias* of the pampas but they are being pushed into reaches further and further from Buenos Aires. A number are employed in huge cattle operations covering thousands of acres, while others work on small family farms, from the rugged brush country of the northwest to the plains of Patagonia.

As with the original gauchos, many of these men are *mestizos*. Generally those in the northeast are of Guaraní stock, while the Araucanians work on the ranches of Patagonia deep in the south. However, over the years there has been a mixing of blood, with everything from Basque to Italian to that of the North American cowboys who came down to work in the 19th century.

Despite the regional differences in nomenclature, dress and blood, these men share the one tradition that makes them all gauchos in spirit, that of excellent horsemanship. A gaucho's pride is still his horse, and as before, he usually does not own much beyond this besides his saddle, his poncho and his knife.

Low wages and poor living conditions have continued to drive these workers into other pursuits. In recent years, many have left to work on hydroelectric projects, and then have drifted to the cities rather than return to the hard life of the *estancias*.

The rodeo: The visitor can be rewarded for a little exploration along the back roads of Argentina, for that is where one can still find the gauchos at work. On a visit to an *estancia*, one might see a *domador* breaking horses, or men riding at breakneck speed with lassoes flying. In small towns it is possible to stop for a drink in the local *boliche* or *pulpería*, where men gather for cards and a little gambling after a hard day.

One of the biggest treats is to see a rodeo. Some of these are large organized events, with an accompanying fiesta of eating, dancing and the singing of traditional songs. Bowlegged men gather at these celebrations, dressed up in their finest hats, *bombachas*, and kerchiefs, with their *chinas* by their sides.

With some investigation and a little luck, it is possible to find more informal rodeos in the villages of the outback, where the gauchos will have come from miles around to compete in rough tests of skill and bravery. Amid flying dust and spirited whooping one will see gauchos barrel racing and lassoing cattle with as much panache and pride as their ancestors ever had.

Left and **right**, gauchitos and gauchos in the distinctive ponchos of the Northwest.

Río de la Plata

JUAN
ANCHORENA

Vicente López

NÚÑEZ

BELGRANO
Hipodromo
QUIZA
Jardín Zoológico
Jardín
Botánico

PARQUE TRES DE
FEBRERO

Av. Del Libertador
Incas
Justo

PALERMO
B. CHACARITA
RECOLETA
LA PATERNAL
Martin
VILLA
CRESPO
CABALLITO
Av. Rivadavia
Entre
La Plata
Rios

CONSTITUCIÓN

ORESTA
ORES
Segurola
Juan

BARRACAS
BOCA
DISTRITO FEDERAL
AIRES

NUEVA
POMPEYA
Parque
Almirante
Guillermo
Brown
BUENOS
Avellaneda

VILLA
LUGANO
VILLA DIAMANTE
SARANDÍ

AVELLANEDA

VILLA DOMÍNICO
Av. Gral

QUILMES
Mitre
DON BOSCO

Lanús

LANÚS
INGENIERO
BUDGE
LOMAS DE
ZAMORA
Lomas de
Zamora
L. Santa
Catalina

REMEDIOS
DE ESCALADA

Camino
General

Quilmes

Av. Gral Mitre
Ezpeleta

Berazategui

BERAZATEGUI
Belgrano

Cintura
General
de

ALMIRANTE
BROWN

Esteban
cheverria
(Monte
Grande)
VILLA
TURDERA
Camino
Roca
Almirante Brown
(Androgue)

FLORENCIO
VARELA

Florencio Varela

Arroyo Platanos

Cancha de Polo

PALERMO

Bulrich
Demaria
Av. Sarmiento
del
Av. Rep. India
Av. Casares
Salguero
Av. Ocampo
Av. Pte
Austria
Castilla
Av. Pte

Juncal
Darragueyra
Cerviño
Ugarteche
Paunero
Libertador

Bonpland Av.
Fitz Roy
Av. Juan B. Justo
Godoy
Cruz
Santa
Fe
Cabello

D JARDÍN ZOOLÓGICO
Plaza Italia
Av. Gral.
Las Heras
French
PARQUE
Pacheco de Melo
Díaz

JARDÍN BOTÁNICO
Juncal
Arenales

Museo de Bellas Artes
Av. del Libertador
Mto. a Carlos M. de Alvear
F. Alcorta
Alvear Palace Hotel
Museo Ferrovi Argenti

Antiguo Convento de los Recoletos
Basílica Menor de Nuestra Señora del Pilar
Museo F. Blanco

PALERMO
Uriarte
Honduras
J. A. Cabrera
Av.
Serrano
Gurruchaga
Nicaragua
Soler
Malabia
Charcas
Paraguay
Caning
Salguero
Bulnes
Cnel.
Av. Austria
Arenales
Juncal

RECOLETA
Pueyrredon
Azcuenaga
P. de Melo
Las Heras
Callao
Av. López
Cementerio de la Recoleta
Jockey Club

AGUERO
Santa

Plaza V. López
Juncal
Arenales
Arenales
Santa
9 de Julio

J. Alvarez
Lavalleja
El Figueroa
Salvador
Honduras
Gorriti
Billinghurst
Aguero
Laprida
Soler
Cabrera

AGUERO
Fe

Teatro Nacional Cervantes

F. A. de
Arganaraz
Cordoba
Av.
J. A.
San
Tucuman
Cordoba
Luis
Puerredon
Viamonte
Tucuman
Paraguay
Av. Cordoba

Plaza Gral. Lavalle
Palacio de Justicia
Obelisco
9 DE JUL

Castillo
Loyola
Israel
Guardia Vieja
Lavalle
Guardia Vieja
Lavalle

Corrientes
Museo de Arte Moderno

Av. Corrientes
Corrientes
Av.
V. Gomez
Sarmiento
Cangallo
Uruguay
Salta
Bartolom

PARQUE CENTENARIO
Estado
Rio de Janeiro
Lambare
MEDRANO
Sarmiento
Salguero
Mario Bravo
Aguero
BALVANERA
Bartolome Mitre
Mto. a los Dos Congresos
Plaza del Congreso
Av. de AV. DE MA
Palacio del Congreso Nacional

Diaz
Bartolome Mitre
Velez
ALMAGRO
Rivadavia
Plaza de Miserere
MISERERE
Av. Rivadavia
H. Yrigoyen
Pichincha
Matheu
Alsina
Moreno
Belgrano

Campichuelo
Ambrosetti
Rio de Janeiro
Avellaneda
H. Yrigoyen
Alsina
Moreno
Catamarca
Jujuy
Saavedra
Venezuela
Mexico
Chile
Combate de los Pozos
Sarandi
Chile
Entre Rios
Independencia
Peña
Virrey

Acoyte
Av. H. Yrigoyen
Rivadavia
Venezuela
Av.
S. de Mexico
Belgrano
Venezuela
Av.
Estados Unidos
Saavedra
Matheu
Pichincha
Humberto I
Unidos
Calvo
Juan
Av.
Cevallos

PARQUE RIVADAVIA
Mexico
Boedo
Independencia
Loria
Carlos
Jujuy
San

CABALLITO
Alberdi
Av. C. Calvo
San Juan
URUQUIZA
Oruro
SAN CRISTOBAL
Av. Juan
Pavon
de
Ga
Pte. L.

AV. JOSE M. MORENO
J. B.
Jose
Av. Pedro Goyena
Directorio
Plata
Av. San Juan
Pavon
Inclan
P. Echague
Rios

Av.
M.
BOEDO
Asamblea
Garay
Inclan
PARQUE PATRICIOS
Oruro
Salcedo
Brasil
PATRICIOS

Pavon
Av. Juan
de
Santander
Moreno
Bell Ville
Balbastro
Plata
Trienta y Tres
Inclan
Salcedo
Boedo
Rondeau
Av.
Chiclana
Monteagudo
Echague
La Rioja
Luca Labarden
Caseros
Santa
Pichincha
Matheu
Catamarca
Jujuy
Luna
PARQUE AMEGHINO
Cruz
Garcia
Sarsfield

PARQUE PATRICIOS

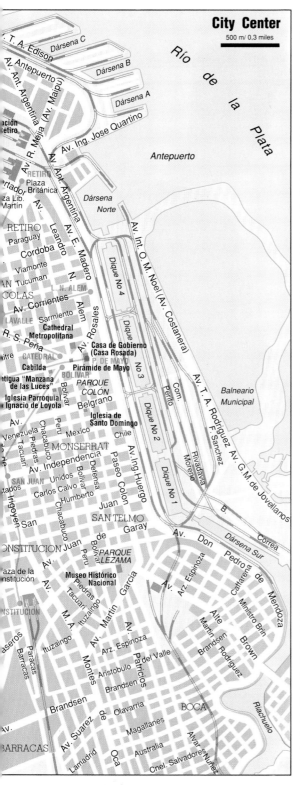

City Center

500 m / 0.3 miles

Río de la Plata

About a third of the 10 million inhabitants of Greater Buenos Aires live in the district known as Capital Federal, whose borders are the highway General Paz, to the north and west, and the Riachuelo to the south. The highway border might strike some observers as imaginary, since blocks of residential streets stretch for kilometers on both sides of General Paz. But for *porteños*, the symbolic demarcation is crucial, for it separates the sophisticated urbanites from the less privileged provincials.

Within the confines of General Paz, the city is a cluster of *barrios*, each with its own strong loyalties and identity.

The *barrio* originally grew up as a parish, centered around the neighborhood church and the Spanish-style plaza which were the two poles of the community. Urban growth melded them together, but the divisions still remain, celebrated in poetry and tango lyrics, reinforced by neighborhood football teams, political affiliations, ethnicity and tradition.

For most visitors, the easternmost sections of the city along the riverbank will be the center of attraction. Hotels, museums, government buildings, shopping and entertainment are generally located in downtown, or *el centro*, Recoleta, Retiro, San Telmo and Monserrat, and La Boca. Palermo and La Costanera offer parks and promenades, gardens and river views.

As for the outlying areas, the most interesting are: Villa Crespo, a traditional Jewish neighborhood and a center of wonderful delicatessens; Chacarita, a location of the world's largest urban cemetery (it's considered to be a less elegant eternal address than Recoleta, but it contains the tombs of General Perón and tango crooner Carlos Gardel); and Flores, a cosy neighborhood of colonial houses traversed by a colorful tramway on Sunday afternoons.

A WALKING TOUR OF BUENOS AIRES

Buenos Aires was a wonderful city for walking, and while I was walking I decided it would be a pleasant city to live in.
— Paul Theroux, *The Old Patagonian Express*

In addition to her nostalgic, old-world beauty, there are two fundamental reasons why Buenos Aires is so inviting to those who enjoy exploring on foot. First, it's a city which evolved as a cluster of almost self-contained villages, each with its own particular airs and ambience. And it's a place where the walk or *paseo* is woven into the fabric of everyday existence. Strolling through a particular quarter will give visitors more than a glimpse of *barrio* life.

This section of the book is divided according to neighborhoods. Each *barrio*'s main interests are highlighted: these include not only museums and monuments but the no less venerable shrines to pastries, wine and pasta.

The first stop is the **city center**, the hub of hotels, restaurants and foreign exchange. The Casa Rosada (Government House) is the area's heart; nearby are the Congress Building, the Colón Opera House, and some of Buenos Aires' stateliest coffee houses, cinemas and bookstores, many of which are open all night.

The *barrio* of **San Telmo** is the city's Soho, a charming quarter where old architecture serves as a backdrop to postmodern art and attitudes. It's a neighborhood of cobbled streets and crumbling villas, of tango and jazz clubs and "underground" theater.

La Boca is the old port area, settled by Italian dock workers at the turn of the century, renowned for its pizza parlors and flashy cantinas. The corrugated tin houses painted in bright primary colors give the neighborhood a carnival atmosphere, but it's a residential neighborhood still strongly influenced by its Italian heritage.

In glittering contrast is **Barrio Norte**, an elegant neighborhood built around a cemetery. This *barrio* of Parisian-style houses, boutiques and continental restaurants was built at the height of Argentina's Golden Age, and retains a good measure of its aristocratic grandeur. Adjacent is **Palermo**, the home of Italianate villas, parks, a turn-of-the-century racetrack and a world-class polo field.

The **Costanera** is the river coastline the city's edge. It's too long to walk the entire route; a pleasant way to see it is to spend a late morning strolling on the old-fashioned promenades, then taking a taxi to one of the riverside restaurants for lunch.

Suggested day or weekend trips from Buenos Aires include an excursion to the villages and ranches of the **pampas**, to the river delta at **Tigre**, or to neighboring **Uruguay** by river ferry.

DOWNTOWN

Inside every *porteño*'s head is a picture of Buenos Aires which resembles the famous *New Yorker* drawing of Manhattan. Looming large in the foreground is his *barrio*, his favorite café and the 24-hour *kiosco* (sweet shop) nearest his front door. On the horizon is **Avenida General Paz**, the city limit, beyond which are endless pampas and foreign countries. In the middle distance is **El Centro**, the city center, where he spends a large amount of his spare time.

Buenos Aires is a city of fervent neighborhood loyalties, but the center belongs to everyone. No matter what the *porteño*'s political persuasion or economic situation, there are certain landmarks – the bright pink Casa del Gobierno, the gilded and crumbling Confitería del Molino, the closet-sized bookstores on Corrientes – which he loves passionately. Never try to tell a *porteño* who is showing you around downtown that the landmarks do not belong to him personally, or that there are other citizens of Buenos Aires who love them equally. He will only smile at you in disbelief. He is not just pointing out buildings, he is telling you his version of the city's history, which is as vivid and as intimate as a wonderful, recurring dream.

The following walking-tour encompasses four important aspects of life in the city center: politics, entertainment, cafés and shopping. Begin at the Plaza de Mayo, follow Avenida de Mayo to the Plaza del Congreso, then double back down Avenida Corrientes and Lavalle to Florida, the main shopping promenade. The walk can be done in about two hours, but obviously can be stretched out to last most of the day, including lunch and lots of coffee breaks. It's meant as an introduction to downtown, because most places will warrant more lingering. This tour also takes advantage of the flow of traffic. So if

need be, you can take a taxi or *colectivo* up Avenida de Mayo and then back down Corrientes to Florida.

The Plaza de Mayo: Buenos Aires began with the Plaza de Mayo. Today it's a strikingly beautiful plaza with its tall palm trees, elaborate flower gardens and central monument, set off by the surrounding colonial buildings. The plaza has been and continues to be the pulsating center of the country. Since its founding in 1580 as the Plaza del Fuerte (fortress) many of the most important historical events have had physical manifestations here.

The most eye-catching structure in the plaza is unquestionably the **Casa Rosada**, the seat of the executive branch of the government. Flanking it are the Banco de la Nación, the Catedral Metropolitana, the Consejo Municipal and the Cabildo.

Pink House: The **Casa Rosada** was originally a fortress overlooking what is now the **Plaza Colón**, but was at that time the river's edge. When the Indian

attacks subsided, the plaza became Plaza del Mercado, a marketplace and social center. The name and role of the plaza changed again with the British invasions of 1806 and 1807, when it became the Plaza de la Victoria. Finally, following the declaration of independence, the plaza assumed its present name, in honor of the month of May, for it was in May 1810 when the city broke away from Spain and became independent.

The date also marks the first mass rally in the plaza, when crowds gathered to celebrate independence. Subsequently, Argentines have poured into the plaza either to protest or to celebrate most of the nation's important events. Political parties, governments (*de facto* and constitutional), and even the trades unions and the Church, use the plaza to make addresses or appeals to the people, and to gather support for their various causes.

Salient events in the history of **Plaza de Mayo** include the 1945 workers' demonstration organized by Eva Perón to protest against her husband's brief detention. Ten years later, the airforce bombed the plaza while thousands of Perón's supporters were rallying to defend his administration from the impending military coup.

In 1982, Argentines flooded the plaza to applaud General Galtieri's invasion of the Malvinas/Falkland Islands. A few months later, they were back, this time threatening to kill the military ruler for having deliberately misled the country about the possibilities of winning the war with the British. In 1986, when Argentina won the World Cup football championship, the entire team, including Diego Maradona, greeted thousands of celebrating fans in the plaza from the famous balconies of the Casa Rosada. And on Easter Sunday 1987, the population responded to President Alfonsín's call to defend democracy against a possible military coup with a turn-out of more than 300,000. More recently, the plaza is the scene of weekly angry protests by retirees, demanding their pen-

Demonstrators gather outside Casa Rosada.

sions owed to them by the government.

The mothers' vigil: But the most famous rallies have been those of the **Mothers of the Plaza de Mayo**, whose Thursday afternoon protests, demanding information on the whereabouts of their "disappeared" children, and punishment for those responsible, still go on today. Their presence in the plaza is perhaps the best illustration of the symbolism of rallying here. During the last years of the military regime, young people accompanying the mothers would chant at the menacing army and anti-demonstration units: "Cowards, this plaza belongs to the mothers..."

Leaders traditionally address the masses from the balconies of the Casa Rosada. This building was constructed on the foundations of earlier structures in 1894. Sixteen years earlier, President Sarmiento had chosen the site for the new Government House. There are several versions of why he had it painted pink, the most credible of which is that it was the only alternative to white in those days. The special tone was achieved by mixing beef fat, blood and lime. Some insist that Sarmiento chose pink to distinguish the building from the US White House. Still others say that pink was selected as a compromise between two feuding parties whose colors were white and red.

The **Museo de la Casa Rosada** is a small gallery, located in the basement, that contains antiques and objects identified with the lives of different national heroes. The entrance is on Hipólito Yrigoyen street, and it is open 11am–6pm every day except Wednesday and Saturday, with guided tours at 4pm.

The Grenadiers Regiment guards the Casa Rosada and the President. This elite army unit was created during the independence wars by General San Martín. They wear the same blue and red uniforms that distinguished them during those times. At sunset each day these soldiers lower the national flag in front of the Government House. On national holidays the Grenadiers often

Changing of the guard at the Government House.

parade on horseback. They also accompany the President during his public appearances.

The other major historic building in the Plaza de Mayo is the **Cabildo** (Town Hall), located at the western end of the plaza. This is perhaps the greatest attraction for Argentine patriots. Schoolchildren are brought here from various parts of Argentina to hear the story of how their forefathers planned the nation's independence in the Cabildo.

The Town Council has had its headquarters at this site ever since the city's founding in 1580, although the present building was constructed only in 1751. Originally, it spanned the plaza with five great archways each side. In 1880, when Avenida de Mayo was built, part of it was demolished. Again, in 1932, the Cabildo was further reduced to its current size with two archways on either side of the central balconies.

The Cabildo also has an historic museum, **Museo del Cabildo**, exhibiting furniture and relics from the colonial period, open Tuesday–Friday 12.30–7pm and Sunday 3–7pm. Behind the museum is a pleasant patio, which features a simple outdoor snack bar and on Thursday and Friday afternoons a small handicrafts fair.

Across Hipolito Yrigoyen, to the south, is the **Consejo Municipal** (City Council), an ornamental old building known for its enormous pentagon-shaped clock on the tower.

The cathedral: The **Catedral Metropolitana** is the next historic building on the plaza. The seat of Buenos Aires' Archbishop, it lies at the northwest corner of the plaza. The cathedral's presence in this highly political plaza is appropriate. The Roman Catholic Church has always been a pillar of Argentine society, and since the city's founding, the church has shared the Plaza de Mayo. A mural at the northern end of Avenida 9 de Julio illustrates the founding of the city, with a spade representing the military, and a priest representing the Church.

Left, on the steps of the cathedral on Flag Day. Below, tomb of General San Martín, father of Argentine independence.

The cathedral, built over the course of several decades, was completed in 1827. It was built, like the Cabildo and the Casa Rosada, upon the foundations of earlier versions. There are 12 severe neoclassical pillars in the front of the cathedral that are said to represent the 12 apostles. The carving above portrays the meeting of Joseph and his father Jacob. This section is considered to be the work of the cathedral architects, yet legend persists that it was created by a prisoner, who was then set free as a result of his beautiful carving.

Inside are some important artworks, including oil paintings attributed to Rubens and beautiful wood engravings by the Portuguese Manuel de Coyte.

For Argentines, the most important aspect of the cathedral is the tomb of General José de San Martín, liberator of Argentina, Chile, Peru, Bolivia and Uruguay. San Martín, who died during his self-imposed exile in England, is one of a handful of national heroes revered by Argentines of all political persuasions.

Illuminated fountain on Avenida 9 de Julio.

Remains of two of his military friends, Generals las Heras and Guido, as well as those of an "unknown soldier" who died during the struggle for independence, are also kept in the cathedral.

Buenos Aires' busy financial district lies just around the corner from the Cathedral, beginning more or less at the intersection of Avenida Rivadavia and the street **San Martín**. To the right down San Martín are the headquarters of some of the country's largest banks, with small *casas de cambio*, or money exchange houses, wedged in between the large buildings.

At the northeastern corner of Plaza de Mayo is the **Banco de la Nación Argentina** (National Bank of Argentina). The old Colón Theater was on this site before it reopened on Lavalle Plaza in 1908. The imposing marble and stone bank was inaugurated in 1888. On the first floor, there is a marvelous fountain called *The Athletes* sculpted by the Uruguayan, Zorrilla de San Martín.

The Plaza de Mayo has a central pyra-

mid that was constructed on the first centennial of the anniversary of the city's independence. It serves as the centerpiece for the Mothers of Plaza de Mayo's weekly rounds.

A Spanish avenue: The view from Plaza de Mayo down Avenida de Mayo to the National Congress is spectacular, and the 15-block walk is a wonderful introduction to the city. The avenue was inaugurated in 1894 as the link between the Executive Branch and the Congress, most of which had been completed by 1906. It was originally designed like a Spanish avenue, with wide sidewalks, gilded lamp posts, *chocolate* and *churros* shops, and *zarzuela* theaters. Today, however, there is a superpositioning of influences and style. No art terms adequately describe the special combination of influences seen here. Nor is there a traditional pattern or coherence from one building to the next; ornate buildings stand side by side with simple and austere ones.

There are several well-known restaurants along the way. One of the oldest is **Pedemonte** (676 Avenida de Mayo), which dates back to the turn of the century. This is a favorite of government functionaries and politicians.

Farther down is the **Café Tortoni**, an historic meeting place for writers and intellectuals. Apart from the famous customers said to have frequented the café, the ornamental interior makes the place worthy of a leisurely coffee-stop. Marble tables, red leather chairs, bronze statues and elaborate mirrors create an almost regal atmosphere. Tortoni has a couple of smaller salons in the back and in the basement, where most evenings one can attend various theater and musical productions, the most common being tango or jazz.

Traditional Spanish restaurants are also a popular feature of Avenida de Mayo. Turn left at the 1200 block onto Salta street for **El Globo** (98 Salta), known for its *paella valenciana* and *puchero* (stew). Similar restaurants are also located both on Avenida de Mayo

Café Tortoni.

120

and down some of the smaller side streets. A well frequented and classic *parrilla* (steakhouse) is **Don Pipón** at 1249 Avenida de Mayo.

World's widest avenue: You could not have missed Avenida 9 de Julio at the 1000 block, which at 140 meters (460 feet), is, the Argentines claim, the world's widest avenue. Everything about it is undeniably big – big billboards, big buildings, looming *palo borrachos* (drunken trees) laden with pink blossoms in summertime, and, of course, the big **Obelisco**.

To build this street, the military government of 1936 demolished rows of beautiful old French-style mansions. Much of that central block is now occupied by parking lots. The only mansion to survive was the French Embassy; its occupants refused to move, claiming it was foreign territory. A barren white wall facing the center of town testifies to the disappearance of its neighbors.

Obelisk jokes: The Obelisco, which marks the intersection of Diagonal Norte, Avenida Corrientes, and Avenida 9 de Julio, was built in 1936 in commemoration of the 400th anniversary of the first founding of the city. Because of its phallic appearance, it became the subject of much public humor. Three years after its creation, the City Council voted 23 to three to tear it down. But apparently even this decision was not taken seriously, for the Obelisk is still standing today.

Certain famous statues seem to crop up wherever you go in the world, lending a certain air of solidity to their host cities. Visitors will be reassured by the familiar sight of Auguste Rodin's *The Thinker*, who in Buenos Aires furrows his brow in **Plaza Lorea**, where Avenida de Mayo dead ends.

Just after Plaza Lorea is the **Plaza del Congreso**. The plaza is a wonderful place to watch people on warm summer evenings. Old and young eat pizza and ice cream on the benches, feeding the pigeons and enjoying the civilized atmosphere. There is a dramatic fountain

The Obelisk.

with sculpted galloping horses and cherubs and, at night, classical music booms out from below the falls. There is a monument above the fountain that honors "two congresses" – the 1813 assembly that abolished slavery, and the 1816 congress that declared the country's independence. These days the plaza serves as a canvas for ever-changing political graffiti, scrawled on almost all the visible surfaces.

The Congressional building houses the Senate, on the south side, and the House of Representatives on the north (Rivadavia entrance). Congressional sessions are open to those with press credentials or a pass provided by a member. The interior is decorated with appropriate pomp: important paintings, bronze and marble sculptures, luxurious red carpets, silk curtains and wood paneling.

Across the street is a new wing of the House of Representatives. Construction began in 1973, but halted with the military coup of 1976. With the return to democracy, building resumed, and it was inaugurated in 1983.

A delicious respite: On the corner of Rivadavia and Callao is the old **Confitería del Molino**, or simply El Molino to *porteños*. The building dates from 1912, and since that time it has been famous as a meeting place for congressmen and their staffs. Along with the requisite coffee and pastries, the café has a gourmet carry-out counter.

Rivadavia is a key street in Buenos Aires. It divides the city in two; street names change at its crossing and numbering begins here. *Porteños* claim that they not only have the widest street in the world, Avenida 9 de Julio, but the longest, Rivadavia, which continues westward into the countryside and out towards Luján.

About 12 blocks up Rivadavia from Congress is the neighborhood known as **Once**. This is the cheapest shopping district in town, particularly for clothes and electronic goods. A traditionally Jewish neighborhood, many of the busi-

Schoolchildren on a field trip to downtown.

nesses are owned by Orthodox Jews and Korean immigrants. The area marked by **Puerreydon**, Corrientes, Rivadavia and **Urquiza** is filled with one-room shops that sell at wholesale prices.

Eating places near Congreso include **Quorum**, located directly behind the congressional building on the street Combate de los Pozos. The location, and the food of course, draw a steady crowd of politicians and business types. Four blocks away is another famous restaurant, **La Cabaña**, at 436 Entre Ríos, the continuation of Callao to the south. It is unfortunately recognized as one of the best *parrillas* in the city and therefore somewhat touristy and overpriced. Still, they have wonderful salads and baby beef.

Three blocks north from Congreso, on the corner of Callao and Sarmiento is the **Fundación Banco Patricios** (312 Callao), an arts center housed in a beautifully renovated classic building. Climbing the majestic staircase from the ground floor are two large galleries which feature painting exhibitions (and views of the street below). The center also has two theater salons with varying productions. The building itself is worth a peek inside.

Movies and books: Continuing one block down Callao you reach **Avenida Corrientes**, another principal street in the lives of *porteños*. It is often introduced to foreigners as the "street that never sleeps" or the "Broadway of Buenos Aires." Indeed, there are neon lights, fast-food restaurants, movie theaters and music stores on Corrientes. But the atmosphere is exceedingly intellectual, rather than gaudy like New York's Broadway. There are tiny bookstores everywhere, newspaper stands with a wide selection of newspapers, magazines and paperbacks, and old cafés where friends gather for long talks. The selection of international and national films reflects the serious interests of the moviegoers.

The bookstores are traditionally one of Corrientes' greatest attractions. They

Human rights demonstration outside Congress.

are single rooms open to the street, selling both secondhand and new books. Some people come to hunt for old treasures or the latest best-seller. Others use the bookstores as meeting places. They stay open way past midnight, and, unlike in many other Buenos Aires shops, one may freely wander in and out without being accosted by aggressive salespeople. There are even *porteños* who claim to have read entire books during successive visits to the bookstores.

An important attraction and center of activity is the **Teatro Municipal General San Martín** at 1532 Corrientes. This chrome and glass building was inaugurated in 1960. It is the largest public theater in Argentina, with five stages and an estimated half a million spectators each year. It has a never-ending agenda of free concerts, theater, film festivals, lectures and musical and dance performances. A small crowd is usually gathered on the sidewalk perusing the long list of programs.

Upon entering the main hall, the box office is to the right and an interesting souvenir and postcard stand is to the left. The elevators, situated just past the souvenir stand, lead up into the vast theater complex, and to two small but interesting museums.

On the 8th floor is the **Museo de Artes Plásticas** and one more flight up is the **Museo de Arte Moderno**. Both are open Tuesday to Sunday noon–8pm. Just above, on the 10th floor is **Leopoldo Lugones**, a film auditorium where rare and interesting film festivals are held.

In the block behind the theater, at 1551 Sarmiento street, is the **Centro Cultural General San Martín**, a sister building with an equally important flurry of cultural activity, including art exhibits, puppet shows, poetry readings, and round tables or seminars on a multitude of topics. In addition, the center is used for press conferences, international meetings and inaugurations. If you enter the Centro Cultural from the main door you pass through an interesting sculpture garden; enter via the theater

Browsing in an all-night bookstore.

from Corrientes, and you will pass through the photo gallery. Also worth a stop is the **City Tourism Bureau**, on the fifth floor, where one can pick up maps and a schedule of free city tours.

The great number and variety of free concerts, seminars and other cultural activities is one of the most striking aspects of Buenos Aires. If anything, activity has gained momentum in recent years, despite the economic crisis, and has undoubtedly been bolstered by the freedom that has come with democracy. For visitors, both these centers are a revealing introduction to the contemporary cultural scene found in the city.

More culture and coffee: Other theaters on Corrientes, which usually feature the big productions, include **Teatro Astral**, **Picadilly Teatro**, **Metropolitan**, and **Teatro Presidente Alvear**.

Directly in front of the Teatro San Martín are the smaller and more bohemian **Liberarte** and **Librería Gandhi**. They are both a combination of bookstore and cafe, and Liberarte also has a performance space. Here the artsy and intellectual set gather to browse for books, sip coffee or take in poetry readings, plays, or music. Thursday through Saturday evenings are a good bet for attending one of the various programs.

At Corrientes 1660 is a fairly recent addition to the theater district, **La Plaza**, which is a multiple-use open air mall, continuing all the way through to the next block. Strolling through, one passes the box office for the five different auditoriums, various boutiques, bookstores and gift shops, and a large modern café enclosed completely in glass where once stood a well known ampitheater.

But for a taste of Corrientes of years past, **La Giralda** on the 1400 block shouldn't be missed. Here waiters in white coats serve the house specialty, *chocolate y churros* (hot chocolate and delicious, sugar-dusted fried dough).

There are many restaurants to choose from for both lunch and dinner right in the heart of this theater district. **Pepito** and **Pippo**, the latter known for its eco-

Coffee and conversation in Café La Paz.

nomical menu, are next door to each other on the 300 block of Montevideo, half a block from Corrientes. At the end of this block, on the corner of Montevideo and Sarmiento is **Chiquilín**, a classic *parrilla*. Continuing down Corrientes towards 9 de Julio is **Los Inmortales**, a famous pizzeria decorated wall to wall with photos, posters and paintings of tango stars.

Plaza Lavalle, with its secondhand bookstalls, crowded park benches and dog walkers, is another center of activity. It is two blocks north on Talcahauna street from Corrientes. The **Palacio de Justicia**, more commonly referred to as Tribunales, is the ancient, weathered court building at one end of the plaza. In the morning, when the courts are in session, the steps are crowded with attorneys, judges, and state employees coming, going and lingering to chat. On the other side of the plaza is the internationally renowned Teatro Colón. The plaza first served as a dumping ground for the unusable parts of cattle butchered for their hides. In the late-19th century, it became the site of the first train station, which later moved to Once.

Opera House: The **Teatro Colón**, Buenos Aires' opera house, occupies the entire block between Viamonte, Lavalle, Libertad, and Cerrito (one of the streets off 9 de Julio). It is the symbol of the city's culture, and part of the reason why Buenos Aires became known early in the century as the "Paris of Latin America." The theater's elaborate European architecture, its acoustics, said to be near perfect, and the quality of the performers appearing here, have made the opera house internationally famous.

Three architects took part in the construction of the building before it was finally finished in 1907. The original blueprint, however, was respected. It is a combination of Italian Renaissance, French and Greek styles. The interior includes great colored glass domes and elaborate chandeliers. The principal auditorium is seven stories high and holds up to 3,500 spectators. There is an

Classical concert in the Teatro Colón.

18 by 34-meter (60 by 110-feet) stage on a revolving disk that permits rapid scenery changes.

Over 1,300 people are employed by the theater. In addition to the opera, the National Symphony Orchestra and the National Ballet are housed here. In a recent rehaul that cost millions of dollars, a huge basement floor was added – creating storage space for the sets, costumes and props and working space for the various departments.

The Colón's season runs approximately from April–November, and there is an interesting guided tour of the opera house Monday–Friday, every hour on the hour, from 9am–4pm, and on Saturdays 9am until noon.

One block from the Colón, on the corner of Libertad and Córdoba, is the **Museo Judío**, open Tuesday and Thursday 4–8pm. The museum is housed inside the historic synagogue Templo de la Congregación Israelita Argentina, and is dedicated to the history of Jewish immigration to Argentina.

Looking up in the Teatro Colón.

Crossing 9 de Julio takes you into the *microcentro*, an area limited on the other three sides by Rivadavia, **Leandro Alem** and **Córdoba**. Traffic is restricted to public transportation during working hours, but do not let this lull you into pedestrian complacency: *colectivo* and taxi drivers are, in the opinion of many, the wildest in the Western hemisphere.

For this reason it is worth going one block over to **Lavalle**, which is a pedestrian walkway. Lavalle is a moviegoer's paradise: there are about 20 theaters in a four-block stretch. Pizza parlors, cafés and ice-cream shops provide sustenance between shows. At 941 Lavalle is **La Estancia**, a *parrilla* easily recognized by its authentic barbeque pit in the front window, and of course *asado* is the thing to order once inside.

Lavalle intersects with **Calle Florida**, also closed to motor vehicles. This promenade is packed with shoppers as well as folk musicians, mimes, preachers and others passing the hat. There is a leisurely pace here and, because of the crowds, it is not a good route for those in a hurry.

Issues of the day: Most intriguing of all are the heated political debates taking place on the street. Sometimes they are intentionally provoked by party activists who have set up campaign tables, but just as often they are begun by groups of older men who seem to have made these discussions their retirement hobby, or they are simply spontaneous arguments over the news of the day.

In all cases, crowds gather around to hear the central players' opinions. Even for visitors unable to follow the conversation fully, it is worth pausing to observe these frequent episodes, for they provide a glimpse of into the vibrant Argentine political scene.

The shopping on Florida is slightly more expensive than other districts outside downtown. As elsewhere, most shops are one-room boutiques, many on interior shopping malls that exit onto adjacent streets. They sell clothes, leather goods, jewelry, toys, and gifts. Leather continues to be the best buy for visitors. Also, there are two tourist information booths located on either end of Florida, one being at Diagonal Roque Sáenz Peña and the other between Córdoba and Paraguay.

One of the most famous malls is the **Galerías Pacífico** between **Viamonte** and Córdoba. It is part of a turn-of-the-century Italian building that was saved from demolition because of the frescoes on the interior of its great dome. Five Argentine painters – Urruchua, Bern, Castagnino, Spilimbergo and Colmeiro – contributed to this vivid, lurid mural of social realism.

The largest bookstore in the country, **El Ateneo**, is at 340 Florida. It's wonderful for browsing, and definitely the best place to find books in English, maps, and guidebooks (check out the basement).

There are two traditional cafés along Florida: the **Richmond**, beloved by middle-aged *porteñas* for its English tea and homemade scones, and **Florida Garden**, a haven for journalists and politicians.

What to take home: Just past Paraguay on the last block of Florida is the **Centro Lincoln** (935 Florida), a library and reading room run by the US Embassy. Here one may read *The New York Times* and *The Washington Post*, as well as major magazines, all in English. Library hours are confined to weekdays from 1.30–5.30pm. The street dead ends at the entrance to **Ruth Benzacar's Gallery** (1000 Florida). It is literally an underground art gallery, dedicated to promoting contemporary artists.

Heading east down towards the river from Florida is **Kelly's**, at 431 Paraguay. It is the best-stocked and cheapest Argentine handicrafts store. It sells traditional artisans' goods from different provinces, including double-layered sheepskin slippers (the inside layer is to wear to bed), brightly-colored wool scarves, leather bags, wooden plates for barbecues, gaucho belts and smaller souvenirs made of native materials.

Spontaneous discussion on Calle Florida.

EATING OUT DOWNTOWN

The variety of choice is overwhelming. From elegant, sophisticated international cuisine to traditional Argentine grilled beef to pasta and pizza to simple sidewalk cafés. The quality and the prices vary greatly, but at midday almost all the places are full.

Any selection of restaurants must necessarily be subjective. If you begin at the southern end of downtown, in traditional Buenos Aires, lunch at **Pedemonte** on Avenida de Mayo is a true belle époque experience. Art nouveau stained glass and attentive service give the simple but well prepared beef and pasta an unexpected glamor. On the first block of Florida just behind the Cabildo is the wood and brick basement restaurant **La Veda**, specializing in grilled beef with a selection of red wines, and featuring dinner with a tango show.

There are numerous *parrillas* downtown, but two of the best are **La Estancia** on Lavalle and **La Chacra** on Córdoba at Suipacha. Both display *asado criollo* in the front window, which are sides of meat skewered and stretched over hot coals, a tradition of the gauchos of the Pampas. If you don't mind a smokey atmosphere, try their *parrillada*, where they set a mini-grill, coals and all, right on your table.

On Paraguay, a block up from Florida, is **Tasca Tancat**. Run by a family from the Catalan region of Spain, the place might best be described as an elegant luncheonette, with its soft lights, jazz, and long, polished wood counter. Some of the specialties include *pulpo español* (Spanish style squid), *tortilla de patatas* (potato omelette), and *champignones a la plancha* (grilled mushrooms). Save room for dessert – homemade creamy Catalan custard with cinnamon.

A couple more blocks up Paraguay towards 9 de Julio is a vegetarian's delight, **Yin Yang**, where health-conscious diners enjoy a respite from Argentina's staple, beef. The front section of the restaurant is cafeteria style, where you chose from a selection of fresh salads, soups and stews, savory pies, and brown rice with stir fried vegetables, all accompanied by homemade bread. Or head to the back and order from the menu in the more formal dining room.

Heading in the opposite direction on Paraguay, towards the river, is the very popular **Filo**, on San Martín. The decor is definitely modern – a kitchy dim-lit bar in front and an attractive dining room splashed with color, avant garde paintings and upbeat music, and even an art gallery in the basement. Here the artsy crowd dine on gourmet pizzas, salads, and fresh, unusual pastas – a light, Italian menu except for the tiramisu for dessert.

Just a couple of blocks away on the small side street Tres Sargentos is a Buenos Aires landmark, **Barbaro**, a lively little bar with an eclectic mix of art-decked brick walls, wooden tables, and young bohemian types seated next to business folk. Midday they serve a simple lunch menu with jazz or tango music and in the evenings lots of beer accompanied by great snack food.

If you prefer to go upscale, there's **Catalinas** around the corner on Reconquista. It's considered one of the top fish and seafood places, where chef Ramiro Rodriquez Pardo wields a mean skillet, in a reserved, elegant atmosphere.

Down on Avenida Leonardo Alem, just a couple of blocks from Retiro and Plaza San Martín, is **Restaurant Dora**. Located in the same spot since 1923 it's a Buenos Aires tradition. The dining room is simple but large and open. The menu features various seafood dishes, but you can also indulge in an enormous beef steak. ■

Welcoming waiter.

Argentina is justly famous for its succulent beef, generally grilled over coals or firewood, and there are literally hundreds of restaurants in Buenos Aires devoted to its preparation. One of the most classic places to indulge is the Costanera Norte, where excellent steakhouses are lined up on the riverside drive. Originally just a row of open air food carts, these cavernous beef emporia are still called *carritos*. The pleasant riverfront is an attraction by itself in warm weather. Other options include the steakhouses of Palermo, where the food is excellent and the atmosphere more casual and cozy, and the downtown restaurants like La Estancia, where gaucho-esque coal spits and skewered beef are displayed in the window.

A matter of terminology: A steak may be a steak in many parts of the world, but in Argentina it is many things under many guises. Making head or tail of the menu in a local *parrilla* (steakhouse) may be child's play for locals, but it can be bewildering to visitors, so here are a few tips to ensure carefree eating.

Local cuts differ greatly from what an American or European butcher would recognize. Argentines don't, for example, distinguish between sirloin, porterhouse and club steak, prime rib and short ribs the way a US butcher does. Rump and round are handled quite differently, and tenderloin has only a passing resemblance to *lomo*.

Bife means a steak prepared from any of the recognized roasting cuts; *churrasco* refers to a steak prepared from a cut not usually used for roasting (for instance, chuck, brisket or shank). *Bife de chorizo*, the most popular cut, is a steak cut off the rib and roughly rump or sirloin in context. A *bife de lomo* is sirloin and a *bife de costilla* corresponds roughly to a T-bone steak. After the *bife de chorizo* the most popular cut is the *tira de asado*, which is a strip of rib roast. If the *tira* is off the grill, it will be a long, fairly thin cut; if it is off the spit, it will be a shorter and much thicker cut.

Two other cuts that will figure on almost any menu are *vacio* and *matambre*. The former is a cut which comprises the bottom part of what in the US is designated as sirloin, porterhouse and the flank. Correctly grilled, it is perhaps the most flavorsome and juicy of all the cuts.

Matambre can come in various guises. Sometimes it is served hot right off the grill. But you'll probably encounter it more often cold and rolled up like a Swiss roll, with a vegetable and hardboiled egg filling. When prepared well, it's quite a treat, served as an appetizer, or at lunch time like a sandwich, squeezed inside fresh french bread.

A proper *parrilla* experience is started off with either *chorizo*, a rather fat and flavorful pork sausage (the one deviant from the beef theme), or *morcilla*, a decadent blood sausage for true carnivores. Both are served hot off the grill, and the main meat course is not far behind. If you like your beef rare ask for it *jugoso*; if medium, ask for it *a punto*; and if well done, *bien hecho*. Whichever way you like it, don't forget the wine.

Although Argentina has become the world's fifth largest producer of wine, its products are still relatively unknown overseas. This is because, until recently, Argentina had managed to drink it all – 91 liters (20 gallons) per head per annum in the 1970s! The recent decline in consumption (to less than 60 liters/13 gallons per head) combined with an almost uniform level of production (an average 20 million hectoliters per annum), has allowed producers to begin to seek foreign markets. But to enjoy the many good wines (and a few exceptional ones) that Argentina makes, you must go there – and know a little about how the country's wine market functions and the terminology used.

Wines are divided into two main types: *vino común* or *vino de mesa,* and *vino fino*. There is also a third, insignificant classification called *vino reserva*, usually regarded as a *vino común*.

A *vino común* is a table wine which can be either modest or dreadful. Unless you are advised by a knowledgeable local, it is best to pass up this type. *Vino fino* is a fine wine and as such is the one which will demand your attention. A good number are generic wines (blends) but many varietals are now making their debut, with great success. In Argentina a varietal must contain a minimum of 80 percent of the base grape, a rule which is in line with that of all other leading wine countries. In the case of white wines the percentage is generally 100, but red wines are more flexible.

Argentine grape varieties are almost entirely of European origin: Chardonnay, Chenin Blanc, Riesling, Cabernet Sauvignon, Merlot and Malbec, are only a small number of the 50-odd varieties cultivated. Almost 75 percent of the total wine production, including about 80 percent of Argentina's fine wine, originates in the province of Mendoza, tucked in the Andean foothills. Mendoza cultivates its vines on desert flatlands made fertile by irrigation water from the icy, crystalline snow which descends from the Andes. Other wine regions of importance are

San Juan, La Rioja and Salta in the Andean foothills, and the valley of the Rio Negro river, to the south.

Although made from European grapes, Argentine wines have a local flavor. This is due to the climate, soil and irrigation methods. In the case of many noble varieties, such as Cabernet, Riesling, Chardonnay and Merlot, the typical flavor is easily distinguishable. However, there are two varieties which can be considered exclusively Argentine for their quality if not their origin.

Above, typical lunch in a *parrilla* or steakhouse.

The first is Malbec, a grape which in France is not particularly distinguished but in Argentina makes what many consider its finest red wine. The second is the Torrontes, an unpopular grape of Spanish origin, which here makes a superb, full, fruity, very sweet white wine.

A few of the most respected and continually reliable wineries include Navarro Correas, La Rural, Escorihuela, Bianchi, and San Telmo. But don't play it safe, there's so much worth tasting, and if you act like an Argentine, both lunch and dinner warrant at least a glass.

The social life, and to a great extent the business and cultural life of Buenos Aires revolves around cafés, or *confiterías* as they are called in Argentina. "Meet me at the *confitería*" is the typical response to an invitation to go to the cinema or the opera as well as to talk over a deal or simply to get together for a chat. A coffee or a cognac in a favorite *confitería* is also the standard ritual for ending a night out on the town.

There are cafés on almost every corner and they range from the most elegant to modest and cozy gathering places where neighbors exchange greetings or employees from nearby offices take a break to read the daily paper. Visitors often comment that only Paris rivals Buenos Aires as a true "café society."

The importance of the café in daily life probably has roots in the necessity of creating meeting places outside the home, which in the Latin view is a private sanctuary. Another reason for the development of the café as an institution was the high proportion of male immigrants who were either single or whose womenfolk had stayed behind. Lonely and living in hotels and pensions, these men found companionship, and, in some cases, domino or parchesi partners in the corner café. The *confitería* as a refuge was not limited to humble immigrants. In one of Argentine literature's most famous novels, *El hombre que está solo y espera,* (*The Man Who Is Alone and Waiting*), published in 1931, author Raúl Scalabrini Ortiz situates his melancholy protagonist in a café on the corner of Corrientes and Esmeralda, site of the old café Royal Keller, a famous meeting place of the era, where Ortiz himself as well as other literary figures often went.

But whatever the social class, the early cafés were definitely a male preserve. In fact, a "*salón de familia,*" which used to be found in some *confiterías*, was a concession to the female population given that it was thought improper for respectable ladies to be directly exposed to men's public habits, such as loud discussions and smoking.

So intimate was the connection between *porteños* and their cafés that many of them became associated with a specific clientele. Each political, artistic, literary, student and social group laid claim to its own café. From the turn of the century up to the present, many of the events that mark Argentine political and intellectual history were first discussed among friends or foes over a *confitería* table.

But the café is also a place to be alone. Its association with loneliness has made the café the setting of many tangos; it is there late at night that the abandoned lover sings of his despair as he drinks "the last coffee" (*El Ultimo Café* tango with lyrics by Catulo Castillo and music by Héctor Stamponi). One of the most famous tango lyricists, Enrique Santos Discepolo, immortalized the café in his *Cafétin de Buenos Aires*, recalling it as "a school of all things" where he learned "philosophy, gambling and cruel poetry, and to think no more of me."

Preserving the past: A few of the most

Left, pondering the meaning of life in the Café Tortoni. **Right**, gilded lamps in the Café El Molino.

famous cafés still exist, little changed from their golden era. In the city center are four *confiterías* that evoke the belle époque, each with its own special flavor and history.

One of the oldest, most historically well known and best preserved of the Buenos Aires cafés is the **Tortoni**, on Avenida de Mayo and Piedras. Its deep red leather chairs and beautiful painted skylights, the luminous billiards room, *salón de familia* and onyx chess and domino tables evoke the epoch, celebrated in the portraits and photographs on the walls, when the Tortoni was a gathering place for the most famous and infamous in the city's active cultural life.

Founded in 1858 by a Frenchman named

and artistic life, with recitals or theater performances almost every night of the week, jazz and tango being the most common. And debates about literature, politics and the meaning of life, spiced by frothy *café con leche* or a cold beer, take place every day, just as they have for more than a century.

Not far away, on Suipacha just off Corrientes, is the **Confitería Ideal**. Right in the heart of the *microcentro*, it is a legendary place for high tea. More than that, for the price of coffee and cake, you can have a taste of life in Argentina's art nouveau past. Elaborate brass fittings embrace the marble columns and, in the late afternoons, an organist plays a medley of classic tunes – waltzes,

Touan, the Tortoni became the epicenter of intellectual life on May 12, 1926, when the painter Benito Quinquela Martín presided over the founding of *La Peña* (The Circle).

Throughout the 1920s, 1930s and 1940s, every distinguished and avant-garde figure in Argentina frequented the Tortoni. In addition, every well-known intellectual or cultural personality that visited Buenos Aires made an appearance at *La Peña*.

The autobiographies, biographies and histories of the period are replete with anecdotes based on incidents that happened in the Tortoni. The café is still a center of musical

tangos, ballads – giving tired shoppers and expectant theatergoers a rest from the crowded downtown streets.

Tea at five: Staying close to the city center, another café that has escaped destruction and/or audacious remodeling is the **Richmond**. Located on Florida between Corrientes and Lavalle, the Richmond has been the place to take tea and scones since the early days of the century. At one time it was, like the Tortoni, a center of literary life, with

Above, teatime in the Café Ideal is a time-honored custom among older *porteños*.

authors and public figures holding court in its Anglophile atmosphere.

Politics and pastries: Politics was always the theme at the other great monument to the Argentine café – **Confitería del Molino** – or simply El Molino to *porteños*. How could it be otherwise? The Molino is just across the street from the Congress and senators and deputies often go there.

"Molino" is the Spanish word for "mill" and the café's name derives from the fact that its original location, at Avenida de Mayo and Rodriguez Peña, just a block away, was across from a flour mill. This is the reason there is a landmark neon windmill on the building's lovely cupola.

El Molino's owner, Cayetano Brenna, saw an opportunity for expansion when work began on the Congress building in 1905, and bought the corner property. By 1914 the Molino was "the place to go," leading Brenna to undertake a vast remodeling that was completed in 1917. Not only did the refurbished *confitería* have the latest belle époque decor, with its imported Walter Scott-inspired vitraux, porcelain and marble fittings, but it also had three underground levels for the preparation of pastries, wine storage and ice making.

In 1979, after four difficult years caused by the closing of Congress by the military government, it was announced that El Molino and the entire building was to be demolished. After months of public outcry, a new corporation formed by descendants of Brenna was able to negotiate its salvation.

El Molino's turn-of-the-century beauty is sadly faded, with its delicate glass mosaic lanterns and windows broken and inoperative, its walls unpainted and its upper floors badly in need of restoration. But one can hope it will prosper and the owners can return it to the splendor of past decades.

In addition to the above *"grande dame"* cafés, there are dozens of others with some special element. At the corner of Rivadavia and Medrano in the heart of Caballito, is the 100-year-old **Las Violetas** which is a more modest version of El Molino. Or if you like having your coffee in the open air there are La Biela and Café de la Paix in the Recoleta. There are also cafés which appeal to the anti-establishment factions of Buenos Aires' intellectual society. A long favored haunt of "café revolutionaries" is the Café **La Paz** on Corrientes, across the street from the San Martín Theater. Decorated in a no-frills 1930s style, the neon-lit café often resembles a library reading-room, as patrons pore over recent purchases from nearby bookstalls. La Paz offers a snack menu as well as the requisite thick black espresso, but it's perfectly acceptable to spend several hours at a table over a single cup of coffee.

During the military government, police routinely raided establishments such as La Paz in search of "subversive elements," but in these more tranquil times, families and dapper elderly couples join the ranks of bearded young *porteños* discussing the state of the world.

Another delightful bohemian spot is **La Giralda** on Corrientes, whose rich Spanish-style chocolate and *churros* (fritters) are famous throughout the city.

On the corner of Paraguay and Paraná is **La Esquina de Troilo**, named for the famous bandoneón player Anibal Troilo. Unchanged through the years, the ancient café is a homage to tango, with photos and clippings covering the walls. If you're curious about where journalists and political "insiders" meet to exchange information, stop in at the **Florida Garden** on the corner of Paraguay and Florida. The 1960s kitchy decor is an amusing contrast to the abundance of cellular phones and deal-making.

El Taller couldn't be more different, with its wooden tables, lofty ceiling, and colorfully painted walls. Right in the heart of Palermo, on the corner of Serrano and Honduras, it's a gathering place for the artistic and bohemian set, with unconventional theater and music performances on weekend nights. A very down-to-earth, cozy café is the **Plaza Dorrego Bar**, a great spot to relax and enjoy a coffee, a glass of wine or a cold beer in the midst of exploring San Telmo. And on the edge of elegant Palermo Chico is the charming **Le Trianon**, nestled in the palace garden of the Museo de Arte Decorativo. In pleasant weather, the shaded patio is a tranquil but refined respite from the hustle and bustle of the city.

The *porteño* passion for cinema has filled Buenos Aires with an overwhelming variety of theaters and supported a new Argentine film industry which is taking prizes at festivals the world over.

More than 70 cinemas are operating in the city center alone. They radiate from three main centers: the pedestrian walkway Lavalle, which clogs with departing audiences after evening sessions until it becomes almost impossible to move; and Avenida Corrientes, where queues a block long can be seen at 1.30am every Saturday, before the *trasnoche* session; and in Barrio Norte, where there are several theaters on Avenida Santa Fe between Callao and Pueyrredon.

Every day, the cinema pages of the newspapers eagerly follow the latest releases in the United States and Europe, which quickly make their way to Buenos Aires. Local critics assess their quality, and gossip columnists follow their stars.

Movie houses: Some of the old theaters on Corrientes are worth visiting for themselves. They include cinema palaces of the 1920s which nobody has had the money or the heart to knock down, with marble staircases and chandeliers. The art deco **Gran Rex** is an old favorite, opposite **El Opera** with its elegant balconies and statues where, when the lights go down, tiny twinkling stars appear on the ceiling. In fact, neither of these relics currently shows films, but have been converted into rock and pop concert venues.

Besides the commercial chains there are a few art-house cinemas which show classic re-releases, plus European, and independent films. The daily *Guía de Espectáculos* in the newspaper *Clarín* is the best place to check the latest offerings. Alternative options include **Leopoldo Lugones** in the San Martín Theater, the **Lorange**, **Losuar**, and **Locra** on Corrientes, two movie houses on Avenida de Mayo – **Gloria** and **Avenida**, and **Cine Club TEA** on Scalabrini Ortiz. Also the universities, cultural centers (especially the **Centro Cultural Ricardo Rojas**), museums and even the commercial theaters are known to sponsor unusual film showings.

Most bohemian of all are the meetings at the **IRCA** (Instituto de Realización Cinematográfica Argentina) cinema, where nearly everyone has to sit on the floor. Film reels are changed by hand on the sole projector available, and every screening is followed by an audience debate.

Porteño film buffs had to catch up on world cinema after years of film censorship under the former military government. Classics such as *Last Tango in Paris* had to wait

until democracy returned to be screened. A bizarre side-effect of this sudden freedom was the tendency to translate foreign film titles more suggestively. *The Sound of Music,* for example, ran under the titillating name of *The Rebel Nun*.

Artistic freedom: The lifting of censorship under democracy was a major impetus behind the Argentine film industry.

"The opening-up after censorship allowed us to experiment with new themes," says critic and Argentine cinema expert Jorge Couselo. "We were able to expose and analyze what had happened in these last years:

the repression, the exiles, the lack of freedom of expression."

This process of revealing the hidden history of the dictatorship was recognized overseas when Luis Puenzo's *La Historia Oficial* (*The Official Story*) won the Academy Award for Best Foreign Film in 1986. It told of the experience of a *porteño* couple who thought that they hád escaped the traumas of the 1970s – only to find that their adopted daughter's real mother was "disappeared" by the military for political reasons.

cinema include *La Pelicula del Rey* (*The King and His Movie*), "a tribute to all failed heroes." It is about a director's colorful but doomed attempt to make a film about a 19th-century Frenchman who declares himself king of the Patagonian Indians. *Hombre Mirando al Sudeste* (*Man Facing Southeast*) by Eliseo Subiela is a touching drama about a saxophone-playing psychologist who is assigned a patient in a mental hospital who insists he is from another planet. *Camila*, directed by María Luisa Bemberg, is based

New films dealing with the dictatorship continue to appear – after all, Italian cinema was still obsessed with fascism 35 years after the war. A highly entertaining classic by Argentine director and political activist Pino Solanas is *El Exilio de Gardel* (*Gardel's Exile*), which looks at Argentine exiles in Paris desperately trying to hold onto their identities through fragile tokens such as *mate* and the tango.

The three other great successes of the new

on the true story of Camila O'Gorman and her affair with a Catholic priest in the mid-1800s, dealing with the church and repression during Rosas' nationalistic government.

Despite its international success at film festivals, Argentine cinema is still struggling to compete in its small local market with the ever-increasing flood of overseas films, and to overcome its chronic shortage of funds.

"You cannot separate the cinema's problems from the economic problems of the country," says Couselo. "But the artistic ingredients are certainly there to ensure continuing success of the industry."

Left, moviegoing on Lavalle. **Above**, scene from the popular film, *The King and His Movie*.

Even those who don't usually make a point of going out of their way to hear classical music while traveling should not miss a night at the **Teatro Colón**.

Settling back in a turn-of-the-century armchair as the great hall reverberates, you can soak up the atmosphere of what has been for more than 80 years one of the world's great opera houses. At the Colón, every performance is still a grand event.

Whether or not they have actually set foot inside, *porteños* always invoke the Colón as climb up almost to the theater's rafters – known as *paraíso*. These few and coveted tickets are available at *precios populares*, or just a few dollars.

After lingering for a suitable spell on the theater's outside steps, the audience make their way into the entrance foyer. Here they savor the splendor which inspired dancer Mikhail Barishnikov to call the Colón "the most beautiful of all the theaters I know."

The performance hall within is even more spectacular. The orchestra consists of 632

proof that their city's remoteness from Europe is a question of geography rather than of culture or style.

The building takes up a whole city block between Plaza Lavalle and Avenida 9 de Julio. At night it is floodlit, providing an irresistible backdrop for Argentine elegance. Taxis and limousines glide to the doorway bearing gentlemen in tuxedos and pomaded hair, and suntanned ladies in fur coats, where they are met by uniformed doormen who furtively pocket their tips.

Meanwhile the more humble arts enthusiasts line up at the side entrance waiting to individual wooden armchairs laid out in careful rows, each padded with mauve velvet. The theater is ringed with six tiers of curtained boxes and gilded gallery seats, allowing the Colón to seat 2,400 or stand 4,000 if a great artist is performing.

At the base of the stage are *baignoires* where *porteños* once heard performances. It now houses the radio equipment used to broadcast every performance live to Buenos Aires. The domed ceiling boasts a mural by Raúl Soldi and a vast chandelier holding 700 light bulbs.

The extravagant plans for the Colón were

first drawn up at the end of the 1880s. The Italian architect Francisco Tamburini hoped for completion within three years. Eighteen years and two architects later, the theater was ready, displaying its curious mix of German 19th-century, Italian Renaissance and French classical styles.

The Colón is currently expanding a small museum which was attached to the entrance foyer, and paid homage to the famous and forgotten artists who have performed here since *Aida* was first presented in 1908. Vaslov

original faded tutu is preserved beneath glass, along with a portrait of Argentine composer Héctor Panizza. The conducting baton of Arturo Toscanini remains the museum's prized possession. The new and larger museum will display even more of the Colón's colorful history, including some original sets, costumes, musical instruments, and photos. It will soon be located in the theater's recently renovated basement.

Yet now, as in the past, more than a month of preparations are needed before the curtain is

Nijinsky and Anna Pavlova have bounded across its stage. Stravinsky, Strauss and Bernstein have conducted here; *porteño* audiences have thrilled to the voices of such greats as Italian tenor Enrico Caruso, Australian soprano Nelly Melba and, more recently, María Callas, Plácido Domingo and Joan Sutherland.

The museum also contains relics from the 1920s, when European opera groups would spend their off-seasons in Buenos Aires. An

finally raised on any production. Beneath the Colón's stage are three floors of underground workshops, where tens of thousands of costumes and wigs are stored. Among the items carefully filed away are 30,000 pairs of shoes, including the proudly displayed leathers once worn by Rudolf Nureyev in *The Nutcracker*.

In these workshops, the entire 1,000-sq. meter (10,000-sq. foot) backdrop to each opera is expertly handpainted by teams of craftspeople. Elsewhere, a subterranean rehearsal room is an exact replica of the stage upstairs, allowing artists to practise while another work is being performed.

Left, the Colón Opera House. **Above**, applause at the Colón Opera House.

On a Saturday night as you walk down the busy street of Corrientes in the heart of Buenos Aires' main entertainment district, someone might well approach you and thrust a slip of paper into your hand. If the piece of paper is not advertising a new vegetarian restaurant or courses in parapsychology, then it's probably promoting some new play or other.

The "Broadway" of Buenos Aires: Corrientes itself is lined with theaters, most of which offer popular plays and musicals by well-

ences are vanishing. Directors, too, complain they are losing good local playwrights to the more lucrative cinema and television industries.

Of course, theater has not always struggled. In the days before anyone knew anything about foreign debt, Argentina built playhouses and a world-famous opera house as monuments to its European past.

The very first theater in Buenos Aires was a large straw-roofed storehouse called *La Rancheria* or The Settlement, because of its

known local, Spanish or international playwrights. The enormous marquees, bright lights and big names attract theatergoers from all over the city and the rest of the country. In addition to these big theaters, "On Corrientes" style productions can be seen in the new theater complex **La Plaza**, with four separate smaller salons, and in the **Fundación Banco Patricios** on Callao.

But, as is happening worldwide, theater is losing out to the video age; and in a country where cinema production is also experiencing a national revival, many theaters are having a difficult time. Not just the audi-

proximity to many new colonizing urban settlements.

Early Argentine theater often covered rural themes and later the lives of those who lived in the city's famous *conventillos* or tenements. In this century, Argentina's theater became particularly well-known for its *Teatro Independiente,* a movement which adapted Arthur Miller-style realism to local themes.

Very "Off-Corrientes": Today the small but active independent theater community experiments with many genres, but is united in its effort to combat the waning of the public's interest which has been ascribed to the coming of the video age.

The **Teatro Del Sur** in Monserrat, run by award-winning director and playwright Alberto Felix Alberto, considers itself a "cultural promoter" – trying to inspire creativity in the younger generation and the city in general. To this end, they have joined a network of theaters from 15 Latin American countries, with the objective of promoting more independent works, facilitating exchanges between artists from different countries, and creating a support system for taking smaller productions on tour. But the Teatro Del Sur is obviously not just about cultural activism – its productions are well produced yet very different from "On Corrientes" offerings, including locally written and avant garde plays.

Other independent art spaces around the city include **Liberarte** and **Librería Ghandi**, two bookstores/cafés which feature a wide variety of entertainment evenings and weekends, from poetry readings to comedy to small musical revues. **La Carbonera** in San Telmo has an interesting space, housed in a renovated antique residence. **Babilonia** offers a mix of productions, as well as **Payro**, located right behind the Galerías Pacífico on San Martín.

State supported theater: Yet another great way to take in the Buenos Aires theater scene is to attend one of the many performances held in the numerous state funded cultural centers or theaters.

The largest by far is the **Teatro San Martín** in the heart of the Corrientes theater district, which features a wide variety of national productions, both theater and dance, as well as hosting numerous international groups which are in Argentina dining the course of their world tours.

The **Centro Cultural Recoleta** has a more bohemian feel, where the alternative set go

to attend experimental, locally produced theater. Even more on the edge is the **Centro Cultural Ricardo Rojas**, affiliated with the University of Buenos Aires, and a magnet for young and open-minded art-lovers. Performers are often from actors' cooperatives, making their living from other full-time jobs, but nevertheless going on stage several nights a week.

The **Nacional Cervantes** just off Plaza Lavalle is an imposing gothic style building completed in 1921. The theater features three

different auditoriums, and on weekdays they offer guided tours to give a closer look at the antique structure.

While live theater may be struggling to survive economically, the choices seem to remain abundant. Not only is there dance at the San Martín, Brecht at the Babilonia, or an avant garde puppet show at the Cervantes, street performers and theater in the city's plazas have become a weekend staple. On a warm Sunday afternoon in Plaza Francia you will encounter jugglers and actors, dancers and acrobats, entertaining the crowds and passing the hat.

Left, innovative, quality theater productions are offered continuously at the Centro Cultural San Martín. Right, mime entertains a crowd.

SAN TELMO AND MONSERRAT

If any place in Buenos Aires confirms that this city has been around for much more than the past century, it's the neighboring *barrios* of Monserrat and San Telmo. To the south of Plaza de Mayo, these historically colorful districts were once the heart of city life and are where virtually all of the pre-20th century buildings can be found. A project to demolish these ancient structures that was dreamed up in the 1950s happily never reached fruition, and since 1979, the area has been protected as a historical zone.

Monserrat, which borders the south side of Plaza de Mayo, is where *porteños* once gathered to watch bullfights before the sport was outlawed at the end of the last century. Today locals go there to buy computers or industrial machinery. But the barrio's legend as a hangout for big-talking knifefighters – *cuchilleros* – lives on, as in this popular verse:

Soy del barrio e' Monserrat
donde relumbra el acero
Lo que digo con el pico
lo sostengo con el cuero.

(I'm from the barrio of Monserrat,
where steel flashes
what I say with my mouth
I enforce with my hide.)

Long knives no longer hold sway in Monserrat, and a stroll through the bustling *barrio* during the daytime should prove quite safe and give a revealing glimpse of another era in the city's life. As always on the city's narrow one-way streets, stick to the sidewalk nearest the passenger side of vehicles to avoid exhaust fumes.

Block of enlightenment: A good starting point is Plaza de Mayo. From there, head up **Avenida Julio A. Roca**, the diagonal street that begins to the left of the old white Cabildo. The big equestrian statue dominating the traffic circle at the end of the block is of General Roca, who distinguished himself massacring the nomadic Indians who resisted westward expansion in the 1860s. The **Ministry of Labor** is to the right, a site of frequent boisterous workers' demonstrations. To the left, on the corner of **Alsina** and **Peru**, is the historic **Manzana de las Luces** or Block of Lights, earlier known as the Block of Intellectuality. Most of the buildings on this block date back to the 18th century. A theater complex run by the municipality occupies the side of the block along Peru. This area once housed the lower house of congress and was earlier headquarters for the Jesuit missions in Argentina.

Turning down Alsina and walking toward **Bolívar**, you'll find the oldest building in Buenos Aires, the **Iglesia de San Ignacio**. This "temple of lights," as it was called by its Jesuit founders, was begun in 1710 and finished in 1734. Like all the other churches in the area, San Ignacio was sacked and burned by Peronist mobs in 1955. But its gilded, carved wood altar survived the attack

and is virtually the only baroque decor to be found in any of the city's churches. Next to the church on Bolívar is the prestigious **Colegio Nacional**, a highly selective state-run school where many of the country's business and political leaders received their secondary education. It also happens to be the *alma mater* of Montonero terrorist leader, Mario Firmenich.

Crossing Bolívar and continuing along Alsina brings you to some fine examples of old residential architecture. At 463 Alsina begin the crumbling remains of a *circa* 1840 residence, whose wrought-iron railed balconies reflect the Italian architectural lines in vogue at the time. The *casona* was once occupied by the widow of the 19th-century dictator Rosas. On the corner is the oldest house in the city, built in 1812. (Older structures collapsed due to infestations of termites.)

Across the street, at 412 Alsina, is the **Museo de la Ciudad,** one flight up. Its historical exhibits of the city are changed every other month, and are housed in what used to be a family dwelling. The museum is open Monday–Friday 11am–7pm and Sunday 3–7pm.

Next to the museum, on the corner, is the **Estrella Farmacia.** The etched shop windows and dark wooden cabinets inside recall turn-of-the-century Buenos Aires, as do the porcelain chamberpots on display, relics from "when *porteños* refused to leave the bedroom." A ceiling fresco inside allegorically portrays "the triumph of pharmacy over disease."

On the corner across Defensa Street are the Basílica and **Convento de San Francisco** completed in 1754. An enormous tapestry which portrays the Virgin Mary (exceeded in size only by a tapestry in Great Britain's Coventry Cathedral) hangs where the main altar stood before it was incinerated during the 1955 Peronist riots.

On the right-hand side of this Franciscan church, towards the back, is a statue of San Benito de Palermo, "the black Franciscan saint," patron of the

Wares at Sunday Antiques Fair in Plaza Dorrego.

needy. (Monserrat was once heavily populated by emancipated black slaves, whose descendants have now virtually disappeared from Buenos Aires.)

If you wish to linger in Alsina, stop in at **Puerto Rico** (number 422), a simple and traditional teahouse.

From Alsina, head south away from Plaza de Mayo up **Calle Defensa.** This street was once the ox-cart thoroughfare for products coming from the south. A block and a half up the street at 372 Defensa is the **Museo Nacional del Grabado,** a museum of printmaking housed in a restored home dating back to the late 1800s. The museum features interesting exhibitions of various contemporary artists, and is open 2–6pm every day except Saturday. Just next door is **Viejos Tiempos,** a pleasant European-style pub also in a renovated colonial-era home, where President Rivadavia once lived. It is open weekdays only, until 9pm, and serves a small lunch menu accompanied by over a dozen imported beers. The seating up-stairs is especially nice with wooden shutters opening onto the street.

Half a block further up Defensa, crossing **Belgrano**, is the **Iglesia Santo Domingo**, built in 1751. The courtyard is dominated by a bier on which rest the remains of General Manuel Belgrano, a hero in the fight for independence and the creator of the Argentine flag.

The upper portion of the belltower on the left side of the church is studded with 19 wooden plugs. Like wounds carefully kept from healing, these plugs supposedly mark where patriots' bullets struck when fired at British troops holed up there in 1806. (It is from this episode, incidentally, that the street Defensa got its name.) Inside the church, behind a shrine to the Virgin on the left-hand side, are four faded and tattered Union Jacks, captured from the British who had tried to seize the city. One of the flags once flew over what was later to become Plaza Britannia (in front of Retiro train station).

From Santo Domingo Church, walk

Left, San Telmo fruit stand. **Right**, fortune-teller poses in her "Magic Corner."

down Belgrano past the old convent and turn right up **Balcarce**. This wide, quiet flagstone street takes you past the former mint, now the **Archivo General del Ejército,** or Army Archives, and various tango bars, asleep during daylight hours but waiting for late night to come alive. Some of the bars located right around the old mint are **La Casablanca**, **Media Luz**, **La Cumparsita**, and **Michelangelo**. Go left on Chile to keep following Balcarce. You are now entering **San Telmo,** once the swankiest part of town and now home to an eclectic mix of artists and musicians, middle-class workers, and some poorer, recent immigrants.

San Telmo: Until the harbor was moved upstream in 1888, San Telmo was a riverport neighborhood, rising above shoals of the River Plate that almost reached what is now **Paseo Colón**. (The incline going down to this broad thoroughfare was once the old riverbank.) Both high and humble society lived here – great landowners and traders dwelt in imposing mansions; fishermen, stevedores, and black slaves in adobe huts. As late as 1838, blacks made up a third of the *barrio*'s population and had their own social center, *La Nación Conga.* White dwellers were, almost without exception, of Spanish birth or descent.

All this changed drastically in 1871, when a ferocious plague of yellow fever killed more than half of San Telmo's inhabitants – more than 13,000 people died during the three-month epidemic. At the time, nobody realized that this disease, indigenous to the Americas, was spread by mosquitoes that proliferated along the riverbank. All who could fled the *barrio* during and after the plague. The rich abandoned their mansions and moved to the burgeoning Barrio Norte, while most of the poor relocated in Monserrat.

San Telmo was quickly repopulated by shiploads of European immigrants, arriving mostly from Genoa, Italy and the Basque region of Spain. They moved

Baroque church of Nuestra Señora de Belén.

into the abandoned mansions, which were subdivided into crowded one- or two-room dwellings.

These squalid *conventillos* still exist in San Telmo, and are today largely inhabited by families from impoverished northern provinces and recent immigrants from Uruguay, Paraguay and Bolivia. These people tend to use the front stoops and sidewalks as an extended living-room in warm weather, giving the *barrio* a lively street life, especially in the evenings – a refreshing change from the somber streets winding through concrete canyons elsewhere in Buenos Aires.

Since being declared a historic zone in the early 1970s, San Telmo has gone through both a commercial and real-estate renaissance to become one of the trendiest neighborhoods in Buenos Aires. Decaying 19th-century homes have been transformed into cozy restaurants and shops that preserve many elements of the original structures.

You can see the inside of a restored *conventillo* by turning to the right up the quiet, charming street **San Lorenzo.** At 319 San Lorenzo is **Los Patios de San Telmo,** which until 1970 was a *conventillo.* Presently it's divided into about 30 artists' studios, with a bar at the entrance that sometimes features live Argentine folk music on weekend nights. A little further up San Lorenzo is **Ultimo Tango,** an old tango bar with a historic plaque marking its entrance.

Tango shrines, cobbles and restaurants: Turning around and continuing down Balcarce is probably the nicest walking route through San Telmo. Crossing Avenida Independencia, the next block is **Pasaje Giuffra,** a quaint little cobblestone street where the largest theater in San Telmo used to be located (it's now a film school). At 371 Giuffra is **La Scala de San Telmo Café,** a popular nightclub which features live music shows in the evenings, usually classical or tango.

Where Giuffra deadends at Defensa street is the **Galería Cecil,** a large in-

Anything can happen at San Telmo's Sunday fair.

door antiques market, with over 30 independent stalls and a pleasant café in the front lobby.

Continuing down Balcarce on the next corner at Estados Unidos is **Bar Sur,** a cozy and not at all upscale tango bar with just a few small wooden tables adorned with candles. Here you are sure to get very close to the performers.

Like churches in a holy land, this neighborhood is populated with such clubs, being a part of that sentimentally sacred terrain of Buenos Aires known loosely as "El Sur." Here is where sharply dressed *guapos* (dandys) adorned with forward-tilted fedoras and long silk scarves used to lean against lamp posts and pick their teeth, slyly waiting for passing women to swoon below their gaze. Or at least that's how the slice-of-life paintings and old tango songs of the era remember them.

At the next block is **Carlos Calvo**, another charming side street. To the right on Calvo are several picturesque restaurants. **La Tasca de los Cuchilleros** has a lovely plant-filled patio with outdoor tables, and offers both Spanish and Argentine cuisine. On the corner of Calvo and Defensa is **La Casa de Esteban de Luca,** the restored colonial-era home of "the poet of the revolution," where the food is good and more reasonably priced.

Just after Calvo, there are two interesting stops on Balcarce. At number 1016 is the home of Argentine painter **Castagnino,** whose murals decorate the ceiling of the shopping mall Galerías Pacífico on Florida street. Since the artist's death, his son has converted the house into an art museum.

Just further down on the right is **Galería del Viejo Hotel** (1053 Balcarce), another old *conventillo* that has been converted into an arts center, with two floors of small art studios surrounding a central courtyard. It is open to the public to wander through, peek at the studios, and of course purchase some of the art work.

Antique shops and Sunday fair: Leaving

Playing *truco* in Lezama Park.

Balcarce and walking back along Defensa brings you to the antique zone, which runs for several blocks in both directions. These shops are usually open after 3pm and their negotiable prices tend to undercut those prevailing in the United States and Europe. Don't be shy about bargaining because almost all the merchants are willing to listen to counter-offers.

At 1066 Defensa is an attractive shopping mall, **Galería El Solar de French.** It was an old residence remodeled in its original colonial style, with beautiful stone floors, plants and bird cages hanging from wrought iron hooks along long patios, and narrow wooden doors.

Here you arrive at what is considered the heart of San Telmo, **Plaza Dorrego.** During the week this is a rather unremarkable square sorely lacking benches. But on Sunday, from 10am to 5pm, it's transformed into a colorful antique and curio fair where you can buy anything from satin underwear to copper-plated milk cans. The Feria de San Telmo is a popular destination for both foreign tourists and jet-set *porteños*, who are also entertained in adjacent streets by poets, dancers, mimes, and itinerant singers and musicians.

A couple of peanut-shells-on-the-floor bars facing the plaza are inviting: **Plaza Dorrego Bar** and **Café de la Feria**, where the tap beer far outflows the coffee. Take a table on the terrace on warm evenings.

Morbid museum: Near the plaza, just down **Humberto Primo**, is one of the more ghoulish attractions Buenos Aires has to offer. It's the **Museo Penitenciario**, housed in a mid-19th century prison that functioned up until the late 1870s. Here you'll find leg-irons attached to cellblock walls and mournful-looking mannequins sporting prison garb from centuries past. All this is explained in numbing detail by cheerful young Spanish-speaking guides from whom you can pick up a surprising number of euphemisms for the word "prisoner."

Just down the street from the jail

Left, trying a hat for size. **Right**, young *porteño*.

museum is a San Telmo landmark, the graceful **Iglesia de Nuestra Señora de Belén**. Its construction, which began in 1805, took another 71 years to complete, mostly for lack of adequate funds from the tight-fisted parishioners.

Not all the locals gave up on San Telmo after the 1871 yellow fever scourge. The Ezeiza family took advantage of rock-bottom land prices when the plague's victims had barely been buried. The large patio-centered home they built on Defensa between Humberto Primo and **San Juan** is now the **Pasaje de la Defensa**, an attractive array of shops selling artisan and manufactured goods. There's also a pricey *cantina* active at the weekend. As with most establishments in San Telmo, it's closed on Monday.

Farther up Defensa, at **Calle Brazil**, you'll find **Parque Lezama**. This is where the Argentine author Ernesto Sábato opens his renowned novel, *On Heroes and Tombs*. The park has seen better days, but remains a popular gathering place for children and the elderly, especially at weekends.

During the summer months there are often free evening concerts in the park's open-air amphitheater. Here is where many mimes and actors made the first stabs at public performances during the former military regime. They were all arrested for their efforts, but they have since flourished under Argentina's civilian government.

The park is believed by many to be the site of the first founding of the city. Later, it was a large private estate belonging to Gregorio Lezama, who made it into a public park. The estate's colonial style mansion is still standing and has been converted into the **Museo Histórico Nacional** (1600 Defensa), or the national history museum. It's open Tuesday–Friday 2.30–6pm.

From Parque Lezama, you can either plunge onward to La Boca, the riverside Italian *barrio* splashed with color, or return by Defensa or Paseo Colón to downtown Buenos Aires.

Antique clothing store in Pasaje de la Defensa.

THE COLECTIVO

Elsewhere in South America, buses are called just that: bus or omnibus. But in Buenos Aires the bus is called a *colectivo* (short for *transporte colectivo* or collective transport).

If you are the kind of person who demands comfort and courteous service, the Argentine *colectivo* is definitely not for you. However if you want to see the entire city of Buenos Aires and the surrounding suburban and industrial area for under a dollar, the *colectivo* is what you want.

Don't be shy about asking at newspaper stands and the ever-present *kioscos* for bus information, it's a common practice even among *porteños*. Be prepared with your fare, which is fifty centavos within Capital Federal, and that's for one ride, no transfers. But it is very unlikely that you would need to take more than one bus to get anywhere, especially from or around the center of town.

However the story changes if you are going to cross General Paz (the city limits), when the fare rises incrementally. Just tell the driver your destination and pay accordingly. As you board at the front end of the bus, there is an automatic coin machine (bills not accepted) where you deposit your fare and it spits out your ticket.

There are more than 140 *colectivo* lines serving Buenos Aires and the greater Buenos Aires area and they run about once every five or 10 minutes throughout most of the day. A number of them run slightly less frequently at night and those that don't, only rest between about midnight and 5am, so it's a pretty good round-the-clock service.

If you don't insist on taking the *colectivo* at peak hours of the day – 8 to 10am and 5 to 9pm – you can plot your own very inexpensive daily tour of different parts of the city. By combining *colectivos* you can reach practically any point of the Greater Buenos Aires area and get from there to just about any other point you choose. And all points lead to the center of the city – eventually.

Taking a bus at rush-hour is an experience that is only for the hardened Buenos Aires resident – a bone-crushing free-for-all in which seats are fully occupied and commuters squeeze three-deep into the narrow center aisle. At this time of day, men and boys hang precariously out the doors of the vehicle and drop running to the pavement as the driver slows, but does not completely come to a halt, at stops.

The typical *colectivo* driver (*colectivero*) is a surly, rude, bossy man who will leave you behind if you don't hurl yourself at his passing vehicle and cling on for dear life. But do pity them. These men (women *colectivo* drivers are few and far between) fight snarled unruly Buenos Aires traffic all day, with many of them driving shifts of up to 14 hours. And they live with inspectors breathing down their necks about staying on schedule. They could hardly not be surly.

But it is the *colectivo* – with its varied and flashy color combinations which distinguish one line from another – that mobilizes the *porteño*.

It's also a surprisingly efficient service. For the traveler with a minimal command of Spanish, it can be an interesting, exhaustive way to see the city. It's a good idea to take a map with you, to make sure that you are heading in the direction you intended.

The buses stop every three or four blocks, so as you approach your destination make your way towards the back to get off. There's a buzzer at the back door that lets the driver know you want to get off at the next stop.

Help is at hand if ever you feel stuck. Do approach your fellow passengers regarding directions, most people will do their best. But most of all, hang on. ∎

A colorful *colectivo*.

For those with expensive tastes, Buenos Aires has plenty of four-fork restaurants where the menus are in Spanish and English and the prices are geared for expense-account living.

But there are also many places for those who prefer good food with few frills.

Probably the most popular eatery in Buenos Aires is **Pippo's**. Actually, there are three Pippo's, all on the same block – one at 356 Paraná, and the other two side by side on the other side of the block at 345 and 346 Montevideo. They're all the same – brightly

Another popular eatery in the same district, but slightly more upscale, is **Chiquilín**, at Montevideo and Sarmiento. The immortal tango crooner, Carlos Gardel, grins under his fedora from a portrait hung at one end of the dining area. Gazing proprietorily from the other side is a brass bust of Anibal "Pichuco" Troilo, the squeeze-box "monster" (as *porteños* call their heroes) who made this restaurant legendary in the tango *Chiquilín de Bachín*. Cured hams hang from the rafters, wine bottles line the walls, sheets of

lit, pale green *trattorias* with white-jacketed waiters rushing around with teetering stacks of dishes. Patrons sit at paper-covered tables (on which waiters used to scribble the bill until printed receipts became mandatory) often elbow-to-elbow with strangers. The food is economical and dependable – "ours is export meat," says the sign; the pasta is made on the premises. Try a steaming platter of *vermicelli mixto:* pesto and tomato sauce on plump noodles. The hearty red house wine comes in carafes and, mixed with ice and soda water (as *porteños* are wont to do), makes a refreshing spritzer.

paper cover the tables, and the cloth napkins will protect the most generous girth. There are no table menus – just a lighted sign hanging in the middle stating the eating options and their reasonable prices.

Grilled beef and pasta are the house specialties. As an appetizer, try a *provoleta* – a thick round slice of provolone cheese grilled with a topping of garlic, oregano and olive oil. The *flan* (egg custard) with whipped cream and *dulce de leche* (a caramel topping) is edible sin.

If you want to try some of the typical dishes of the Argentine Northwest, visit **El**

Ceíbal, with two locations, one in Palermo and another in Belgrano. *Locro* is a thick corn chowder with chunks of beef or sausage, onions and other seasonings. *Humitas* are an Argentine version of *tamales*, which come freshly steamed inside a corn husk, some with an added beef filling to the usual sweet corn meal. And of course they have tasty oven baked *empanadas*.

El Trapiche is a typical neighborhood *parrilla* located in Palermo, a few blocks from Plaza Italia. Red tablecloths deck the

Pizza is quite good and deservedly popular in Buenos Aires, where *pizzerias* abound. One that's especially enticing is **Guerrín**, on Corrientes. Its garish panoply of multi-colored wall tiles complements perfectly the amazing variety of pizzas you can order there. Among the more than 90 options is one that comes with mozzarella, hearts of palm and strawberries; another is mozzarella, asparagus and hard-boiled eggs; and there's a camembert cheese pizza topped with mouth-watering chunks of octopus.

long communal tables and the daily specials adorn the walls. The portions are ample and quite affordable, and the menu offers a lot more than *asado* or a juicy *bife de chorizo*. They serve a variety of seafood, including numerous squid dishes (*pulpo a la gallega*), and delicious *ñoquis*, the traditional potato filled pasta. Appetizers and fresh salads round out the enormous menu, and of course tempting desserts, if you have any room left.

Left, young couple enjoy *vermicelli mixto* at Pippo's. <u>Above</u>, the ubiquitous steak, served at almost every meal.

For good pizza but also a tasty sampling of regional foods, there's **La Americana** at 77 Callao, near Bartolome Mitre. A large sign boasts this is "the queen of the *empanadas*" – no small claim in a land renowned for these snacks. The large meat-filled pastries come spicy (*salteña*) or bland (*criolla*).

There are countless other good and inexpensive eateries. Unless you're dying for familiar food, it makes sense to avoid the fast-food hamburger franchises – after all, why eat rubbery burgers and limp French fries when you can eat just as economically in places with considerably more character?

Presumably, the bad news about the possible effects on health of caffeine and sugar has not reached Buenos Aires. The typical *porteño* day is broken up by an infinite number of short breaks for strong coffee and a sweet morsel. A Spanish poet who visited Argentina at the turn of the century reckoned that the *porteño* sweet tooth was a legacy of their Spanish-Arab ancestors. In any case, you never have to look far in Buenos Aires for something delicious to eat.

Virtually every street has at least one sweets and soft drinks vendor who works out of the hole-in-the-wall sidewalk stalls called *kioskos.* There you can find candy bars (*Shot* chocolate and *Mantecol* wafer-covered peanut nougat bars are among the favorites), chewing gum (generically called "chiclets"), hard candies (*caramelos*), and lollipops (*chupetines*).

A *kiosko* is also the place to get the great Argentine hunger postponer, the *alfajor.* This consists of two cookies which sandwich a creamy filling, usually either chocolate or *dulce de leche,* that soft caramel which Argentines also spread on their morning toast. Although the *alfajor* is usually bathed in white or dark chocolate, eating one without a glass of milk at hand can prove a mouth-drying experience. Those made by Terrabusi and Havanna are best.

Candy-coated peanuts cooked on the spot in copper kettles are a common snack on street corners. Popcorn sold by the same vendors, though, tends to be rubbery.

Ice-cream in Buenos Aires is the stuff fond memories are made of. To all but the most disciplined, it can quickly become addictive, and there are plenty of shops there to tempt you. Almost all churn out their own ice-creams on the premises, and they can offer a bewildering variety. If you visit one of the trendy Freddo shops, try a cone (*cucurrucho*) of the house specialty, a nougat cream called *torrocino.* The mint-chocolate chip is also compelling. Other flavors include *sambayón*

Left, a coffee break in a sidewalk café.

(eggs and rum), *dulce de leche* (caramel) and *crema rusa* (nuts and cream). It's all right to ask for several flavors even for a single scoop.

In winter months many ice-cream parlors offer thick hot chocolate and *churros,* deep-fried ridged fritters about the size of a fat cigar. (For real excess, try the *churros* injected with *dulce de leche.*)

Argentines tend to fill the cafés and bars as the afternoon wanes and their stomachs whine. This is the hour of *la merienda,* the secret of how Argentines make it from midday lunches to late-night suppers.

If you want only coffee, remember it comes in a *demi-tasse* unless you request a *café doble.* If you want it with a bit of milk, ask for a *café cortado,* or if you prefer a lot of milk, a *café con leche.*

With your coffee, try the local version of croissants: *media lunas*, or half moons. *Media lunas* usually come in threesomes and are more compact and chewy than their French cousins. They are made either of butter (*de manteca*) or lard (*de grasa*).

Sweet pastries called *facturas* are also served for *la merienda,* as are plates of little cakes called *masas.* Don't let the mound of sweets intimidate you – you pay only for what you eat.

Sandwiches tend to be rather on the dainty side. There are the sandwiches *de miga*, prefabricated crustless squares stacked high on counter tops for your inspection. Try them toasted (*tostadas*).

There are also more substantial sandwiches in buns called *pebetes.* Prosciutto (*jamón crudo*) and slices of meat rolled with vegetables (*matambre*) are popular fillings.

A refreshing respite from coffee is a *licuado,* a milk based fruit shake, or *jugo exprimido*, fresh squeezed juice.

For a variety of savories, try a *picada*. This tray full of treats always includes peanuts and potato chips, and sometimes cheese cubes, salami slices, and olives. *Picadas* are usually served alongside *tragos* (cocktails), *cerveza* (beer), or a *gaseosa* (cold soda).

MATE: ARGENTINA'S NATIONAL DRINK

Yerba mate, the green Paraguayan herb which is drunk as an infusion in a variety of different ways, is something of a national passion, especially among the less affluent portion of the population, and particularly so in the country, outside the more sophisticated and bustling cities. (And if Argentines think they are *mate* fans, they should see how the Uruguayans treat it! Uruguayans are seldom seen without a thermos flask under their arm and a *mate* gourd in their hands.)

To drink *mate* the traditional way you require four things: a hollow gourd, a long metal pipe or straw called a *bombilla, yerba mate* (the dried leaves and stalk which provide the infusion) and hot but not boiling water. The gourd is two-thirds filled with *yerba*, which is moistened with a little cold water and the mixture is then allowed to stand for a minute.

The hot water is then poured in until the gourd is full to the brim. A generous froth should cover the surface. Sugar can be added or not. If it is used, it is placed in the gourd first, before the *yerba*. On being poured the *mate* is sucked through the *bombilla* until all the water has gone. The gourd is then filled with more water and passed to the next drinker, who repeats the process and passes on the gourd to the next person. Everyone uses the same *bombilla,* which has a perforated bulb at the end which acts as a strainer. *Bombillas* can be simple metal straws, or they can be elaborate objects of silver or silver and gold.

The gourds can be dried, hollow squashes, a simple rounded cup carved out of wood, or ornately embellished affairs of silver artistry. You will surely notice the latter in some of the local museums and the silver shops in San Telmo.

Mate contains about the same amount of caffeine as a cup of coffee; it is refreshing and stimulating and helps stem the pangs of hunger. It is also a great remedy for mild stomach and intestinal upsets.

Right, drinking *mate* in the traditional manner.

The tango is something of a paradox in Buenos Aires: it is both everywhere and nowhere. Visitors who have their hearts set on spending every night in dark, glamorous clubs enthralled by local couples dramatically re-enacting the tango's primitive ritual are likely to be disappointed. On the other hand, those who are attentive to the city's more muted melodies that suddenly break through a surface of urban sound to reveal its soul, will hear tangos in taxis, cafés, and floating out of upstairs windows.

The tango, which had its origins at the beginning of this century, has both traveled far and stayed close to home. A number of clubs located in San Telmo feature tango music and professional dancers who provide tourists with the variety of tango flavors which made the dance a successful exotic export. On the other hand, in some of the more plebeian social clubs and dance halls, the tango can be heard and seen very much as it was 50 years ago.

Immigrant roots: As the tango is Argentina's most authentic form of popular music, its history and the history of the country are intertwined. Edmundo Rivera, one of the great tango singers, said: "When all is said and done, the tango is no more than a reflection of our daily reality."

Tango's reality began somewhere in the 19th century, when Argentina was consolidating after a series of bloody civil wars and a frontier war against the local Indians. Buenos Aires was becoming a thriving commercial center. The growth of the city created an impression of endless opportunity. Discharged soldiers, along with *criollos* from the economically declining interior provinces, sought to put down roots in the semi-rural areas around the city. They were joined by thousands of European immigrants who arrived hoping to "*hacer la America*" (to make it in America). Argentina, like the United States, became a great melting-pot.

This polyglot immigrant mixture, composed mainly of Italians, Spaniards, Jews and Eastern Europeans, encountered the native *criollos* and descendants of African slaves in the growing number of *conventillos* (tenements) and in the outlying part of the city called the *arrabal*. Each group brought to the tenement patios and *barrio* street corners its own cultural voice in its most transportable form: music. The haunting laments of Spain's flamenco, the rhythms of Africa's

candombles, and the lilting *milongas* of the creoles came together. The disparate sounds were forged into one by the shared nostalgia for an irrecoverable past and hope for an uncertain future. The tango was the product of this fusion.

Lascivious dance: Beyond a general knowledge of its family tree, the tango's birth is a mystery: exactly when, where and which group of progenitors contributed what are questions that are still hotly debated. What is known is that the tango was first a dance and only later did lyrics appear. Even then the words were mostly improvised and seldom

Left, 1930s tango singer and movie heart throb Carlos Gardel. **Right**, doing the tango in La Boca.

written down. In part, that is explained by the shady character of one of the main branches of the tango's family tree.

Bordellos played a major role in launching the tango. Brothels and rough-and-tumble cafés attracted Argentina's predominantly male immigrants. There men escaped their loneliness and poverty, spending evenings listening to the bawdy lyrics of the early anonymous *tanguistas* and dancing among themselves.

By day these workmen shared the crowded tenements in the southern area of the city with their womenfolk and before long the tango, both as a dance and as song, had also

ments altered, adding the sound that marks the tango to this day.

A type of accordion, the *bandoneón* (concertina), was added to the previous combination of guitar, flute, violin, and, when it was available, piano. Manufactured in Germany until the 1920s, bandoneóns are only available secondhand today, and are passed from generation to generation with reverence. Its most renowned repair specialists are found here in Buenos Aires. So essential to the tango is this strange instrument with its haunting tone, that one famous lyricist, Homero Manzi, paid homage to it in a well-known tango, *Che bandoneón!*

found a place in the patios, fiestas and plebeian theatrical productions called *sainetes*. By 1904, the popular magazine *Caras y Caretas* was heralding this new cultural phenomena in an article titled "The Stylish Dance." Only the culturally conservative upper classes remained aloof from what the author called this "madness" for the "lascivious dance" with lyrics "that would redden the face of a policeman."

As the new century opened, the tango, like the city that gave it birth, was in a process of rapid change. Not only was its audience expanding, but the configuration of instru-

In the madcap days before the outbreak of World War I, the tango appeared in European cafés, scandalizing its upper classes. Kaiser Wilhelm prohibited the dance among his officials and Queen Mary refused to attend parties if there were to be tangos. But for everyone else, it was the rage. The tango's success in Europe gave it the seal of approval back home where even among the aristocracy the tango came to represent national creativity.

The magic of Gardel: With its acceptance by the monied classes and the introduction of recordings, the tango entered a new stage.

Fancy clubs and records made possible the appearance of tango "stars" and the development of a mass audience. When, in 1917, Victor recorded the voice of a little known singer named Carlos Gardel singing a song called *Mi Noche Triste* the tango hit the big time all over Latin America.

Gardel is unquestionably tango's biggest superstar and the symbol of its golden era. He is to tango what Frank Sinatra was to North America's swing era ballad. Like the tango itself, Gardel's origins are a matter of debate among aficionados, some of whom claim that he was born in Lyons, France. Others have suggested that he was born in

simultaneously wrenched the tango away from its traditional working-class and neighborhood roots. The new audiences were demanding more romantic and sentimental tunes and were looking for a dashing vocalist to sing them. Gardel, who met all these requirements, had no equal. His fame was spread by a series of movies made from 1929 to 1935. With luck, you might catch one on television during your stay.

Many tango devotees still insist that "every day he sings better" and posters of Gardel can still be seen to this day all over Buenos Aires. The romance of Gardel was heightened with his tragic death in a plane crash

Montevideo, Uruguay, tango's other well-spring. With exotic good looks, dubious connections in the marginal world of brothels, clubs and political bosses, Gardel was rescued from obscurity by his clear tenor voice which, by 1912, had secured him a spot on the hill in the most elegant nightspots of Buenos Aires.

What catapulted Carlos Gardel into the public's heart was his success in the new media – recordings, radio, cinema – that

during a 1935 tour of Colombia. Thousands of sobbing fans met the boat containing Gardel's body at Buenos Aires' harbor. And right up to the present time, his shrine in the Chacarita Cemetery is always adorned with fresh flowers.

But Gardel's truest memorial is the widespread adoption of his gestures and singing style in the clubs of Buenos Aires. His success and impact were so great that they have become part of common language. If a *porteño* wants to say someone has attained a peak of achievement, they are likely to remark that the person is "Gardel."

Left, tango on San Telmo street. **Right**, hand-painted *filete* recalls a well-known tango melody.

Unfortunately, the tango itself has had a different history. Always related to the well-being of its main audience, the working classes, the tango flourished during the 1940s when Peronism provided a sense of promise among the Argentine masses.

By the end of the 1950s the tango entered a crisis from which it is just now emerging. Competition from newer musical forms, mainly rock-and-roll derived ballads, and its own inability or reluctance to evolve pushed the tango to the sidelines of the contemporary entertainment world.

However, even as the great names of yesteryear disappeared from the playbills and marquees of Avenida Corrientes (the Boulevard of Tango), some innovative forces were at work. Argentine musicians who have either traveled abroad or been influenced by other musical forms have created a current that could be called "neo-tango." The most important and best known of these modernizers is Astor Piazzola.

Piazzola's training as a classical and jazz musician has led him to produce fascinating experiences in fusion. Piazzola's – and incidentally Gardel's – broad appeal was demonstrated again in 1987 by the success of his soundtrack for the prize-winning Argentine film, *El Exilio de Gardel*.

In recent years tango has made a comeback. It is not the shared social idiom of today's Argentine youth, as it was in previous generations, but the universities now offer tango dance classes, which fill up rather quickly. There is a popular all-tango radio station called *FM Tango*, and recently *Todo Tango* was launched on cable television with rave reviews. The touring dance show *Tango Argentino* has been received enthusiastically in Europe and the United States, and today you can find crowded tango clubs in Berlin, Amsterdam, New York and Paris.

Where to hear and see the tango: Thanks to this recent revival, Buenos Aires is once again full of dance halls, small smokey tango clubs, and as always, the made-for-tourist revue shows. They break into distinct categories. Dinner shows (*cena show*) are the most touristy, but can be enjoyable and a good place to see some of the best performers. For a set price you are fed and then enter-

tained by musicians, singers and dancers. **La Veda**, an upscale steakhouse on Florida, has shows most evenings, or try **El Querandí** in Monserrat.

Another option is to skip dinner and still take in a full show complete with dancers and cocktails (*show + copa*). Probably the most attractive spot, and with excellent artists, is **Cafe Homero** in Palermo. **Casablanca** in San Telmo is a tourist institution, but has a good reputation and a reliable, steady line up of shows. Also in San Telmo but much less elegant is **Bar Sur**, which has the authentic feel of a tango bar of years past.

A casual outing could include listening to a live tango set in one of the following bars or cafés, which often come up with interesting variations on the theme. The vintage **Tortoni** hosts some good shows, as does **Clasica y Moderna**, an attractive café on Callao with a cultured atmosphere. Close to Café Homero in Palermo is the **Club del Vino**, and in San Telmo is **La Cumparsita**, named after the famous tango.

But you don't have to be limited to sitting and watching a performance. The *milongas* are probably as authentic as it gets – no glitz, no glamor, but on weekend nights these old dance halls fill up with older (and recently younger as well) dance enthusiasts who glide gracefully across the floor for hours. **La Argentina** just off Corrientes has a devoted Saturday night crowd, or try **Club Sin Rumbo**, or **Club Almagro**, similar but a little bit more off the beaten path. At **La Trastienda** in Monserrat they hold a combination tango class/show/dance hall one night a week called **Zapatos Rojos** (Red Shoes), a great way to get in an impromptu lesson and then dance the night away.

Ask at your hotel if there are any special shows in town during your stay. You might catch one of the big names, like Adriana Varela, the Sexteto Mayor, or the fabulous full orchestra, **Orquesta de Tango de Buenos Aires**. Also check the *espectáculos* section in the big newspapers for the latest in what's playing around town. The difficulty these days isn't finding tango in Buenos Aires, it's choosing where to go.

Right, accordion player at a tango club.

LA BOCA

The working-class neighborhood of La Boca is at the southern tip of the city, along the **Riachuelo Canal.** The *barrio* is famous for its sheet-iron houses painted in bright colors, and for its history as a residential area for the Genovese sailors and dock workers during the 19th century.

La Boca came to life with the mid-19th-century surge in international trade and the accompanying increase in port activity. In the 1870s, meat salting plants and warehouses were built, as well as a tramway to bring workers into the area. With the expansion of the city's ports, the Riachuelo was dug out to permit entrance of deep-water ships. La Boca became a bustling dock, and sailors and longshoremen, most of whom were Italian immigrants, began to settle with their families in the area. Today the impression given by the names in the

Buenos Aires telephone directory is that of an Italian city.

For many years La Boca was also a center of tango. Unfortunately, this is no longer the case. However, one *cantina*, as the combination restaurant/music halls are called, has a homey tango touch. At the **Cantina Feli Cudi** (corner of Suarez and Hernandaria streets) families of old and young alike dance and sing along with a bandoneón player, giving us a nostalgic reminder of tango's homespun roots.

The sheet-iron houses which can still be seen throughout La Boca and across the canal in **Avellaneda** were originally built from materials taken from the interiors of abandoned ships. The idea apparently came with the settlers from Genoa. The style, as well as the bohemian play on colors so unusual in the rest of decorous Buenos Aires, became a tradition in this part of town.

Local artist: The famous Argentine painter Benito Quinquela Martín also influenced the use of color in the neighborhood. Quinquela was an orphan, adopted by a longshoreman's family in La Boca at the turn of the century. As an artist, he dedicated his life to capturing the essence of this working-class neighborhood. He painted dark stooped figures scurrying like ants against the florid background of the docks.

In one painting, which, according to popular legend, Benito Mussolini unsuccessfully tried to buy with a blank check, men hurriedly unload a burning ship against an immense background splashed with bright orange, blue and black. In later years, Quinquela used whimsical pastels to represent the fabric of life in La Boca, making a subtle social protest.

Neighborhood residents took pride in their local artist, and were influenced by his vision of their lives. They chose even wilder colors for their own homes, and a unique dialogue grew between residents and the artist.

Quinquela took over an alleyway known as the **Caminito**, decorated it with murals and sculpture, and established an open-air market to promote local artists. The brightly painted houses and strings of laundry and hanging birdcages give the Caminito the look of a stage setting, but the modest lives of the people here are quite real.

There is an uncomfortable contrast in this *barrio* between tourists with their cameras, and gaudy souvenir shops which cater to them, and the humble local stores, and children begging for coins.

A stroll through La Boca begins at the Caminito. Heading north from the river on the alley, it is worth walking around the block and back to the riverside to get a sense of one of the residential streets.

The colorful houses look like toys, but they are in fact fairly solid homes. Most of them have long corridors, lined with wood paneling leading to interior apartments. The cobblestone streets are lined with tall and imposing sycamore trees; and elevated sidewalks foretell rainy season flooding.

Ship's graveyard: The **Vuelta de Rocha**, where the Caminito begins, consists of a small triangular plaza with a ship's mast. It overlooks the port area, which might be more accurately described as a decaying shipyard. More boats lie half sunken on their sides than upright and functioning.

Depending on which way the wind is blowing, visitors may be accosted by the rude odors coming up from the canal which is so polluted that reputedly there is no life whatsoever in its waters. Residents blame the old slaughterhouses upriver, which in the past dumped wastes into the canal.

East along **Pedro de Mendoza**, the avenue parallel to the canal, is the **Museo de Bellas Artes de La Boca**, La Boca's own fine arts museum at 1835 Mendoza. It's open Tuesday–Friday 9am–5.30pm and Saturday 9am–noon and 2–6pm. The top floor was used by Quinquela as an apartment studio. Many of his most important paintings are here, and you can also see the flat he used in his last

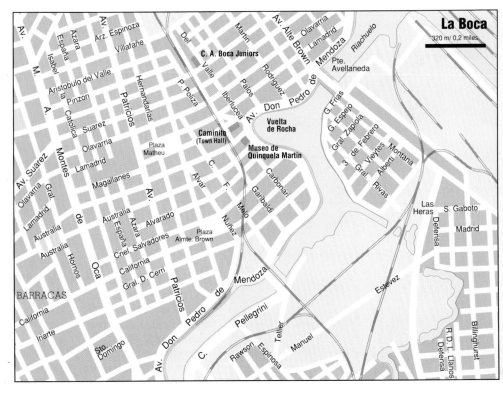

years. The museum is an interesting stop if only to get a view of the shipyard from the window of the studio, the same shipyard depicted in his paintings.

About three blocks further down Pedro de Mendoza is the **Puente Nicolás Avellaneda**, a bridge used by commuters living south of the city. There is a rickety old escalator that takes local pedestrians and game visitors up to the bridge, where you can experience a rush of agoraphobia and get a view of the neighborhood.

A night on the town: Just past the bridge is **Calle Necochea**, whose rowdy *cantinas* provide an atmosphere that seems part gameshow, part eatery and dancehall. These were originally sailors' mess halls and in their new manifestation are enjoyed by both locals and visitors for their garish decor, fresh seafood, and rather corny floor shows.

Bright flashing lights, speakers set out on the sidewalk blaring loud music, and the aggressive doormen may remind some visitors of San Francisco's

North Beach strip joints, but the scene is not as seedy as it appears. Families from the interior of the country are there for a festive night out. Old people are singing their favorite tunes and dancing amidst balloons and ribbons.

The traditional idea that a night out on Necochea is a celebration of sailors returning home is definitely still preserved. Most of the action of a La Boca non-stop night tends to take place on Necochea between **Calle Brandsen** and **Calle Suárez**.

Pizza break: Two blocks to the west is **Avenida Almirante Brown**, the main thoroughfare in La Boca. The avenue holds no particular charm for the tourist were it not for its excellent pizzerias. *Porteños* come from all over the city to eat pizza *a la piedra,* a thin dough pizza baked in a brick oven, and *faina,* a chick pea dough which is eaten on top of pizza. Wash it down with a bottle of Argentinian wine, or even a refreshing beer, and contemplate your next move in this sprawling city.

Traditional balcony on corrugated tin house.

Towering above the wood and corrugated metal dwellings and old brick warehouses of La Boca is the giant stadium of one of Argentina's leading professional soccer clubs, Boca Juniors. **La Bombonera** (the chocolate box) is an imposing and austere rectangle of concrete about 60 meters (180 feet) high that covers two full blocks and becomes a cauldron of working-class passion on match days, marked by the famous ticker-tape welcome the fans give their team and by off-the-cuff verses chanted to the tunes of pop songs, sung to their glory or to the damnation of their team's rivals.

Boca Juniors and arch-rival River Plate are clubs founded on the waterside at the turn of the century, when British immigrants spread the game throughout the country.

River Plate moved out in the 1920s and went on to become a middle-class club with a wide range of sports. In the 1970s, after many years without winning a national championship, River spent an unprecedented amount of money purchasing the best players from around the country. Thanks to this buying spree, River gained the nickname the Millionaires. Not by coincidence, they have won the most national championships. Boca Juniors stayed behind, rooted in the working-class harbor area. But they too quickly joined the world of big money football, starting with the purchase of Diego Maradona in 1981 for almost $10 million.

Both have vied for dominance ever since, and their rivalry overshadows all others. Boca claims to belong to "half the country plus one," enjoying a following that spreads from the northern tropical provinces to the vast Patagonian wasteland in the south.

Passionate loyalties: Many ardent fans who grew up supporting big teams in the capital have seldom seen them play and have never been to the Bombonera, or to River Plate's **Monumental** stadium, where the 1978 World Cup final was played.

The passion for soccer in Argentina knows no boundaries, pervading family and *barrio* life. Every member of a family roots for a team, and not always for the same one. In a city with eight first-division clubs, four more in the suburbs and twice that number in the second division, the neighborhood in which a fan is born or raised is the decisive factor in choosing which team to support.

But the passion takes root at an early age, and the choice can be influenced by many factors, such as which team is the champion at the time, or a persuasive older kid next door: "You're for Boca or else!" ... "Never mind if your Dad supports San Lorenzo."

Soccer is something you learn as a natural part of growing up. The traveler will find no published procedure for going to matches, and ticket information and recommended games are most easily obtained by word of mouth. But Argentines are very willing to help with advice on one of their favorite topics. Most visitors naturally would like to see good soccer in a packed stadium full of atmosphere. Anyone, from the hotel concierge to the waiter at the corner café, is likely to be remarkably well-informed about what good derbies are taking place on any given weekend or if one of the teams is playing an important cup match against another South American country.

The average weekend game is easy. There is seldom a full house, but the uninitiated must go armed with words such as *tribuna visitante* (visitors' stand) or, if you feel you will be safer among the home crowd and are prepared to pay extra to rub elbows with the club members, ask for the *tribuna local.* The cheap seats are called *populares.*

The teams: Traditionally Boca was known for its strength of spirit and physical commitment rather than technique. In contrast, River Plate was known for technical skill and offensive tactics. But nowadays these differences have faded, as a result of the buying and selling of players, and changing coaches. But the loyalties and rivalries remain.

Independiente, just across the murky Riachuelo in the southern suburb of Avellaneda (and owners of the oldest concrete stadium in the country) has a pair of nicknames. First and most common is Red Devils, which refers to their red jerseys. But they are also referred to as the King of Cups, because they have won more international championships than any other Argentine team. Their neighbors and arch-rivals, Racing Club, built a beautiful stadium a stone's throw away. Unfortunately, structural damage and lack of funds to make the necessary repairs, have kept fans away.

San Lorenzo, in red and blue jerseys, hail from Almagro, an old tango neighborhood. But they sold their stadium in the midst of a financial crisis, and now a huge supermarket occupies the space. After years of having to

working-class district of the city, Villa Fiorito, on the fringes of Lanus borough. Before drug convictions forced him off the field, he became the world's best-paid player.

Maradona was exceptional in having made his first-division debut at the age of 15, and his first full international match at 16. But his story is like that of so many Argentine youngsters whose only way out of poverty is through professional sport. Argentina is an endless conveyor belt of soccer talent. Half the boys tried out by the clubs fail to make the grade, but mainly for temperamental reasons, especially those from the provinces, who cannot stand the loneliness of the big city.

rent out other teams' stadiums, they have built a new one in the south of the Capital called the **Nuevo Gasómetro**.

Argentina's soccer fortunes have gone the way of the country, but the game has survived the worst economic crises.

Fame and fortune: It is on this foundation that Argentina gave the world Diego Maradona. Maradona, like so many Buenos Aires kids, was discovered by a scout for the small first-division club Argentinos Juniors, while playing in games on vacant lots in a poor

Above, Diego Maradona celebrates another goal.

Maradona entertained crowds at half-time with ball-juggling feats when he was in his teens, but this sort of extra act is rare nowadays. Nevertheless the atmosphere is to be savored, provided it is not ruined by fighting.

Maradona was not exceptional in having pursued a more lucrative career abroad. Especially during times of crisis, when sportsmen's salaries are below those on the world market, it has become common for the best to move to teams in Europe for huge fees. But Argentina, with World Cup victories in 1978 and 1986, seems to produce talented replacements to keep the fans' interest alive.

Buenos Aires has a great deal to offer visitors interested in the visual arts; there are probably more painters and schools of painting here than anywhere else on the continent. The city that proudly calls itself the Paris of South America has traditionally looked to Europe for technique and inspiration. Nevertheless, the geography and social realities of Argentina have added a rich dimension to the lessons of the Old World masters.

In the 1830s, as soon as Buenos Aires had established itself as the main and most southern port in South America, the first painters emerged. A young Italian engineer, Carlos Enrique Pellegrini, decided to become a painter when his first portraits and landscapes became successful. Until his death, his paintings, portraits, and lithographs of the city of Buenos Aires were acclaimed and sought after. They are fascinating documentation of the society of that period.

In the middle of the 19th century another painter, Pirilidiano Puerreydon, stood out. His paintings, portraits and landscapes demonstrate a profound professionalism. Puerreydon's portrait of *Manuela de Rosas y Ezcurra* has a fine quality and the use of red tones (the color of Federalism which was imposed by Manuela's father, Juan Manuel de Rosas, governor of the Province of Buenos Aires) is superbly accomplished.

At the end of the 19th century and beginning of the 20th, the best-known painters were Eduardo Sivori, whose *La Pampa en Olavarria* is one of many paintings that depict the placid life in the Argentine countryside (the pampas); and Ernesto de la Carcova, whose paintings deal with Buenos Aires and its people, particularly its poor, as in one entitled *Sin Pan y Sin Trabajo* (*No Bread and No Work*). He made use of background light, as did Fernando Fader in his beautiful landscape paintings.

Social realism: During the 1920s Buenos Aires became an important city due to its industrial development, which consequently also gave the arts new life. The outstanding painter of this period was Benito Quinquela Martín, who was born and raised in the southern port quarter of Buenos Aires called La Boca. He was a stevedore when he decided to put his life and La Boca on canvas. His paintings are strong and full of vigor. La Boca has always been a place where artists lived and worked. Even now, on weekends, on a street called **Caminito**, painters can be seen working and selling typical scenes of La Boca (*see pages 169–70*).

Social realism was expressed most heavily by such artists as Lino Eneas Spilimbergo (known for his strong, impassioned and expressive work, his figures, his still lifes, and his landscapes), and Antonio Berni (whose large paintings of workers and, later, his collages of two main characters typical of the city's poor and neglected). These collages are a major expression of Argentine art. Both of these artists were also accomplished printmakers.

The work of Juan Carlos Castagnino, another expression of this style, gives a lighter and more beautiful treatment to the same subject matter (the poor). Perhaps the largest and most expressive works of these three artists are their 1946 murals which can still be seen in the **Galerías Pacífico**, the shopping mall on Calle Florida.

An artist of a slightly younger generation is Carlos Alonso, painter, printmaker and illustrator, with a different lyrical and poetic touch. Alonso's characters include both those which populate the city of Buenos Aires, and the gauchos in the countryside (as in his illustrations for *Martín Fierro*.)

Surrealism influenced many Argentine printers, including Xul Solar. His old home on Laprida 1212 has been converted to a museum with a collection of over 80 of his paintings, personal objects and publications. Raquel Forner followed a few years later, and Roberto Aizenberg is known for his neo-surrealist works.

There is also a significant Argentine group of non-figurative artists – Vicente Forté, Leopoldo Presas, and Luis Seoane, to name just a few; as well as the more contemporary neo-figurative artists like Antonio Segui, Romulo Maccio and Felipe Noe.

The **Museo Nacional de Bellas Artes**, the national fine arts museum, has an impressive collection by Argentine painters, from the early 1800s to contemporary figures. You could also visit the **Museo de Arte Moderno** and the **Museo de Artes Plásticas**, two small but interesting galleries located inside the San Martín Theater.

Printmaking: As in the rest of South America, printmaking is an important visual expression in Argentina. Woodcuts, linocuts, lithographs, etchings, silkscreens and even experimental printmaking have strong tradi-

Company was established in Buenos Aires. C.H. Bacle and his wife, E. Pellegrini (who printed a series called "Remembrances of the River Plate"), Onslow, and others produced an amazing quantity of work: the first illustrated newspapers, a series entitled "Picturesque Customs of Buenos Aires" (*see illustration, page 39*), as well as the official list of all the important cattle brands for the Rosas government.

At the end of the 19th century, a new period emerged with the etchings of E. Argelo and Eduardo Sivori, the pioneers of Argentine etching. Their work deals with life in the countryside as the titles suggest: *Ombúes*

tions and contemporary practitioners. The first prints and woodcuts to be found in what is now Argentina were done by the Guaraní Indians who lived in the Jesuit missions in the northeast of the country. They were excellent craftsmen and their prints depicted mostly religious themes due to their Spanish Jesuit education.

In 1828, the first important lithographic printmaking workshop, called Bacle and

Above, *Sin Pan y Sin Trabajo* (*No Bread and No Work*) was one of the first Argentine paintings to portray social conflicts.

(typical tree-like plant of the pampas), *Las Carretas* (the ox-carts), and others.

Giving graphic arts a new spirit, in 1915, was a group called The Artists of the People, formed by Hebequer, Arato, Vigo and Belloca, among others. Their images dealt with the social reality of the poor and neglected, and addressed the eternal themes of rebellion and hope.

In the late 1980s, the works of many Argentine printmakers were organized to form part of the basic collection of the **Museo del Grabado** (Museum of Printmaking) of the city of Buenos Aires.

BARRIO NORTE

In Buenos Aires, **Barrio Norte** is home to many affluent Argentines. But this wasn't always the case. In the city's early days, a large slaughterhouse occupied the northern part of the barrio, the **Recoleta**. It was said that a ravine was filled up with cattle heads and that people dreaded the onset of the rainy season on account of the floating heads.

Barrio Norte acquired some much-needed tone when a yellow fever epidemic hit the city in 1870. Wealthy *porteños,* convinced that the river fogs were causing the deaths, fled from the southern lowlands near San Telmo for the higher ground to the north.

Over the next few decades, Argentina's upper classes spared no expense in making Barrio Norte into a miniature Paris. Here, more than anywhere else in the city, it's easy to imagine what Buenos Aires was like when it was the capital of one of the richest countries on earth. At the ever-fashionable Café La Biela, you may see a handsome businessman in a well-cut Italian suit. His head may be tilted back to take advantage of the sun as a white-jacketed waiter takes his order, another man shines his shoes and a third, a street artist, sketches his likeness.

A wonderful death: Today, Barrio Norte is an enormous neighborhood, stretching from downtown to Palermo, and from the river to Once. But it is possible to do a walking tour concentrating on the Recoleta and Retiro, the nicest areas. A good starting point is where the privileged Argentines end, the **Cementerio de La Recoleta**.

In a city that devotes itself to distinctions of class and military rank, the Recoleta is Buenos Aires' marble heart. To be buried in one of these ornate crypts, you must be related to one of Argentina's "name" families. A general or two in the family tree would also help. The allure of the necropolis is such that even mourners have the air of apartment hunters, doggedly searching out immortality with a view. As one Argentine writer put it, the inhabitants of Recoleta are "more dead and less dead than the ordinary deceased."

This is true of no one more than Eva Perón, reviled and revered wife of the dictator Juan Perón, whose body disappeared for 16 years before it finally came to rest in a black crypt marked simply "Eva Duarte." Her inscription reads *Volveré y seré millones* ("I will return and be millions"), a populist sentiment that does not sit well with many of the families who pay respect at the neighboring tombs.

Although Evita expressed scorn for Argentina's oligarchy, she was hurt when the society ladies didn't invite her to become head of an exclusive charity organization, the *Sociedad de Beneficiencia,* as was the usual prerogative of Argentine First Ladies. She lies among them now, in a supposedly unrobbable grave under 2 meters (6 feet) of concrete.

Preceding pages: aristocratic "*barrio* of the dead." Left, Basilica of Nuestra Señora del Pilar.

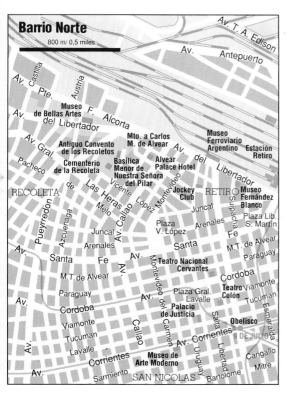

Barrio Norte

800 m/ 0,5 miles

Next door to the cemetery stand the **Basílica de Nuestra Señora del Pilar** and the adjoining convent, both completed in 1732 by the Recoletan monks (a Franciscan order) who give the area its name.

For anyone familiar with the imposing stone exterior of Latin American cathedrals, the basilica's mustard and white stucco seems almost cheery. Children play in a nearby playground, and on weekends artisans gather to sell *mate* gourds and handmade leather goods in the plaza. The basilica houses a baroque silver altar, and woodwork attributed to the Spanish artist and mystic Alonso Cano, yet on a sunny day at Recoleta, you could imagine that they fold the basilica into a box when the circus gets ready to leave town.

The russet-red convent has been converted to the **Centro Cultural Recoleta,** a cultural center which displays cutting edge examples of contemporary Argentine art. In one recent exhibition, *Las Historietas de Hierro* (*Cartoons of Iron*),

visitors were greeted by a highly realistic representation of a dead steelworker crumpled in the entrance hallway. The center's young artists often traffic in images that are violent, grotesque and explicitly sexual. It also hosts dance, theater and music productions. Located in the entrance hall is an art bookshop, information desk, and a tourist kiosk. The **Museo Participativo de Ciencias**, a hands-on science museum for kids or playful adults, is on the second floor off the patio.

Coffee with a view: After exploring the cemetery and cultural center, it's time to wander the streets of the Recoleta. Head south directly opposite the church towards the enormous rubber trees and colorful billboards. Here the street **Quintana** deadends at the plaza, and facing each other are two cafés – **La Biela** and **Café de la Paix**. This is the place to see and be seen while having a coffee on the outdoor patios. They are the portals to the posh neighborhood of the Recoleta. To the right down **Ortiz** is

Tomb of Eva Perón in the Duarte crypt, which belongs to her father's family.

a long row of upscale restaurants and bars, most with outdoor patios as well. And down Quintana one block, at the corner of Ayacucho, is some of the best ice-cream in the city, at **Freddo**, the most popular flavors being *chocolate amargo* (dark chocolate) and *dulce de leche* (caramel).

Heading east down Ayacucho towards the river will take you to the most interesting street in the neighborhood, **Avenida Alvear**. You will witness a sumptuousness that has faded from many quarters of Buenos Aires but which has been retained here. Have a look inside the **Alvear Palace Hotel**, where the gleaming lobby is a favorite spot for afternoon tea. Also inside is the **Galería Promenade**, an excellent example of the Recoleta's swank boutiques.

Jockey Club and old silver: Walking south down Alvear, you pass a number of the city's finest apartment buildings, scrupulously copied from the French; there is no choicer spot in Buenos Aires. Gaze upon the French and Brazilian embassies, and, more importantly, the **Jockey Club**, the citadel of Argentine Anglophilia. The doors of the Jockey Club open for no man who cannot produce impeccable references and an equally impeccable suit; women are allowed only in the dining-room. Here, at the corner of Arroyo and 9 de Julio, is **Plaza Cataluña,** a striking piece of urban redesign consisting of a mural by Josep Niebla painted in great slashes of color across the sides of several Dickensian-looking houses.

Plaza San Martín: The only way to enter Plaza San Martín is from **Avenida Santa Fe**, three blocks to the right from Arroyo. Described by one Argentine writer as a "prolongation" of New York or Paris, Santa Fe offers everything imaginable in leather, and will satisfy a reasonable number of other desires as well. Most of the Santa Fe stores and malls are north of Avenida 9 de Julio, continuing all the way to Callao. *Porteños* spend a lot of time window shopping, crowding the sidewalks.

Taking the sun in Café La Biela.

Browsing southward on Santa Fé, the avenue opens up into the Plaza San Martín, a palm-fringed greensward dominated by the bronze statue of San Martín upon his horse. Built in 1862, the statue is Argentina's monument to a lost cause. The general had left his base near the present-day plaza to wage a war of continental liberation against Spain. He returned to Argentina triumphant, only to discover that internal bickering had undone his vision of a liberal, unified South America.

The area around the plaza is an upscale mix of travel agencies, government buildings and hotels. On one side is the **Palacio San Martín,** an old mansion now used by the Foreign Ministry to welcome and entertain diplomats. Just across from it on the corner of Maipú and Santa Fe is a stately old residence, now painted white and used as a social club by the military, in addition to housing an arms museum. The recently refurbished and elegant **Plaza Hotel** is on the Florida street side of the plaza.

Heading southeast and downhill to **Avenida del Libertador,** there is a view of the British Clocktower (renamed after the Malvinas/Falklands War) in the middle of **Plaza Fuerza Aérea Argentina**, or Air Force Plaza, flanked by the **Sheraton Hotel** and the **Retiro** station.

North on Libertador, at the 400 block is a hidden gem of Argentine history, the **Museo Nacional Ferroviario**, a must for train enthusiasts. Before the federal government recently shut down the majority of lines due to financial woes, Argentines traveled from one end of the country to the other in a very efficient and quite elegant British-built railway system. The charming museum is housed in an old, brick workshop, part of the Retiro complex, where you can see model trains, photos, bells, lamps and ancient telegraphs.

A couple of blocks further you can't miss one of Buenos Aires' landmarks, El Rulero, or the haircurler, the circular glass building which houses the offices of Fiat and Peugeot. To escape the mass

Sinister show at the San Martín Gallery in Recoleta.

L. Aro

ilustrador

of automobiles on Libertador, here at the intersection with 9 de Julio take a left up the avenue and a quick right on **Posadas**. Just on the other side of a modern shopping area is the very posh hotel, the **Park Hyatt**. Continue north on Posadas to wander back through the Recoleta, passing small, elegant antique stores, sidewalk cafés, and some finely preserved apartment buildings. At the 1200 block is **Patio Bullrich,** a very new and very exclusive shopping mall that extends all the way through to Avenida del Libertador.

Just a few blocks further is a wonderful art gallery, the **Palais de Glace,** at 1725 Posadas. This mustard-colored, dome topped building was constructed in 1911 and served originally as an ice skating rink for the elite of the Recoleta, hence its circular form and its name. Later it was a swank tango dancehall. Today the gallery is one of the best in Buenos Aires, hosting exhibitions of artists from all over the world. On the first floor is an interesting gift shop, the **Mercado Nacional de Artesanía,** where you can find wall hangings, silver items, carved wood, and ceramics.

Fine arts: Here Posadas deadends at the **Plaza Alvear,** right in front of the Recoleta cultural center. Cutting across the plaza and crossing the avenue you arrive at the **Museo Nacional de Bellas Artes,** the national fine arts museum, at 1437 Avenida del Libertador, a dark red, columned, classical building.

On the first floor are nudes by Rodin, Gauguin, Manet and others.

The second floor of the Bellas Artes is more interesting than the first since you won't find its like in London or New York. There are various portraits of the Argentine aristocracy, painted with all the solemnity that was imported with European convention; in another room, folkloric canvases romanticizing the hard men of the pampas; and in another, panoramic paintings by Cándido Lopez (1840–1902) detailing the glorious carnage of historic military campaigns against South American neighbors.

Walking pure bred dogs in Recoleta.

DINING OUT IN RECOLETA

It is not often that a cemetery is connected with fine dining, but in the case of La Recoleta, restaurants and sidewalk cafés go hand in hand with tombs and masoleums.

An enormous number of eating establishments are concentrated in a very small area. Beginning on Ortiz near the corner of Quintana is **Munich,** which features a continental menu with some German-style dishes. The food is solid and simple; what it lacks in sophistication is made up for by the portions. In contrast is **Lola,** a few doors down on the corner of Ortiz and Guido. The restaurant is decorated in muted, floral tones and the walls are adorned with paintings of 20th-century personalities. The menu features better than average French cooking, including duck, lamb and rabbit dishes.

On the next block, where Ortiz becomes Junín, is **Harper's**, a delightful restaurant, also strongly orientated towards the French tradition, with a pleasant decor and superb food. A couple of doors down is **El Gato Dumas**, probably the best known of these restaurants locally, mainly due to its flamboyant owner and chef, Juan Carlos "Gato" Dumas. Many of the dishes are personal creations and show considerable imagination and skill. Colorful fabrics billow around tall columns in the dining room.

At the end of the block Junín intersects Vicente Lopez, and here on the corner is **Rodi Bar**, definitely in a different class from the Recoleta gourmet norm. Here locals from the neighborhood dine on simple but delicious homemade food. Choose a table in the tableclothed section of the restaurant.

Down the block on Vicente Lopez is **Au Bec Fin**, in an elegant turn-of-the-century mansion. The cooking is also French and the antique atmosphere is marvelous. Also on Vicente Lopez in the other direction, facing one of the cemetery walls, is **Mora X**. The tall ceiling and mural-size paintings give the place a posh gallery feel. The menu is informally French, with pastas and grilled beef.

Right, the maître d' of Fileto shows off appetizers.

Scattered among the Cacharel and Benetton shops in the fashionable Santa Fe and Florida districts are a preponderance of jewelry stores specializing in silver objects. At the **Sunday Antiques Market** in San Telmo, it's still possible to find (often for reasonable prices) old-fashioned pieces such as silver-handled daggers (*facones*), horn-shaped water canteens (*chifles*) and *mate* gourds.

Silver has long had a totemic importance in Argentina. The wealth of silver in the

An obsession with precious metals was perhaps the only thing the native South Americans and the Spanish conquistadors had in common. Spanish priests found Indian silversmiths skilful and intelligent in their use of silver, and accustomed to treating it as a sacred metal. Native motifs combined with Catholic imagery and Spanish plateresque style created a colonial religious art that was truly hallucinatory. While much of Argentina's mission art was lost in the

humblest colonial chapels helped underscore the power of the Catholic Church, while on the pampas the jingling silver ornaments, bridles, stirrups and spurs proclaimed the gaucho's worshipful love of his horse. Many beautiful silver pieces from the gaucho era are preserved at the **Museo de Motivos Argentinos "Jose Hernández"**. Silver *mates* are now collector's items rather than tableware, but this unique and elaborate art emerged at a time when Creole settlers were anxious to make the Indian habits they'd acquired in the New World appear more elegant and European.

colonial wars with Portugal, two splendid relics of that period remain: the votive lamp and sacrarium in the **Museo de Arte Hispanoamericano "Fernández Blanco"**.

As with many South American capitals, the Spanish thirst for silver was the impetus behind the founding of Buenos Aires. Pedro de Mendoza's settlement on the banks of the Rio de la Plata (literally, the River of Silver) was meant to be the first leg of an expedition into the Andes to find a legendary mountain of silver. As it turned out, there was almost no silver in Argentine soil, but the Bolivian border was a mere symbol until 1776, and the richest silver mines in the world were on the other side.

European silversmiths began settling in Buenos Aires; by the beginning of the 18th century there were 38 silversmiths serving a population of 20,000. During the struggle for independence the lavish use of silver was a means of patriotic expression, but as it became more common it fell out of fashion; rich *porteños* didn't want locally made silver plates and goblets – they preferred imported crystal and china.

Mechanization and art deco dealt a final blow to the silversmiths' art in the first half of this century, but during the 1960s there began a revival of interest in silver.

The Pallarols workshop: Through seven generations of changing fortunes and fashions in Argentina, the Pallarols family has maintained its silver workshop in Buenos Aires, using many of the same tools and methods brought from Barcelona in 1804.

The silverwork of Juan Carlos Pallarols, now the head of the family business, is very much in demand. In recent years he has been commissioned to design a *facon* for King Juan Carlos of Spain, a silver and gold chalice to commemorate the Pope's visit, and the presidential baton for Raúl Alfonsín. When Pallarols was learning his trade in the 1950s, however, he never imagined he'd be able to make a living. "But I didn't want to do anything else," he says. "I believe every human being has the soul of an artisan."

The workshop, with its 19th-century lathes and chisels worn silky by generations of use, is completely self-sufficient. Here they twist their own silver wire, heat the furnace with coal, and use the light streaming in through the French doors facing the **Plaza Dorrego**. When he moved to the neighborhood in 1970, San Telmo was far from being the South American Soho it has become today, but Pallarols liked the village feeling of the

barrio, the plaza full of old men playing Spanish card games in the shade. Now the Plaza Dorrego is full of artisans and Pallarols' waiting-list is usually several months long, but a sense of timelessness nevertheless pervades the workshop.

Pallarols and his assistants, two of whom are his sons, work long but tranquil hours. They tinker with a piece for a while, sketch something and wander back and forth between the workshop and the adjoining house.

Most commissions are modest orders for christenings, weddings and birthdays. Even with a small order, such as a silver bookmark, Pallarols discusses his designs with his client. His house is filled with things he's loved making: a silver sugar bowl, a picture frame, a wrought-iron staircase which throws lacy patterns against the wall.

As his own father did with him, Pallarols brings home scrap pieces of metal for his small daughter to pound with a toy hammer. But she isn't sure she wants to be the first female Pallarols silversmith. "Right now," she says, "I prefer to work with bronze."

Left, silversmith Juan Carlos Pallarols at home in his workshop. **Right**, silver *mate* gourd in the form of a ñandu bird.

PALERMO

Palermo is a neighborhood of parks and gardens, of embassies and cattle shows, of a world-class polo field and a turn-of-the-century racetrack. Argentine writer Martinez Estrada called it "the most poetic spot in the city." Certainly its mossy cobbled streets and crumbling Italianate villas have inspired countless poets, including Palermo native Jorge Luis Borges, to meditate on Buenos Aires' frayed expectations.

If neighborhoods were fictional characters, Palermo might be Dickens' Miss Havisham: a mad old lady in a musty bridal gown, who stopped her clocks when her fiancé failed to show up. The frothy marble monuments at the intersections which look like wedding cakes, and the countless dowagers feeding stray cats in the botanical garden, give the landscape an air of eccentricity.

Rosas slept here: Juan Manuel de Rosas, the 19th-century president, was a neighborhood pioneer who built a magnificent estate in the middle of what were then swamps and thistles. Like many Argentine rulers, Rosas arouses passionate controversy long after his death: he is credited with unifying the country and accused of making death squads a grim feature of Argentine politics. One contemporary admirer, bent on demonstrating his leader's sense of humor, wrote of how Rosas enlivened one of his daughter's tea parties by letting his wild puma loose on the lawn. The women screamed and the animal fled to the river, causing the president to exclaim jovially, "How savage those women must be, to frighten my puma!"

Sunday in the park: The best time to visit Palermo is on a Sunday afternoon. While most of the neighborhood's residential section is resolutely middle class, the parks in Palermo are truly for every-

Preceding pages: park benches in Palermo.
Left, sharing a cracker at Palermo zoo.

one. On a sunny day *porteños* converge from all parts of the city to picnic, drink *mate*, kiss in the grass, jog, play soccer, win political converts, and drive pedal boats around the lake. Families stroll en masse through the sumptuous subtropical gardens. Even the most casually dressed are combed and natty; children are the adored center of every group.

A tour of the area might begin with **Palermo Chico**, a neighborhood of the rich and famous just around the bend from Recoleta. In fact, you must weave around several bends to get a sense of the elegant *barrio*. This cozy nest of palaces appears to exclude the rest of the city, with its tangled web of streets and its armed guards around some of the mansions. But it is well worth winding your way through to admire the French-style houses and the spotless gardens.

The area was built in the 1880s. Many of the old palaces are now used as embassies, since the original owners could not maintain them. However, there are plenty of brand-new estates in the 20th-century Southern California style, built to order by Argentine sports heroes and television stars. Palermo Chico is bordered by Avenida del Libertador, continuing across Figueroa Alcorta towards the river, and the two smaller streets Tagle and Salguero.

An excellent way to get a look inside one of these magnificent palaces is to visit the **Museo Nacional de Arte Decorativo**, located at 1902 Avenida del Libertador, directly in front of the **Plaza de Chile**. This enormous palace was started by the Errázuriz family in 1911 and took seven years to complete. In 1936 it was donated to the state on the condition that it was converted into a public museum, and today it remains a frozen testimony to Argentina's glorious years. On the first floor are three main galleries full of French antiques, Chinese porcelain, and original European oil paintings.

Up the marble staircase in the entry hall is a beautiful mezzanine looking down on the rooms below. Here is the

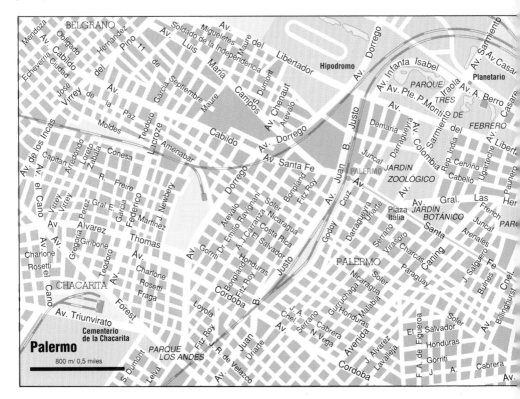

Museo Nacional de Arte Oriental. This small but interesting museum attracts exhibitions from all over the East, from Chinese dolls to Hindu silkscreening.

Upon entering the iron gates of the palace is a charming and intimate restaurant **La Trianon,** which has a shady outdoor patio around the back. Here in the palace's garden is probably one of the nicest spots in the city to relax and have lunch or a coffee.

Sports and suntans: From Palermo Chico, those willing to set off on a lengthy jaunt can walk six blocks along **Figueroa Alcorta** into Palermo's dense green heart: **Parque 3 de Febrero**, which covers some 400 hectares (10,000 acres).

Approaching **Avenida Sarmiento** (not to be confused with the downtown street Sarmiento) on the left crossing the avenue is the **Jardín Japonés**. The traditional Japanese garden is a tranquil rest spot and a nice place for strolling. Ponds full of carp and exotic vegetation create a peaceful atmosphere, and on any warm afternoon you are likely to spot half a dozen young *porteños* posing for bridal pictures among the colorful frangipani.

Avenida Sarmiento intersects with Figueroa Alcorta at an enormous statue of General Urquiza, the president who in 1852 overthrew Rosas in a bloody battle just outside the capital.

To the right on Sarmiento is the **Planetario Galileo Galilei**, which sits next to a small artificial lake. The planetarium features a changing astronomy show on Saturday and Sunday at 3 and 4.30pm. To the left on Sarmiento from Alcorta, the small street **Avenida Iraola** bends to the right, winding through the park to the main lake in Palermo. Here you can rent pedal boats, and wander through the pretty gardens and over quaint pedestrian bridges.

Avenida Iraola weaves around the lake and back to Libertador and Sarmiento, where yet another large white monument, this one donated by Spain, graces the intersection.

Pedal boats on lake in park.

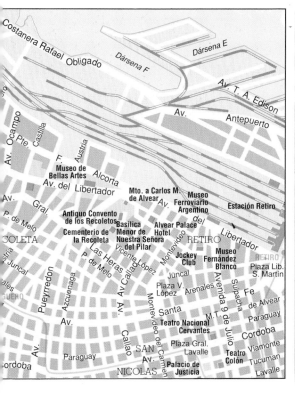

Now you are at the back corner of the 19th-century **Jardín Zoológico**. At the time of its construction in 1874, it was the last word in enlightened zookeeping – the cages were built in the architectural style of the animals' country of origin, and the grounds were sprinkled with marble reproductions of the Venus de Milo and Bacchus. Now, however, the buildings are sadly decayed.

The entrance to the zoo is one long block up Avenida Sarmiento, where the street dea ends at **Plaza Italia**. Also on the plaza, just across Avenida Las Heras, is the **Jardín Botánico**, which lies between Las Heras and Santa Fe, stretching four blocks towards downtown. The botanical garden is not as extensive or well-kept as it could be, but it does have many beautiful trees and plants, and is a lovely place to take a walk, soak in the sun on the many beaches, and admire the various fountains and many stray cats wandering around.

Directly across from the zoo to the other side is the **Sociedad Rural,** an exhibitions complex run by the powerful association of Argentina's large-scale farmers. The society was founded in 1866 under the motto "to cultivate the earth is to serve the fatherland." Its first president was Don Jose Martínez de Hoz, a rancher and political figure. Beef made Argentina rich, and cattle ranchers were a powerful group throughout much of the society's history.

Although times have changed and the price of beef has fallen, the society's annual **Exposición Rural** is still a major event on the Buenos Aires' events calendar, where pure bred cattle, prize-winning horses, and the newest in farming equipment are displayed and celebrated with all due ceremony. Don't miss it if you happen to be in town in August. The Rural Society also rents out their grounds for other events, from auto shows to foreign country festivals. All the exhibitions are open to the public for a small fee.

Handicrafts and neighborhood life: Plaza Italia itself holds no particular charm when empty, but on weekends it becomes the center of a lively street market. On adjacent blocks is a market known to *porteños* as the "hippy fair" – the products are often made and sold by bearded artisans and women in tie-dyed dresses. It's a good spot to buy inexpensive leather goods, such as belts and handbags, as well as leather-covered *mates*. There are also ceramics, handmade jewelry, embroidered clothes, and, on the last block, secondhand books.

If you'd like to explore a bit of the residential side of Palermo, just take one of the side streets off Santa Fe right across from Plaza Italia, heading west, away from the parks. Scattered along the tree lined streets are fruit stands, bakeries, small businesses, butcher's shops, lots of apartment buildings, and the further from Santa Fe you walk, more and more old, quaint houses of Palermo Viejo. Amongst these, **Calle Serrano** is a nice choice – nine blocks down is a pleasant plaza surrounded by cafés and restaurants.

Below, exercise class in Palermo Park. Right, shopping for a feather duster.

Etiquette once dictated that an Argentine gentleman should don a coat and tie for an evening at the movies or an afternoon at the racetrack. Today, a T-shirt and jeans suffice for the cinema, but a piece of old Buenos Aires has been preserved at the **Hipódromo Argentino de Palermo**, on Avenida del Libertador at Dorrego. The racetrack still enforces its coat and tie dress code for the center grandstand.

The five grandstands themselves have changed little since 1882, when they were built by the Jockey Club, the bastion of Argentina's landed aristocracy. They were divided into four distinct categories, thus sparing high society from rubbing shoulders with the common people. The national lottery now runs the track, but the divisions remain. The *tribuna oficial* has the prime location in front of the finish line. Seats cost between $5 and $10, but don't forget the obligatory coat and tie. In order of price and proximity to the finish line, comes by the paddock section, with seats for $3, and finally the *tribuna especia,* a mere dollar. Of course no matter where you sit, the betting is the same. The minimum stake is just $2.

Despite the differences in price and location, all of the grandstands offer the same type of benches and a roof overhead. The gentlemen sitting on those benches share many common features themselves: tweed sportscoats, felt hats, and grey hair combed straight back with hair tonic. Any resident of Buenos Aires can be called a *porteño*, but these men at the Hipódromo, like those who can be seen playing dominoes in the plaza, are distinguished as classic *porteños*.

The racing fans of the Hipódromo Argentino also distinguish themselves as true gentlemen, according to Alfredo Rapán, who has followed the races in Palermo for 55 years. "The same guy who's causing trouble at the soccer stadium changes when he comes

here. If he bumps into you slightly he'll say, 'excuse me, I'm sorry.' If I ask to look at someone's magazine, he'll hand it to me. It's a special kind of people."

Roque Larrocca, a newcomer with only 20 years of watching the races, agrees. "At soccer they yell, say bad words – that's what the young people like today," he says, adding that horse racing is for the more civilized. Civilized, that is, until the horses are thundering down the home stretch.

The horse-racing season never ends in Palermo. The two most important events, the *Gran Premio República Argentina*, held every January, and the *Gran Premio Nacional* in November, can attract as many as 60,000 spectators, as well as horses from other racing countries in South America.

Almost every day of the year is a racing day somewhere in Buenos Aires. The Palermo Hipódromo is open every Friday with afternoon and evening races, and frequently on Sunday and Monday. The track in the elite northern suburb of San Isidro holds races on Wednesday and Saturday.

Left, at the racetrack in Palermo. **Right**, punters watching the final stretch.

Although Argentine polo players continually travel all over the world to play, they rarely do so as a team. To see the best polo in the world played by Argentine teams, one has to come to Argentina, more particularly Buenos Aires where the top tournaments are played in October and November.

Polo is played almost all year in Argentina, but the big tournaments are played in the spring. The main ones are the Hurlingham Open at the fashionable Hurlingham Club and then the Argentine Open on the picturesque polo fields in Palermo in the center of town. However, games frequently have to be postponed due to rain and wet fields and it is quite usual that they are still being played in December.

Polo, although originally started in India, was brought to Argentina by Britons as were most other sports. There are references to it being played in the province of Santa Fe by British farmers as early as 1875 and at the Hurlingham Club since 1888. The first Argentine Open Championship was won by Hurlingham in 1893.

The locals soon took up the game. Many Argentines, especially those living in the country, were practically born on a horse and, as such, any game on horseback naturally attracted them.

By 1924, when polo was included in the Olympic Games for the first time, Argentina was represented by a team of home-born players, though some of them of English descent. The team of Arturo Kenny, Juan Nelson, Enrique Padilla and Juan B. Miles walked off with the medals.

Reigning champions: Argentina is the reigning Olympic champion. When polo was again included in the Olympic Games for the last time in 1936, they also won the title. Only once was an open world championship held – in Buenos Aires in 1949 – and Argentina won that also.

The United States is the only other country whose polo is anywhere near the standard of Argentina's. A trophy, the America Cup, is occasionally played between the two countries and Argentina's success rate in winning it is enviable. Today nobody disputes Argentina's superiority in the game, although they get few chances to show it. They just do not have any real rivals.

The upkeep of horses (of which a regular player needs at least 20) and playing kit is expensive, so the game is for the rich and upper middle classes. It is, nevertheless, very popular in Argentina mainly because people know their players are the best in the world and because of heavy coverage in the press.

Many leading Argentine players are also in the curious position of being amateurs at home and professionals abroad.

Nobody gets paid for playing in Argentina. In fact the players have to spend quite a bit of money to be able to play. When they go to play abroad, however, they usually do so at the invitation of some wealthy player or fan who pays them to play on his team. The players also take their own horses with them and invariably sell them abroad at a far better price than they would fetch at home.

Argentine polo horses are much sought after all over the world. The phrase may still be "polo ponies," but in actual fact ponies have not been used for the game in Argentina for a very long time. Fully-grown horses are used for speed, stamina and strength. The game has become very fast and horses must be strong to withstand the pushing which takes place during a game.

A horse needs special training for polo and nobody can do this better than certain stable hands, known as *petiseros,* at the *estancias* (ranches). The skill for this job tends to run in families and it is often said that teams depend a lot not only on the quality of their horses, but on their *petiseros.*

Polo has a set of rules designed to eliminate danger as far as is humanly possible. In spite of the vigor with which the game is played, nasty accidents to horse and rider are remarkably rare.

<u>Left</u>, **Argentine polo players are regarded as the world's best.**

Following the game: Basically, teams of four players hit a wooden ball about the size of an orange with a wooden mallet in order to shoot it into the opposing team's goal, which is formed by two posts at each end of the field. To avoid crashing into each other at top speed, the rules forbid a player from crossing the line of the ball (the direction in which the ball is going) and the horseman riding towards it. And when two players ride towards each other, both must give way to the left.

There are penalty shots at goal from different distances for a variety of infringements. The teams change ends after each goal and at the end of each period when a bell sounds. Other than that, play continues until a natural stoppage for a goal, an infringement or when the ball goes out of the field. Each period is called a chukker and lasts seven minutes. Games are composed of six to eight chukkers, depending on who's playing whom.

There are over 6,000 registered polo players in Argentina today which means they have a handicap according to their standard and they play in tournaments. There are also tournaments for youngsters in various age groups from below 10 to 21. Women also play, and have their own annual tournament.

To a large extent, the game runs in families with generation after generation playing it. Sons of leading polo players start to ride and hit a polo ball around almost before they can walk. By the time they are in their teens, they are good enough to rank among the top players in any country.

The Heguy clan, for example, owns a farm 640 km (400 miles) west of Buenos Aires. Of the eight sons of two brothers, five are top players and two more are close behind. "As children, we would spend whole holidays on horseback," says one son, Horacio Heguy. "When one horse was tired, we would find another. No helmets, no boots. My father shouted at us a lot, but he never put pressure on us. He taught us to play good polo – fast, aggressive, smart."

If you attend a polo match in Buenos Aires, you will rub elbows with relatives and friends of the players themselves. They are landed gentry for the most part, "beautiful people" who divide their time between the family *estancia* and elegant apartments in the city.

Their dress code is casual elegance – sportscoats, designer jeans, crisp skirts – and they watch the matches with the reserved demeanor of a crowd at a garden show. It is certainly a world removed from the boisterous and sometimes violent crowds that can all too often be found in the soccer stadiums. It is a world of belonging, one most Argentines have heard about but few have actually experienced, a world where one mingles between matches with players in dusty breeches while eating finger sandwiches under the grandstand.

Pato: A cross between polo and basketball, *pato* is an authentic Argentine sport probably played by the Indians before white settlers set foot in South America, and certainly by the gauchos as far back as the 16th century. It has a colorful history, starting with its name, which is Spanish for duck. The duck certainly got the worst of it during the formative period of *pato*.

A leather basket with handles and a duck inside it was placed midway between two *estancias* or Indian encampments. Two teams of horsemen, either ranch workers or members of Indian tribes, lined up at their respective homes. At a given signal, they raced across the countryside towards the duck. The object was to grab it and carry it home. There was no limit to the number of participants.

The sportsmanship between horsemen wildly tugging at the basket's handles is exciting to watch. As one would be pulled off his horse (with the likely fate of being trampled to death) and another would let go to avoid falling, a third would manage to get away with the duck's basket and ride at full speed for home. The rest would race after him in hot pursuit.

There were no holds barred, from lassooing an opponent to cutting his saddle free. The only unbreakable rule was that the man in possession of the *pato* had to ride holding it in his outstretched right hand, offering it to an opponent to grab if he was caught up. This would invariably produce another tug- of-war. The winning team was the one which managed to get the duck's basket back to their own farm or village.

The game was played after a feast which would include the inevitable barbecue and which would ensure that most of the participants were the worse off for drink. It was followed by a dance at the winner's farm or village for those still able to stand.

Excommunication for pato players: In fact, the games so often ended in fights and disorders that the Catholic Church tried to ban them in 1796 under the threat of excommunication for anyone who took part. The Church was not very successful, but the government was when it banned *pato* by law in 1822. The punishment was one month's hard labor.

As a result, fewer games were played, but the sport, if one can call it that, continued to

Today *pato* is played by teams of four horsemen. The duck's basket has been replaced by a leather ball the size of a soccer ball with six handles. The playing area is approximately 200 meters long and 90 meters wide (650 by 300 feet). At each end is a basket, with the opening facing the field, about 3 meters (10 feet) from the ground. The ball must be thrown into the basket to score a "goal." Games are played in six periods of eight minutes each.

One of the few links with the past is that players wear gaucho costumes. Unlike the past though, they now wear protective headgear. Players must still ride with the ball in an

flourish in the more remote areas. The passage of time did what government and Church were unable to do. As people became more civilized, they turned to less dangerous sports and *pato* virtually died out.

It was left to Alberto del Castillo Posse, a great champion of Argentine tradition, to revive the game in 1937 by first drawing up proper rules. Then he arranged exhibition games and a year later, the Argentine Pato Federation was formed.

Above, the traditional duck in the Argentine game of *pato* has been replaced by a leather ball.

outstretched hand. They punch or throw it to each other. When it falls to the ground, they must pick it up at full speed, which requires outstanding horsemanship.

The game is still played mostly in the provinces on the larger *estancias*, but in October and November the teams come to Buenos Aires for weekend games at the Campo de Mayo, a military base west of Greater Buenos Aires, just off Route 8. After two months of playoffs, the Argentine Open is held in mid-December at the Palermo polo fields, which if you are in Buenos Aires at that time should not be missed.

THE PORT AND COSTANERA

The European and North American tourists who traveled by ship to Argentina in the early 20th century imagined a coastal city that would greet them after their long journey. Many wrote of their initial disappointment as they approached the Buenos Aires ports, an area deserted except for the normal dock activities of a large city. Unlike Montevideo, on the other side of the river, Buenos Aires became known as the "city with its back to the river."

While the residential section of the city is still farther inland, the coastal area, over the years, has been built up as a recreational as well as a commercial district. The **Costanera Sur** and the **Costanera Norte** are both lined with *parrilla* (grill) restaurants and open spaces for sunbathers (swimming is not recommended), joggers, and fishermen. A tall stone wall prevents flooding. There are wide promenades where families set up lawn chairs to enjoy the sun, watch each other, drink their afternoon *mate* and eat *facturas* (pastries). A high-pitched whistle calls attention to the old man pushing a cart of hot sugared peanuts and bags of sweet popcorn.

There are four major ports in the city: **Riachuelo**, which includes **Barracas** and La Boca; **Dock Sud**; **Puerto Madero**, built in 1887; and **Puerto Nuevo**, the newest, built in 1914 and extensively renovated.

National ports: Historically, the ports of Buenos Aires have controlled over 70 percent of the country's international commerce. Produce is transported overland by railways built by the British in the 19th century. Those who favor the decentralization of the economy point out that the system is a holdover from colonial times and that it continues to reinforce the dominance of the capital over the rest of the country. One of the best ways to see the coast is with the free tours organized by the city's tourism bureau, located on the fifth floor in the Centro Cultural San Martín, at 1551 Sarmiento. Most of the people who sign up are *porteños* exploring their own city. Depending on your tour guide, you may wind up singing old tangos and Spanish and Italian songs along with the rest of the passengers.

Alternatively, a taxi ride from La Boca to the Costanera Sur, then on to the Costanera Norte to Ciudad Universitaria costs between $15 and $20 and gives you a quick view of the port and the adjacent parks.

But walking, of course, is also a wonderful way to see the area. Two separate walking tours cover the nicest spots along the river.

Costanera Sur: Avenida Belgrano descends east out of the city center, crossing the large avenues and the docks below, and enters the Costanera Sur. You will pass right through the heart of Puerto Madero, one of the old ports made up of more than a dozen large, brick buildings that overlook the enor-

Preceding pages: the Mississippi steamboat *Delta Queen* is a popular Costanera restaurant. **Left,** rigging an old schooner. **Right,** an Arabian ship docked in Catalinas harbor.

mous cement docks. The long-abandoned port buildings have been converted into a popular commercial area, featuring offices and lofts, and elegant cafés and restaurants. Turning to the left you can stroll along the pleasant pedestrian walkway between the buildings and the docks for about 12 blocks.

An oasis of sun and silence at the edge of the bustle and exhaust fumes of the banking district, the four-story 19th-century brick warehouses extend from Córdoba to Brasil avenues. With their backs to the traffic, the dock buildings face onto the placid waters of the inner port and are an ideal place for a stroll in the early morning or late afternoon. Sitting at a café on the tastefully designed promenade overlooking the water is an ideal way to wait out the rush hour before returning home.

Along the way are two preserved antique navy sailboats, now museum pieces open to the public to explore for a small entrance fee. The **Fragata A.R.A. Presidente Sarmiento**, at the intersec-tion of Avenida Perón, was constructed in England in 1897 and was used to train Argentine navy cadets until 1961, sailing the seas for a distance equal to 42 trips around the world. Further down at the end of the port and Viamonte is the **Corbeta A.R.A. Uruguay**, which arrived in Argentina in 1874, and was also used as a naval school, although it is most famous for its many historical trips to Antarctica.

Avenida Belgrano deadends in the heart of the Costanera Sur. Sunbathers and picnickers (in season), beautiful tall trees, handsome statues, elegant walkways and old stone arches covered with vines all evoke turn-of-the-century Sunday promenades.

Taking a right off Belgrano, a wide boulevard leads to two interesting attractions, both within a few blocks. Down on the left is the **Reserva Ecológica Costanera Sur**, a large protected area with lagoons, abundant birdlife, and thick bushes. Sandy footpaths crisscross the reserve, and you can

Dock workers in Costanera Sur.

walk right out to the edge for splendid views of the river and the port, and for downtown skylines.

Continuing south on the boulevard, there is a small grassy plaza on the right, and just beyond it is the **Escuela de Bellas Artes**, the fine arts school, which houses a small museum featuring copies of famous sculptures. Behind the school is a lovely courtyard with a café and garden. Both the museum and the courtyard are open to the public at weekends. Past this point to the south the area becomes rather stark and industrial, and not really worth exploring.

From Avenida Belgrano to the left is the charming **Museo de Telecomunicaciones**, housed in what used to be an old café-bar called Munich. Built by a Hungarian architect in 1927, it has a somewhat fairyland look to it, with playful stained-glass windows and carvings of gnomes in the walls. The museum took over the building in 1980, and features different galleries dedicated to radio, television and the telephone, all,

of course, with lots of old relics and memorabilia. The museum is open Friday to Sunday 2–6pm, and on Saturday at 3pm they host varying dance, music or theater productions.

You can continue walking north down these two parallel coastal boulevards. It's lovely for strolling, stretching for blocks until Viamonte street, where you will leave the parks behind. Coming out, back onto the main thoroughfares, you can continue further by taking a right down **Avenida Antártida Argentina**, passing more of the port area and eventually arriving at the plaza in front of the Retiro train station. Or by taking Viamonte across the avenues and up a few blocks, you will once again enter downtown.

Costanera Norte: The northern stretch of the coast begins where Salguero street intersects **Avenida Costanera Rafael Obligado,** which runs right along the wide brown river. On a clear day you can sometimes pick out the Uruguayan coastline in the distance. Out at the end

View of the promenade along the Costanera Norte.

of a long pier is what appears to be a large country home. It is actually an elegant fishing club, although people do most of their fishing by throwing their lines right off the stone wall running along the river.

Just further up on the left is **Aeroparque Jorge Newbery**, the city airport, where all domestic flights and some planes to bordering countries come and go. The boulevard is also populated by large sports complexes, where young *porteños* go to play tennis, swim and work on their tans.

But the Costanera Norte is most famous for its *parrilla* restaurants, dozens of which line the road about a mile north of the airport. Feasting on a steak here is a typical event for Saturday night (the restaurants start to fill late evening) or Sunday afternoon on. Part of the ritual is cruising by slowly in a car to contemplate the choices, as the enticing smell of grilled beef wafts around.

Ignore the young parking attendants waving the cars in, and look to see if there is a terrace, if you like the view of the river, if you are amused by the restaurant's name, and whether the people inside look as though they are happy with their choice. But actually the restaurants are mostly very similar. **Los Años Locos** is the spot usually recommended to foreign visitors, and **Los Patitos** is a local favorite.

The last stop along the coast is the **Ciudad Universitaria**, just one of the University of Buenos Aires' campuses. It is comprised of three enormous institutional looking buildings on the river's edge, housing the science, architecture and urban planning departments. Construction of the campus began in 1960, the original plan being to move the entire university to this site. It was never completed due to lack of funds, and different campuses remain scattered about the city.

<u>**Right**</u>, restored warehousing at Puerto Madero, with the Catalinas business district in the background.

THE PAMPAS

Too much time in the big city can give both residents and visitors an overdose of neon, concrete, and pollution. The only known cure is some green grass, a wide sky, and a herd of cattle on the horizon, so many residents head for *el campo* (the country) for a day or week-end. For visitors in need of the same remedy, three especially effective prescriptions are a tour of an *estancia* (ranch) or a visit to the towns of Luján or San Antonio de Areco.

Buenos Aires is a sprawling metropolis, so the first signs of the *campo* are well outside the city limits, in the province of Buenos Aires. About 45 minutes west of the city, the concrete sprouts into grass, and paved side streets fade into dusty lanes. The garbage collectors here still make their rounds in horsecarts. The roadside is littered with outdoor grill restaurants, often no more than a few card tables and a portable kitchen – a barbeque trailer spewing smoke.

About an hour out of town appear the first pastures dotted with cattle – the driving force behind the history and wealth of Buenos Aires. In addition to grazing land, wealthy city-dwellers own luxurious weekend and vacation homes at elite clubs which offer facilities such as golf courses, swimming pools and tennis courts.

The road continues another hour before it reaches the classic scenery of the pampas: endless pastures of rough grass, broken only by cattle, clumps of trees, and the occasional *estancia* house. A rancher's home is typically a broad, low building painted either white or pink, and preceded by a long, tree-lined drive.

The easiest way to get a closer look at an *estancia* is to take a tour from downtown Buenos Aires. This excursion, often called a *fiesta gaucha*, is a whole day outing at a real *estancia*, set up to handle tourists. Though the tour may head to any one of several *estancias*, the basic

itinerary is the same: plenty of food and wine, a show of regional singing and dancing, horse-riding, demonstrations of gaucho sports, relaxation, and fresh air. Check with the City Tourism Board at Sarmiento 1551, 5th floor, or major travel agencies for information. Tour options are abundant.

The tour begins with a trip of two or more hours west or northwest, making the gradual transition from one of the largest cities in the world to the wide open pampas. Upon arrival, the eating begins with *empanadas,* the traditional Argentine meat pies. After an opportunity to stroll around the grounds of the *estancia,* ride one of the horses, and settle into the slower pace of life, the word arrives that lunch is ready in the semi-open shelter.

The main event: As with any true meal in the pampas, the main event is meat. *Asado de tira* arrives first. These beef ribs are roasted outdoors on stakes next to a wood fire, just as the gauchos prepared them 200 years ago. They are

Preceding pages: drinking *mate* and listening to tangos on an outing to the provinces; the pampas. **Left**, the cathedral in Luján. **Right**, riding a bull calf in San Antonio de Areco.

followed by steaks, sausages, kidneys, and other offal, all grilled over wood coals. Anyone who still has room for more is welcome to second helpings. Bread, salad and a dessert of *pastelito,* a traditional crispy pastry filled with jam, add variety to the meaty meal. And of course, the long tables come with bottles of wine and soft drinks.

During and after lunch, a pair of dancers flirt and stomp the *gato, zamba,* and *escondido,* accompanied by guitar and accordion. Both singing and dancing are in the gaucho style, especially the *malambo de boleadora,* a rhythmical feat of coordination performed by whirling a *bola,* a gaucho lasso with weighted balls on the ends. As the music speeds up, the *boleador* keeps rhythm with the tapping of the *bola* against the floor until the *malambo* ends in a frenzy.

The gauchos are most skilful in the outdoors, so after lunch has settled a little, the entertainment moves onto a field for *sortija, pato* and calf-riding. *Sortija* requires a horseman with a steady hand. Riding at full speed, the competitor tries to aim a needle-like stick through a ring *(sortija)* hanging from a pole. *Pato* is a team sport played on horseback with what looks like a soccer ball with handles – a humane substitute for the duck *(pato)* originally used by gauchos *(see pages 200–1).*

Pampas horsemen: Though the men at the *estancia* maintain some of the dress and customs of the gauchos, these horsemen of the pampas disappeared in the 19th century. They made their living by hunting the plentiful wild cattle and the ostrich-like *ñandu,* selling the hides and feathers, and eating as much meat as they wanted, leaving the rest to rot. As the pampas were divided into huge *estancias,* the mixed-blood, fiercely independent gauchos were seen as good-for-nothing thieves by the "civilized" men of rural Argentina. Barbed-wire fences dealt the final death blow to the gauchos. Deprived of the open plains and wild cattle, they had no choice but to work for wages on the *estancias.* Since their demise, the gauchos have been symbols of Argentine freedom and independence.

The citizens and streets of **San Antonio de Areco** have preserved a bit of the image of the gaucho and his times. Though Areco is less than two and a half hours from Buenos Aires by bus, in 1725 and the following decades, its fort marked the frontier between land settled by Europeans and the land of the Indians. As well as a stage-coach stop on the **Camino Real** from Buenos Aires to Peru, Areco was a common meeting place for gauchos.

One of the *pulperías,* where the gauchos met to drink and buy supplies, has been preserved as part of the gaucho museum in Areco. The museum also features a replica of an *estancia* house, containing paintings and artefacts from gaucho and ranch life. The museum is named for Ricardo Guiraldes, the novelist who made Areco famous with his *Don Segundo Sombra,* a *gauchesco* novel about a man from the area.

The memory of Don Segundo Sombra and reverence for the gaucho live on in one of Areco's better-known citizens, artist Osvaldo Gasparini. He sketches gaucho scenes with pen and ink and sells them for a song to the schoolchildren and tourists who visit his studio and gallery. The attraction, as much as the drawings, is Gasparini himself. He dresses as a gaucho, and loves to tell stories about his life, especially the few years in the 1930s when Don Segundo Sombra looked after him.

San Antonio de Areco has many craftsmen like Gasparini. In fact, just a block down the street, Homero Tapia fashions stirrups from ram horns, a traditional craft of the pampas. Another couple of blocks down, Juan José Draghi works in silver, using original designs from the region for knives, belts, and horse tack.

City of pilgrimage: Luján was also a frontier town in colonial Argentina, but today it is better known as the holy city of Argentina. The images of the Virgin Mary that can be seen in any subway station in Buenos Aires and in shrines across the country are replicas of the Virgin of Luján, housed in the basilica there. Though the city has a lovely river and a large museum complex, Luján rates as one of Argentina's most visited cities, primarily because of the basilica and the Virgin.

The story goes that, in 1630, a man was carrying two small statues of the Virgin from Brazil to Peru. When crossing a river not far from Luján, his cart got stuck in the mud. The cart finally moved when one of the statues was taken off, so the man decided it wanted to stay. A shrine grew up around the Virgin of Luján, and was later moved to its present site.

Today, the original statue stands above the altar of a grand gothic **Basílica Nuestra Señora de Luján**, finished in 1935. In the interior of the basilica hang many silver medallions given in thanks to the Virgin of Luján for illnesses cured and petitions granted. The medallions are in the shapes of arms, legs, torsos, and internal organs, depending on the part of the body healed.

Twice each year, hundreds of thousands of pilgrims walk the 60 km (40 miles) between the city of Buenos Aires and Luján. The pilgrimage ends with an open-air Mass in the plaza facing the basilica. Less hardy visitors can cut the trip down to about two hours by taking the bus or train from Once station.

After the basilica, the **Complejo Museográfico Enrique Udaondo** deserves a visit. One of the most complete museums in Argentina, it covers not only the local history of the Virgin, Indians, gauchos and *estancias,* but also the history of the entire country from the colonial period to recent years. The building itself is a museum piece, which served as the *cabildo,* or town hall, of Luján two centuries ago.

After visiting the museum, it is time for a relaxing, scenic boat ride on the river, and time to breathe in the pure air and to enjoy a meal at one of the outdoor restaurants along the banks.

A visit to an *estancia* involves an outdoor *asado* (barbeque) and a ride across the pampas.

TIGRE

For over 100 years, the streams and canals of the **Tigre Delta** have been a favorite weekend refuge for *porteños*. Every Sunday afternoon, thousands make the hour-long journey to the delta to relax among the elegant monuments to the faded glories of Argentina.

Trains for Tigre leave regularly from the Victorian cast-iron **Retiro** station, and dozens of small wooden ferries leave the wharves across the road to service the waterway-veins of the region.

A tree-lined promenade follows the murky-brown main river. Weeping willows reach to the water in between the open-air restaurants and cafés, while assorted food vendors, soapbox politicians and charlatans crowd the footpaths. Across the river are the ostentatious clubhouses of English-style rowing clubs. In March and November, the waterways are taken over by regattas.

If you want to walk before embarking, there are a couple of pleasant options. A few blocks away from the station is the **Puerto de Frutos** (green signs indicate the path). This was once a bustling trading port for produce and other goods coming down river, but these days the activity is at the weekend handicrafts market, the specialty being baskets made from local delta reeds.

Along the Rio Luján is the **Paseo Victorica**, more relaxed than the main thoroughfare near the train station and boat docks. Here, people stroll by the river, picnic and sunbathe. At the 600 block is the interesting **Museo Naval**, housed in a 19th-century navy workshop, the exhibits include photos, models, and antique boats.

Boating on the delta: Meanwhile, every other type of sailing craft seems to ply the Tigre Delta. The boats may be more modern, but the atmosphere has changed little since the homesick English traveler John Hammerton recorded in his 1920s travel guide that Tigre awakens

Boating on the river delta in Tigre.

memories of the Upper Thames on summer days: "Crews practising in outriggers; lonely canoeists; launches scurrying along, well-laden with passengers and delightfully oblivious of the 'rules of the road'; and the gilded youth showing the paces of his new motorboat and translating his Florida swagger into terms of the river."

Numerous boats and ferries head farther out into the delta to quieter zones for lunch, passing various homes along the way: turn-of-the-century stone mansions, English cottages, Italian villas, and little wooden shacks painted bright blue and green. Ferries stop at many of the broken-down piers to drop off newspapers and pick up mail.

In the midst of the docks is the **Estación Fluvial,** where the boat and ferry lines offer information and book trips for passengers. Restaurants in the delta include upscale **El Gato Blanco** and the more modest **Paso El Toro**.

Faded elegance: By far the most original excursion is that to the **Hotel El Tropezón** in the farthest reaches of the delta, where visitors come for lunch or a cheap overnight stay, and to get a taste of 1920s elegance. The hotel is at the intersection of the major boat routes to Paraguay and Uruguay, in what is jokingly called "the Buenos Aires jungle."

Built in the late 1920s at the peak of Argentina's wealth, the hotel has tried to maintain its style and standards despite the country's declining fortunes. El Tropezón (the blunder) was named by its original owner, but the hotel was in fact a raging success, luring the most fashionable *porteños* away from the city. Today, it is run by the founder's five unmarried daughters.

The wooden hotel is painted beige. On the wrought-iron fence around its patio, are sculpted tiny red flowers. Real flowers fill the garden, where the grass is so lush it seems to glow. The centerpiece is a twisted cactus flanked by dysfunctional art nouveau lamp-posts.

A set lunch is eaten on the patio among dozens of tables which will never be filled. Drinks can be ordered in a dark wooden bar next to which is an ancient looking icebox and a framed picture of Jesus of the Sacred Heart. Outside, the ocean-going cargo ships are slowly squeezing their way through the river.

The clean spartan rooms have beds with what feel like original 1920s mattresses. The bathrooms have glistening tiles and polished brass fittings, but the pipes which burst years ago have not been repaired so there is no hot water.

An indoor games room still has its wooden piano and faded photographs of fishermen displaying their hauls alongside grinning chubby girls clad in shorts. At the back of the room is a print of national heroes San Martín and Belgrano with the heroic figure of Freedom carrying the Argentina flag. The emblem reads: "There Arose Upon the Face Of the Earth a Great and Glorious Nation."

At dusk, the ferries start making their way back to the Tigre terminal where trains carry the visitor back to the present, and the bright lights of Buenos Aires.

A warm afternoon on the delta.

ON THE BEACH

When the summer heat smothers Buenos Aires, Buenos Aires migrates to **Mar del Plata**. By the million, *porteños* flock to this Atlantic City of Argentina, fleeing the heat and the hustle of the city – but not the crowds.

On a typical Friday in January or February, six trains, 14 planes, hundreds of buses, and a traffic-jam full of cars leave Buenos Aires for Mar del Plata 400 km (250 miles) away. The city of 500,000 permanent residents swells with three million tourists in those two months. Mar del Plata has enough beaches to absorb such numbers, but as one visitor commented: "You just can't see the sand."

Mar del Plata was an exclusive resort graced with vacation mansions belonging to the Argentine elite at the turn of the century. Today, though the wealthy and their mansions remain, middle-class Argentines, and workers who pay special rates in union-owned hotels, make up the tourist majority.

Most visitors rent an apartment or house for two weeks or a month in Mar del Plata. Many also rent one of the beach tents lined up in colorful rows, where they spend their days chatting, eating and relaxing. If a cold spell strikes, the bathers can take long walks on the ramblas along the beach or go downtown to shop for local sweaters and *alfajores* (sweet cakes). Nightlife is supplied by casinos, discotheques, and theatrical productions, which all follow the migration from Buenos Aires.

Those left back home are constantly reminded, by broadcasts from Mar del Plata and photographs of scantily-clad beachgoers in magazines and newspapers, of the beach they are missing. Even sports and political news have Mar del Plata datelines, since the games and politicians migrate too. The only consolation in Buenos Aires is the lack of crowds. They're at the beach.

Preceding pages: threatening day near Mar del Plata. Below, marble lion in resort village of Piriapolis.

Punta del Este: For most of the year, Punta del Este is a quiet Uruguayan town. The top crust of Montevideo may drive out for a weekend at their ocean home, but usually the long beaches are stirred only by the surf.

Then, suddenly, cars with Argentine license plates are jamming the streets. Buenos Aires newspapers are outselling Uruguayan dailies three to one. Neighbors on the sidewalk are gabbing in *porteño*. When Argentines are released for summer vacation, Punta del Este becomes a second Argentina.

Only a select group of Argentines can afford Punta del Este (probably the most expensive city in Latin America) and most of them prefer to keep things that way. They already complain that their resort "isn't what it used to be" – 20-story condominiums, which offer more affordable rates, are replacing the summer estates that dominated the point for most of the 20th century. But one of the taxi companies which operates in Punta del Este still uses exclusively Mercedes-Benzes, so there must be some spare cash still around.

In the previous century, the village lived off the plentiful fish, whales, sealions and salt found at the point where the Rio de la Plata blends into the Atlantic Ocean. The endless sand created such a nuisance that camels had to pull the salt carts, and forests were planted to halt the advancing dunes.

Now it is the Argentines who are advancing on Punta del Este, to enjoy the sand rather than fight it. Off the sand, vacationers enjoy Uruguay's most exclusive little shopping district. Several sweater stores sell the country's famous hand-knits, some so intricate they resemble tapestries.

When the cool breezes that blow across the point become winter's colder winds, the shutters close on most of the town. Only a few small hotels, shops, and restaurants stay open. It is time for long walks on empty beaches and afternoons at quiet cafés. It is time to return Punta del Este to Uruguay.

Buenos Aires moves to the beach at Mar del Plata in December.

COLONIA DEL SACRAMENTO

An easy day's escape from the pace and crowds of Buenos Aires is the old Portuguese settlement of **Colonia del Sacramento**, across the muddy Rio de la Plata in neighboring Uruguay. It is one of the few surviving colonial relics in the southern zone of South America.

The Portuguese presence in this otherwise Hispanic country is the result of Spanish greed. The explorer Juan Diaz de Solis landed near Colonia in 1516 thinking he was on the way to the riches of the Orient. Unfortunately, he took only six men ashore with him. Instead of finding gold, they were ambushed by Indians and, according to contemporary reports, eaten.

History: Later explorers refused to bother with Uruguay, being much more interested in the stories told by shipwrecked sailors of a "white king" who ruled a fabulously rich land to the north.

While the Spaniards were chasing their dreams of gold, the Portuguese slipped down from Brazil in 1680 to found Colonia for the far more profitable purpose of smuggling.

Although Colonia was founded by the Portuguese as a rival to Buenos Aires, it is difficult to imagine two more different towns. A short hydrofoil ride or a more leisurely trip by ferry takes travelers across the river to a slower and completely different world.

Dreamlike: Arriving in Colonia at lunch-time from the Argentine capital can be an unnerving and dreamlike experience. There are only 20,000 people in the town and few of them are in the streets. The only signs of activity are dogs wandering aimlessly and old men sitting in the shade of sycamores, sucking *mate* through silver straws.

The colonial part of the town is largely intact or restored, jutting into the Rio de la Plata so that water is at the end of every street. With the scattered palm trees, it would be an idyllic semi-tropi-

The steamer arriving in Colonia.

cal setting except for the odd color of the river. The Rio de la Plata looks like silver in the morning, copper in the afternoon and gold at dusk.

While the buildings of Buenos Aires are often extravagant and indulgent, the lines of the Portuguese architecture are clean and symmetrical. An old parochial church has plain twin towers and a simple clock. There is a plaza with neat gardens and ancient trees, usually with more gardeners than visitors. Crooked streets with crumbling whitewashed houses lead down to the water where a lighthouse warns of the dangers of Uruguay's treacherous coastline.

The streets may be deserted but the restaurants are packed and noisy. Lunch in Colonia is long and relaxed. The tables have plastic cloths, the walls are decorated with religious paintings, and a television blares a soccer match. Vegetarians should beware: even more than in Argentina, meat is difficult to avoid at any meal. Even the Hotel Italiano in this Portuguese enclave of an ex-Spanish colony sells steaks which dwarf the plate on which they're served.

An extended walk should follow lunch along the riverside to the remains of colonial fortifications and groups of weeping willows. There is a 30-meter (200-foot) stretch of beach around which the local soccer club seems to be endlessly jogging. The sun bounces from the white buildings and there are no sounds but the cicadas and the wind.

Museums, churches, bikes and chevvies: The large and shaded **Plaza Mayor** is a good place to start exploring. Around the plaza you will find the ruins of the **Convento de San Francisco**, with a colonial era lighthouse looming overhead. Here there are also two museums. The **Museo Portugués** has a fine collection of 18th-century furniture, carved from mahogany and with cordovan upholstery, and nearby is the **Museo Municipal**. On Sunday, be sure to check out the market in the plaza.

From here a nice strolling street is Paseo de San Gabriel, which runs along the water. You will pass the old **Jesuit Chapel**, and if you keep walking, will eventually reach the old port, **Puerto Viejo**. Heading back into town is the **Plaza de Armas**, with the oldest church in the country, the **Iglesia Matriz**. And the **Museo Español** is worth a visit, if only for the restored colonial building.

A nice activity in Colonia is to rent a bicycle and explore the quiet town and surrounding beaches. Also, 4 km (2½ miles) from the center in Real de San Carlos is a colossal and lavish bullring which was built at the turn of the century with no expense spared, but which has not been used for decades. When you arrive look for the tourist office at the ferry docks for more detailed information, maps and walking tours.

Towards evening, a few bicyclists and horse-drawn carts appear in the streets. Many of the town's cars are antique Fords and Chevrolets, including crank-starters in working condition. There used to be many more, but foreign museums snapped them all up.

Colonia's colonial lighthouse.

MONTEVIDEO

In his ode, *Montevideo*, the Argentine writer Jorge Luis Borges wrote of Uruguay's capital: "You are the Buenos Aires we once had, that slipped away quietly over the years, you are ours and all revelers, like the star mirrored in the waters. False door in time, your streets contemplate a lighter past."

Borges' nostalgic recollection of **Montevideo** is shared by many who've been there: a city that looks like Buenos Aires might have looked several decades ago, when life moved more slowly and locals never strayed far from home without a vacuum jug of hot water and a *yerba mate* gourd in hand.

A ferry ride: A side trip to Montevideo is easily made from Buenos Aires, and there are two options for getting there, plane or ferry. The planes take about 15 minutes and leave from the city airport at the Costanera Norte, Aeroparque Jorge Newbery. Aerolíneas Argentinas flies daily as well as PLUNA, the Uruguayan airline. But more interesting and economical is a ferry ride across the Río de la Plata.

Only one company, **Buquebus**, at 867 Córdoba street, offers direct ferry service to Montevideo. The journey across the river takes two and a half hours and round-trip tickets cost about $75. But you can also take a ferry to Colonia and then make a bus connection to Montevideo, the bus trip taking a little under two hours. **Ferry Líneas Argentinas**, at the corner of Córdoba and Maipú, offers the combination ferry/bus trip, as well as Buquebus. Both companies have two different types of ferries that go to Colonia, a hydrofoil which crosses in 45 minutes and costs about $50 round trip, or an older, cheaper and slower ferryboat that takes 3 hours.

Unfortunately, with the combination ferry/bus to Colonia-Montevideo you are not allowed to split the trip up. The connection is made immediately from

Approaching Montevideo after a night-time river crossing.

the dock onto the bus, no sightseeing in between. If you want to visit both places, the easiest option is to go round trip on the ferry to Colonia or Montevideo direct, and purchase round-trip bus tickets separately between the two cities.

Ask about special cruises which serve lunch or dinner if you want to enhance your crossing. Late afternoon and evening are a good time if you enjoy sunsets and night skylines. Only the older ferries have outside decks for enjoying the river and the views.

As the ferries approach Montevideo, you can see the large rise which inspired a Galician navigator's exclamation, *Monte vi eu!* (I saw a hill!), a remark that reportedly inspired the city's name.

South American Switzerland: Landing in the Montevideo harbor may give you the sensation of having traveled back in time. On sycamore-shaded streets, old British Leyland buses maneuver around spark-showering trolley buses, scooters, motorcycles, bicyclists and masses of pedestrians. Ancient automobiles, spared the rust of harsher climates, mix with recent models on the city's streets.

Uruguayans form an older population than the Argentines, a consequence of small families and an exodus of younger Uruguayans during a period of military rule that lasted from 1973 until 1985. One and a half million Uruguayans – half the country's population – live in or around Montevideo.

Generally, Uruguayans are regarded by visitors as less pretentious and more friendly than Argentina's *porteños*. Perhaps because this is such a small country – the smallest Spanish-speaking nation on the continent – they are passionately interested in their nation's affairs.

Uruguay was South America's first welfare state early in this century, earning the somewhat misleading title of "the Switzerland of South America." The agricultural wealth that financed the wide array of social services provided by the state has been spread increasingly thinly over the decades, and Montevideo now looks a little shabby.

Leaving Buenos Aires on the ferry for Montevideo.

Its charm lies in the Old World dignity and graciousness of its people. Montevideans still find time for the afternoon siesta, and, like Argentines, they like lingering lunches and dinners.

Argentina, in fact, has always been Uruguayans' cultural point of reference – they call Uruguay the Eastern Republic of Uruguay, and talk of themselves as Easterners (*Orientales*), in reference to the colossus to the west. Some liken the relationship to the slightly edgy one which Canada has with the United States. Yet you'll quickly notice some significant differences between Montevideo and Buenos Aires.

Perhaps the most striking change from Buenos Aires is the racial mixture in Montevideo. While its inhabitants are predominantly of European descent, there are also many of African origins. Montevideo's blacks have kept alive the rhythms of *candomble* music, first developed in the southern barrios of neighboring Buenos Aires before that city's black population disappeared. You can often hear the drumming of *candomble* in Montevideo's plazas and street markets, as well as during the annual New Year and pre-Lenten carnival street celebrations.

A more subtle difference from Buenos Aires is Uruguay's fiercely laic tradition. The Catholic Church plays no role in the state, and religious holidays have all been given secular names: Christmas is the Feast of the Family, Holy Week is Tourism Week.

Montevideo can be seen in a day or two. You may want to make the rounds in a day and catch the 9pm ferry back, or else take a bus (two hours) to Colonia, the picturesque port opposite Buenos Aires (*see pages 224–5*), then take a pleasant ferry ride back to town.

A stroll through town: A good place to start seeing Montevideo is by going to **Plaza Cagancha** (also called Plaza Libertad) on the city's main thoroughfare, **Avenida 18 de Julio**. There you'll find the main tourism office with plenty of brochures and free maps of the city

Plaza de la Constitución in the colonial quarter of Montevideo.

and surroundings (Montevideo is, after all, a resort town and promotes tourism with great skill).

From Plaza Cagancha it's an easy walk down 18 de Julio to the city's main square, **Plaza Independencia**. Along the way are several shopping arcades filled with boutiques, and a series of bustling coffeehouses in the avenue.

Strolling along 18 de Julio and window-shopping is a popular pastime for the gregarious Montevideans. Economic difficulties in recent years have made window shopping a necessity as well as a form of entertainment.

Plaza Independencia is at the beginning of 18 de Julio. The antennae-peaked scalloped tower to the left as you approach the square is the famous **Palacio Salvo**, for some a monumental eyesore and for others an endearing symbol of the city on a par with the Obelisco in Buenos Aires.

In the middle of the square is the **Mausoleo de Artigas**, the subterranean tomb of General José Artigas, leader of Uruguay's fight for independence from both the Portuguese and the Spanish. The cream-colored palatial building on the south side of the square is the 18th-century **Palacio Estévez**. Once the main government house, today it serves only as the ceremonial presidential office.

Further down the south side, just off the square, stands the city's cultural palace, the stately **Teatro Solis**. Even if you don't attend one of its plays or concerts, it's still worth a look inside.

The arch at the west end of Plaza Independencia marks the entrance to the **Ciudad Vieja**, or old city. This port-flanked peninsula has the city's oldest and most picturesque buildings. **Plaza Constitución**, at Ituzaingo and Sarandí, is a pleasant place to stop. Facing the plaza on one side is the **Iglesia Matriz**, or cathedral, the oldest public building in Montevideo. On another side is the ancient **Cabildo**, or town hall, which dates back to 1812 and houses a historic museum. The stock exchange building called **La Bolsa**, the **Banco de la**

República, and the imposing **Aduana,** or customs house, are all north of the plaza and worth seeing.

Also in the Old City is the **Museo Histórico Nacional**, housed in four different 18th-century colonial homes, most of which belonged to Uruguayan national heroes. They are the **Casa Lavalleja**, **Casa Rivera**, **Casa de Garibaldi**, and the **Museo Romántico**.

Look for the **Mercado del Puerto** on **Calle Piedras**, near the Aduana. This is a congenial place for a leisurely lunch or dinner, with restaurants inside and on the fringes of the market. Succulent seafood is available at several places; grilled beef, almost everywhere. And on Saturday there is a lively street fair, complete with handicrafts and street performers.

Buying wool and leather: Shopping is best in terms of woolen or leather goods. A knitting cooperative called **Manos del Uruguay** has several shops with beautifully knitted and woven woolens made for export. (As the country's major export, Uruguayan wool is generally of high quality – usually better than anything to be found in Argentina.)

Leather prices are generally lower than they are in Buenos Aires. Details such as zippers and buttons on clothing articles also tend to be sturdier than those used for Argentine leather goods.

If it's warm, visit Montevideo's beaches. They're clean, broad expanses of sand that are popular sunning spots on weekends. Also worth visiting are several large parks not far from downtown. There is the rambling **Parque Rodó,** which has a small lake, an amusement park and the **Museo Nacional de Bellas Artes,** a fine arts museum. **Parque El Prado** features a large rose garden and the municipal fine art and history museums. The pleasant **Parque Batlle y Ordóñez** was named after the great social reformer president who pioneered the welfare state. And don't miss the beautiful **Palacio Legislativo**, constructed almost entirely from domestic pink marble.

A TRIP TO CÓRDOBA

The city of Córdoba, an hour's plane ride or 650km (400 miles) from Buenos Aires, dates back to colonial times. One of the oldest cities in the country, it was founded by Jeronimo Luis de Cabrera in 1573. Cabrera came from Santiago del Estero in the north, following the Dulce River, and settled his people by the Suquia River. It is interesting to note that when information about these new, not yet settled areas was recounted in Peru by the early adventurous surveyors, some of the characteristics that have made Córdoba attractive were already mentioned. It was said that these lands had low mountains, plenty of fish in the many streams and rivers, an abundance of wild birds and animals (South American ostriches, deer, pumas, armadillos, otters, hares, partridges and much more) beautiful views, and weather like Spain.

In these few words lay the allure, the charm of the Córdoba region, the same charm which draws Argentines to visit the hundreds of little towns, inns, and campgrounds every year.

When Cabrera arrived in the Córdoba region in 1573, it was populated by three principal Indian groups: the Sanavirones in the northeast, the Comechingones in the west and the Pampas in the plains.

Though a few confrontations did take place between the Spanish and the Indians, the latter were labeled "peaceful and cooperative" by the Spaniards, a commentary dictated by the contrast between these groups and other very bellicose tribes of the northwest, south and east of the country.

One hundred years after its foundation, Córdoba manifested the characteristics which are still seen as its trademark. The little village had flourished religiously and culturally. By that time it boasted an astonishing number of churches, chapels and convents erected by the Jesuits, the Franciscans, the Carmelites and others; it had a Jesuit-run

Preceding pages: Córdoban facade. Below, the cathedral exterior.

232

university, the oldest in the country, erected in 1621 (now called the Universidad Nacional de Córdoba); the local economy was supported by a variety of agricultural products (corn, wheat, beans, potatoes, peaches, apricots, grapes and pears) and by extensive and ever-growing herds of wild cattle.

The tree: In Córdoba one finds the stark juxtaposition of the impossibly flat pampas with the rolling sierras, the first mountain chain one encounters when moving west towards the Andes. As one approaches across the plain, the hills appear as great waves breaking on a beach.

There are three chains of mountains in the western part of the province of Córdoba, all of which run parallel to each other, from north to south. They are the Sierras Chicas in the east, the Sierras Grandes in the center and the Sierras del Pocho (which turn into the Sierras de Guasapampa) in the west. The highest peak in the province is Champaqui, which reaches a height of 2,884 meters (9,517 feet).

The Sierras de Córdoba are neither as high nor as extensive as many of the other mountain formations east of the Andes. Their easy accessibility, their beauty, their dry weather, magnificent views, and good roads, as well as the myriad of small rivers and water courses have established for Córdoba a strong reputation as an ideal spot for rest and recuperation.

Bird songs: The fauna of the region is not as rich as when the Spaniards first arrived, but is still plentiful enough in some hidden areas to support seasonal hunting. Pumas or American lions still roam the hills but are few and isolated. Guanacos are not a common sight around most of the vacation resorts but can be seen toward the higher western areas. Hares abound and are hunted and eaten, as are partridges and vizcachas. Several types of snakes can be found, including rattlesnakes and coral snakes, but the steady invasion of most places in the mountains by residents and visitors has decreased their numbers. Foxes are also occasionally seen. The countless spe-

The Jesuit church, with university students in the foreground.

cies of birds, including condors, in the area are a source of attraction and delight for many people.

Córdoba has a continental climate. Though the summer, with its hot days and cool nights, is the favorite season for most visitors, the winter is not without its charm. Because the rains are seasonal, occurring in spring and summer, the views change dramatically.

Across the flats: The easiest access to the city and province of Córdoba is from the south and east. Buses are fast, offer a wide variety of schedules and are all new, spacious and comfortable units. There are several companies that make the Buenos Aires–Córdoba run with options to stop in Rosario and a few other large towns (the "express" takes about 9 to 9½ hours). The two principal airlines, Aerolíneas Argentinas and Austral, have several daily flights to Córdoba which take about an hour.

If the trip from Buenos Aires is made by land, there are two main ways to go to Córdoba. The shortest is via Rosario, a city of 1 million inhabitants located 300 km (185 miles) from Buenos Aires, using Route 9. The other choice is using Route 8, a slightly longer but quieter and quainter road. In both cases, the visitor will pass through miles and miles of pampas (plain, flat and very rich terrain) dotted with small towns and huge plots planted with corn, wheat, soya and sunflower. Everywhere there are enormous herds of cattle (Aberdeen Angus, Hereford, Holando-Argentina) and horses. The roads are quite good and offer the basic commodities (hotels, small restaurants, cafés, gas stations) in almost every town along the way. Córdoba can also be reached easily from the west (either Santiago de Chile or Mendoza) by plane and bus and from the north (Santiago del Estero, Salta, Tucumán, Jujuy) by plane, bus and train.

Spanish grid: The city of **Córdoba** is one of the largest in the country, with a population of approximately 1,200,000. The basis of its economy is agriculture, cattle and the automotive industry. Its key location in the country, at the crossroads of many of the main routes, estab-

One of Córdoba's central walkways.

lished its early importance and fostered its rapid growth. Although Buenos Aires, with its excessive absorption of power and people, has always tended to overshadow the rest of the country, Córdoba and its zone of influence is the strongest nucleus of resistance found in the vast interior of Argentina.

Córdoba, like most Spanish-settled cities, was designed with a rectangular grid of streets, with the main plaza (in this case Plaza San Martín), the cathedral and the main city buildings in the center of town. It is therefore easy for travelers to find on a map the different sites of historical, architectural or artistic interest within the city.

Because many of the early buildings of Córdoba were either religious or educational, time and progress have spared a great number of them, leaving visitors and residents with a rich treasure-trove of colonial chapels, churches, convents and public buildings amid the modern surroundings.

There are several different tourist offices, including downtown, at the air-port and inside the bus terminal. The main office for city tourism is located in the Recova del Cabildo, Independencia 30, with information about walking tours, special events, museum exhibits, maps and historical background. If planning a trip to the countryside, make sure to visit the provincial tourist office at Tucumán 360, which offers a wide range of information about the nearby sierras.

Church circuit: The religious *circuito* (circuits being the various tours that are recommended) covers most of the oldest colonial religious buildings. Alone or with a guide the traveler can visit the following:

The cathedral: Though its site was decided on in 1577, the final consecration took place in 1784, after collapses, interruptions and changes. These delays account for the many artistic styles visible in the architecture. It has been described by the architect J. Roca as having a classic Renaissance portico and a baroque dome and steeple, with influences of indigenous origin. A large wrought-iron gate completes the picture.

The Candonga church, in the Córdoba hills.

The interior of the church is divided into three large naves, separated from each other by wide, thick columns (which replaced the smaller original columns which were not strong enough to support the building).

The main altar, made of silver, is from the 19th century; it replaced the original baroque altar which is now in the church of Tulumba.

The cathedral is located across from **Plaza San Martín**.

The Jesuit complex: This complex is located on the spot where there was originally a small shrine, dating from 1589. It is located on Caseros Street, two blocks from the cathedral.

The group of buildings is made up of the church, the Domestic Chapel and the living quarters. Originally it also encompassed the Colegio Maximo and the university, both of which are now national institutions.

The church dates to the 17th century. One of its outstanding details is an arch made of Paraguayan cedar, in the shape of an inverted boat's hull, fitted with wooden pegs. The church interior is lined with cedar beams and the roof is made up of beams and tiles. The tiles were joined with a special glue, which after 300 years is still tightly weatherproof. Many of the baroque altars, including the one made of cedar, date to the 18th century and the Carrara marble work on the walls is 19th century.

The Domestic Chapel (with its entrance on Caseros Street) is also from the 17th century. Here, the ceiling was constructed of wooden beams, and canes tied with rawhide, which were placed between the beams and then plastered and covered with painted cloth.

The Jesuits and their work occupy a special place in the history of Argentina and the rest of South America, up to the time of their expulsion in 1768 by the Spanish Crown. Córdoba has its share of their legacy, and for those interested in Jesuit lore and work, visits to the **Santa Ana Chapel** in the city, and the towns of **Alta Gracia**, **Colonia Caroya**, **Estancia La Candelaria** and **Jesus Maria** are recommended.

A river through the sierras.

236

The Church and Monastery of the Carmelite Nuns (also called Las Teresas) was founded in the early 17th century. It was heavily renovated during the 18th century and many of the buildings date to this later period. The main altar has a large baroque sculpture of Saint Teresa of Jesus and the wooden choir is an example of fine woodwork. In the monastery there is a religious art museum, in which many of the objects once belonging to the cathedral are now exhibited. The entrance is on Independencia Street and the complex is located opposite the cathedral.

The Church and Convent of Saint Francis: The land for the church was given to the Franciscan Order by the founder of the city, Jeronimo Luis de Cabrera. The first chapel was built in 1575; this original chapel and a second one which replaced it no longer exist. The current structure was initiated in 1796 and finished in 1813. Within the complex, a room named Salon de Profundis is original.

The church is located at the corner of Buenos Aires and Entre Rios streets and is only two and a half blocks from the cathedral.

The La Merced Basilica: Located in the corner of 25 de Mayo and Rivadavia, only three blocks from the cathedral, the present building was finished in 1826 over foundations from the 1600s.

The main altar, executed in 1890, and the polychrome wooden pulpit from the 18th century are two of the outstanding attractions of the interior.

Also worth mentioning is the **Sobremonte Historical Museum**, an outstanding example of colonial residential architecture. It hosts a very comprehensive collection of Indian and gaucho artifacts, old musical instruments, ceramics and furniture.

It is located on Rosario de Santa Fe and Ituizango Streets, three blocks from the cathedral.

The contemporary city: Córdoba might be better known for its historical and colonial charm, but the modern city also has much to offer visitors. A few blocks from the city center is **La Cañada**, the

The golf club at La Cumbre.

tree-lined canal that runs through town, a lovely place to walk in the evening or when there is not too much traffic. On Saturday and Sunday there is an art and crafts fair on the corner of La Cañada and A. Rodriguez.

The Rincon de los Pintores (the Painters' Corner) is a gallery devoted to the work of local painters, located downtown inside the Centro Muncipal de Exposiciones Obispo Mercadillo at Rosario de Santa Fe 39.

The *peatonales* (pedestrian streets) in the city center are lined with cafés, bookstores and boutiques, and many students coming and going from the university. This is a good place to sit and relax, do some window shopping and watch the people strolling by. Also close by are numerous movie theaters featuring current releases.

Village fiestas: Once the city of Córdoba has been explored, a trip to the surrounding countryside is highly recommended for those with the time. The local tourism authorities have laid out a number of routes which will lead the dedicated traveler up into the mountains, along paved and unpaved roads to lakes, streams, campsites and spectacular views. While these routes can be done by bus, a car is necessary to really explore the area.

One of the most popular areas is **El Valle de la Punilla**, which extends north from the city of Córdoba on Route 38 towards **Cruz del Eje**. This route passes through or near most of the small resort towns of the region.

The first stop is **Carlos Paz**, famous for its night life, its casinos, restaurants and clubs, and the sports activities centered around Lake San Roque. This town surprises the visitor with its handsome chalets, comfortable hotels and streets packed day and night with tourists (if one visits during the high season).

Eighteen km (11 miles) directly north of Carlos Paz is **Cosquin**, a quaint village famous for its Argentine and Latin American folk music and dance festival in the second half of January. Another 15 km (9 miles) north along the narrow but well-paved road brings one to the

An Oktoberfest in the village of General Belgrano.

village of **La Falda**, which holds a festival celebrating the folk music of Argentina's immigrants, along with the tango, in the first week of February.

About 11 km (7 miles) further north lies **La Cumbre**. This town boasts excellent trout fishing from November to April (as do many other towns in the area) as well as facilities for golf, tennis and swimming. Its altitude of 1,142 meters (3,768 feet) makes the climate extremely pleasant and for that reason, as well as for its serenity, it has become known as a writers' haven.

Another 15 km (9 miles) along the same road (now one has traveled 106 km/66 miles from Córdoba) will take the visitor to **Capilla del Monte**, a town which celebrates its Spanish Festival in February. One can enjoy hiking, rock climbing, swimming and serenity in this town in the heart of the sierras.

By taking Route 5 south of Córdoba the traveler will find another tourist haven, **El Valle de Calamuchita**, which lies between Las Sierras Chicas and Las Sierras Grandes.

Chalets and cakes: Arriving in **Alta Gracia**, one finds a charming, prosperous town which welcomes tourists but does not live off them, so one is not overwhelmed by the kinds of crowds or tourist establishments found in Carlos Paz. Life seems to move at a very slow pace here, with shops closing at 12.30pm for lunch and opening again at 4pm. There are a number of modest but clean hotels and several decent restaurants. One of the main attractions is the **Jesuit Church and Monastery**, veritable jewels of colonial architecture.

A short excursion into the hills behind Alta Gracia toward **La Isla**, on the **Anizacate River**, leads over a passable dirt road, past small farms and spectacular views of the beautiful river.

With luck, somewhere along this route, or another in the Sierra region, the visitor just might come upon a group of locals branding their cattle and be invited to eat a barbecue (*asado*), drink strong red wine and throw the *taba* (a gaucho game of chance played with the left knee bone of a horse) with some rough looking but friendly country people. Traditionally, when the meal is over, a simple gourd is packed with *mate* (Argentine green tea) and drunk through a silver straw with the same seriousness and enjoyment with which New York bankers would sip cognac after a meal.

Leaving Alta Gracia behind and returning to the main route, one continues on south and enters the Sierras on a well-paved, but winding road. Twenty picturesque kilometers (12 miles) later the **Los Molinos Dam** and **Lake** appear. This is a favorite spot for the people of the region to practice various aquatic sports. One can eat a decent meal overlooking the dam, high above the lake.

Another 20 km (12 miles) brings one to **Villa General Belgrano**, a town purportedly founded by seamen from the ill-fated battleship *Graf Spee* (and whose name has also appeared on another unfortunate vessel) who chose not to return to Germany. The town has a decidedly German character, with its charming chalets and well-kept gardens. As might be expected, the town celebrates an Oktoberfest during the first week of that month. And don't leave without sampling the famous homemade cakes.

The tiny town of **La Cumbrecita** is nestled at the foot of Las Sierras Grandes, 40 km (25 miles) down an unpaved road west of Villa Belgrano. Visitors will find many nature paths just outside town, crossing small rivers and waterfalls, and meandering among varied plant life, including a small forest of cedar, pine and cypress trees. On the road between Villa Belgrano and La Cumbrecita there's a view of Champaqui, at 2,800 meters (9,186 feet), the highest peak in the sierras of Córdoba.

A less developed and more tranquil part of the sierras is Traslasierra (which means behind the mountains), reached by taking **El Camino de las Altas Cumbres** to the west, on the other side of the mountains from the valleys La Punilla and Calamuchita. Some of the towns worth visiting are **Mina Clavero**, **San Javier**, and **Cura Brochero**.

The Sierras of Córdoba offer infinite possibilities to explore off the main tourist routes, following dirt roads to quiet villages in the mountains.

INSIGHT GUIDES
Travel Tips

FOR THOSE
WITH MORE THAN
A PASSING INTEREST
IN TIME...

Before you put your name down for a Patek Philippe watch *fig. 1,* there are a few basic things you might like to know, without knowing exactly whom to ask. In addressing such issues as accuracy, reliability and value for money, we would like to demonstrate why the watch we will make for you will be quite unlike any other watch currently produced.

"Punctuality", Louis XVIII was fond of saying, "is the politeness of kings."

We believe that in the matter of punctuality, we can rise to the occasion by making you a mechanical timepiece that will keep its rendezvous with the Gregorian calendar at the end of every century, omitting the leap-years in 2100, 2200 and 2300 and recording them in 2000 and 2400 *fig. 2.* Nevertheless, such a watch does need the occasional adjustment. Every 3333 years and 122 days you should remember to set it forward one day to the true time of the celestial clock. We suspect, however, that you are simply content to observe the politeness of kings. Be assured, therefore, that when you order your watch, we will be exploring for you the physical—if not the metaphysical— limits of precision.

Does everything have to depend on how much?

Consider, if you will, the motives of collectors who set record prices at auction to acquire a Patek Philippe. They may be paying for rarity, for looks or for micromechanical ingenuity. But we believe that behind each $500,000-plus

bid is the conviction that a Patek Philippe, even if 50 years old or older, can be expected to work perfectly for future generations.

In case your ambitions to own a Patek Philippe are somewhat discouraged by the scale of the sacrifice involved, may we hasten to point out that the watch we will make for you today will certainly be a technical improvement on the Pateks bought at auction? In keeping with our tradition of inventing new mechanical solutions for greater reliability and better time-keeping, we will bring to your watch innovations *fig. 3* inconceivable to our watchmakers who created the supreme wristwatches of 50 years ago *fig. 4.* At the same time, we will of course do our utmost to avoid placing undue strain on your financial resources.

Can it really be mine?

May we turn your thoughts to the day you take delivery of your watch? Sealed within its case is your watchmaker's tribute to the mysterious process of time. He has decorated each wheel with a chamfer carved into its hub and polished into a shining circle. Delicate ribbing flows over the plates and bridges of gold and rare alloys. Millimetric surfaces are bevelled and burnished to exactitudes measured in microns. Rubies are transformed into jewels that triumph over friction. And after many months—or even years—of work, your watchmaker stamps a small badge into the mainbridge of your watch. The Geneva Seal—the highest possible attestation of fine watchmaking *fig. 5.*

Looks that speak of inner grace *fig. 6.*

When you order your watch, you will no doubt like its outward appearance to reflect the harmony and elegance of the movement within. You may therefore find it helpful to know that we are uniquely able to cater for any special decorative needs you might like to express. For example, our engravers will delight in conjuring a subtle play of light and shadow on the gold case-back of one of our rare pocket-watches *fig. 7.* If you bring us your favourite picture, our enamellers will reproduce it in a brilliant miniature of hair-breadth detail *fig. 8.* The perfect execution of a double hobnail pattern on the bezel of a wristwatch is the pride of our casemakers and the satisfaction of our designers, while our chainsmiths will weave for you a rich brocade in gold *figs. 9 & 10.* May we also recommend the artistry of our goldsmiths and the experience of our lapidaries in the selection and setting of the finest gemstones? *figs. 11 & 12.*

How to enjoy your watch before you own it.

As you will appreciate, the very nature of our watches imposes a limit on the number we can make available. (The four Calibre 89 time-pieces we are now making will take up to nine years to complete). We cannot therefore promise instant gratification, but while you look forward to the day on which you take delivery of your Patek Philippe *fig. 13,* you will have the pleasure of reflecting that time is a universal and everlasting commodity, freely available to be enjoyed by all.

Should you require information on any particular Patek Philippe watch, or even on watchmaking in general, we would be delighted to reply to your letter of enquiry. And if you send us

fig. 1: The classic face of Patek Philippe.

fig. 4: Complicated wristwatches circa 1930 (left) and 1990. The golden age of watchmaking will always be with us.

fig. 6: Your pleasure in owning a Patek Philippe is the purpose of those who made it for you.

fig. 9: Harmony of design is executed in a work of simplicity and perfection in a lady's Calatrava wristwatch.

fig. 2: One of the 33 complications of the Calibre 89 astronomical clock-watch is a satellite wheel that completes one revolution every 400 years.

fig. 5: The Geneva Seal is awarded only to watches which achieve the standards of horological purity laid down in the laws of Geneva. These rules define the supreme quality of watchmaking.

fig. 7: Arabesques come to life on a gold case-back.

fig. 10: The chainsmith's hands impart strength and delicacy to a tracery of gold.

fig. 11: Circles in gold: symbols of perfection in the making.

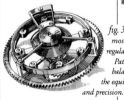

fig. 3: Recognized as the most advanced mechanical regulating device to date, Patek Philippe's Gyromax balance wheel demonstrates the equivalence of simplicity and precision.

fig. 8: An artist working six hours a day takes about four months to complete a miniature in enamel on the case of a pocket-watch.

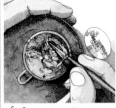

fig. 12: The test of a master lapidary is his ability to express the splendour of precious gemstones.

PATEK PHILIPPE
GENEVE
fig. 13: The discreet sign of those who value their time.

your card marked "book catalogue" we shall post you a catalogue of our publications. Patek Philippe, 41 rue du Rhône, 1204 Geneva, Switzerland, Tel. +41 22/310 03 66.

Reality check. Call home.

—— *AT&T USADirect® and World Connect®. The fast, easy way to call most anywhere.* ——

Take out AT&T Calling Card or your local calling card.** Lift phone. Dial AT&T Access Number for country you're calling from. Connect to English-speaking operator or voice prompt. Reach the States or over 200 countries. Talk. Say goodbye. Hang up. Resume vacation.

Argentina♦	001-800-200-1111	**Guyana***††	**165**
Belize♦	555	Honduras †	123
Bolivia*	**0-800-1112**	**Mexico**◊◊◊	**95-800-462-4240**
Brazil	**000-8010**	**Nicaragua**	**174**
Chile	**1-23-0-0311**	**Panama**■	**109**
Colombia	**980-11-0010**	Paraguay (Asuncion City)†	0081-800
Costa Rica*■	**0-800-0-114-114**	**Peru**†	**171**
Ecuador*†	**999-119**	**Suriname**†	**156**
El Salvador*■	**190**	Uruguay	00-0410
Guatemala*	190	**Venezuela***■	**80-011-120**

AT&T
Your True Choice

You can also call collect or use most U.S. local calling cards. Countries in bold face permit country-to-country calling in addition to calls to the U.S. World Connect® prices consist of USADirect® rates plus an additional charge based on the country you are calling. Collect calling available to the U.S. only. *Public phones require deposit of coin or phone card. †May not be available from every phone. ††Collect calling only. ♦Not available from public phones. ◊◊◊When calling from public phones, use phones marked "Ladatel". ■ **World Connect calls can only be placed *to* this country. ©1995 AT&T.

For a free wallet sized card of all AT&T Access Numbers, call: 1-800-241-5555.

Getting Acquainted

The Place

Area: 3.6 million sq. km (1.4 million sq. miles)
Location: On the Rio de la Plata estuary opposite Uruguay
Population: More than 3 million, with a further 8 million in the surrounding metropolitan area.
Language: Argentinean Spanish
Religion: Roman Catholic
Time Zone:
Currency: *peso*
Weights and Measures: metric
Electricity: 220 volts with 50 cycles AC
International dialing code: 54 (1)

Orientation

Buenos Aires, the second largest city in the southern hemisphere, is among the world's 10 biggest metropolitan areas.

Because the country's resources were becoming alarmingly concentrated in Buenos Aires, Congress decided in 1987 to move the many of the capital's functions to the Patagonian twin cities of Viedma and Carmen de Patagones.

Buenos Aires has 16 museums and around 40 theaters, including the world-famous opera house Teatro Colón, and is the home of the national ballet and symphony. Palermo Park, the city's oldest park, covers about 1,500 acres (600 hectares).

Climate

Buenos Aires' climate is a slave of the Rio de la Plata (River Plate). It is a city of an average humidity of 45–60 percent in the summer months (December to March) and as high as 70–95 percent in the winter (June to September). Humidity is to such an extent the star of the show in BA that a coin expression goes, *Lo que mata es la humedad* (the killer is the humidity), as opposed to temperature which in the mild climate

zone of Buenos Aires is an average of 50°F–65°F (10°C–18°C) in winter and around 90°F (32°C) in the summer. The river moderates the climate of the city and sprawling suburbs.

The People

Natives, who call themselves *porteños*, ("people of the port"), are mainly European in origin, with Italy strongly represented. But large-scale immigration towards the end of the 19th century also produced communities of English, French, and Germans, with a sprinkling of Poles, Russians, Portuguese, Turks, and other South Americans.

Culture

Most *porteños* are of Spanish or Italian descent, and customs generally follow those of Southern Europe. Breakfast consists of coffee and croissants; lunch is the main meal and is served between 1pm and 3pm. Dinner tends to be quite late.

On weekends restaurants are jammed at midnight. Restaurants portions, particularly meat, are often enormous; it's all right to order one dish for two.

It is also customary for women and acquaintances of the opposite sex to kiss (one cheek) on meeting.

It's also still common for quite decent-looking men to murmur suggestive comments to women on the street. Ignoring all such remarks is best.

Economy

The city relies on both manufacturing and service industries. Industrial products include textiles, cars, chemicals, metal products, and foodstuffs. The port itself, through which foodstuffs, wool, and flax are exported, is a big employer.

Government

Buenos Aires, the federal district of Argentina, has 46 administrative districts and is controlled by the country's president, who appoints the mayor. The National Congress is responsible for the city's legislative affairs.

Planning the Trip

What to Bring

Dressing in Buenos Aires tends to be quite formal, especially during the winter months.

Fashion is very important, and people are always up-to-date with the latest styles from Europe. Dressing for dinner is customary. Men will want to bring along a jacket and tie; women a skirt and stocking. Umbrellas and waterproof footwear are advisable year-round; in winter a warm jacket, scarf and gloves are essential. Many *porteña* women wear fur coats.

Entry Regulations
Visas & Passports

You will need a passport and a tourist visa to enter Argentina, unless you are a resident of one of the bordering countries of Brazil, Uruguay, Paraguay, or Chile. In this case, a national ID card is sufficient. Travelers must fill out a card at customs to be surrendered on departure. Don't lose it! For customs regulations, contact your travel agent. Proper clearance for special equipment such as videos recorders, computers, and tape recorders may be arranged through your travel agent.

Argentina visas are good for four years of multiple entries, but each visit to the country is limited to three months. For an extension, apply to the National Directorate of Migration.

Be sure to have your entry card on hand; you will not be allowed to leave the country without it. Also, don't forget to save enough cash for the airport departure tax.

Currency

To combat the hyperinflation of the late 80s and early 90s, the Argentine government has marked their *peso* to the US dollar, one for one. This makes the math very simple but prices rather high compared to other Latin American countries. US dollars are definitely the preferred foreign currency and are easily changed in banks (*bancos*), exchange houses (*casas de cambio*), or hotels, and in some instances dollars are accepted outright. Travelers' checks are not accepted directly as payment, but are also easily changed in the major banks or exchange houses, the majority of which are located downtown near the Plaza de Mayo and on the street San Martìn. Major credit cards are widely used, Visa and Mastercard by far the most popular, American Express and Diners also accepted. Beware, however, that credit cards are sometimes subject to minimum amounts or surcharges.

Your best bet is to bring along one major credit card, travelers' checks, and a small supply of US dollars in greenbacks – easier to exchange on weekends or bank holidays.

Public Holidays

All government agencies, as well as banks and most businesses, close on public holidays. Note that except for Christmas, New Year's and Good Friday, the holidays are actually observed on the closest Monday to allow for long weekends.

New Year's Day (*Año Nuevo*): January 1

Good Friday (*Viernes Santo*): Friday before Easter

Labor Day (*Dìa del Trabajador*): May 1

Commemoration of First Government (*Revolución de Mayo*): May 25

Malvinas Day (*Dìa de las Malvinas*): June 10

Flag Day (*Dìa de la Bandera*): June 20

Independence Day (*Dìa de la Independencia*): July 9

Anniversary of San Martìn's death (*Dìa de San Martìn*): August 17

Columbus Day (*Dìa de la Raza*): October 12

Christmas Day (*Navidad*): December 25

Getting There
By Air

From New York, fly Aerolineas Argentinas, Eastern, LAN-Chile, Varig. From Miami: same. From Toronto, Montreal and Vancouver: Canadian Pacific airlines. From Europe: KLM, Swissair, Alitalia, Lufthansa, Iberia, Aerolineas Argentinas, Varig, etc. Charter flights, tours prove a good buy, since services are greatly improved. Argentine travel agents are making a major effort to deliver the goods on schedule in a bid to reach a long-sought-after international standing.

By Sea

Major world carriers visit Buenos Aires periodically. For those with time and money, Prudential Lines, to name one, sails its luxury liners from Vancouver to Buenos Aires with stops in Tacoma, San Francisco, Los Angeles, Buenaventura, Guayaquil, Callao and Valparaiso, passing through the Straits of Magellan. The liners accommodate about 120 passengers. The return route goes through Santos, Rio de Janeiro, La Guaira (Venezuela) and the Panama Canal.

By Road

Several all-comfort luxury buses feature daily and (in many cases) hourly trips joining BA to major cities in the neighboring countries of Uruguay, Paraguay, Brazil, Bolivia and Chile.

Argentine railways are run by the government, sometimes not to the tightest of schedules or to the greatest physical comfort of the traveler. But they get there, and they are very inexpensive. A good way to travel the great expanses of Argentina. Main train terminals in BA are Retiro (northern lines), Once (western line) and Constitución (southern line).

Remember, whether you get in to Buenos Aires by train, bus or plane, your best friend is the Tourism Secretariat, and do steer away from the "friendly" limousine, or taxicab driver or that smiling promoter of downtown hotels and restaurants.

Useful Addresses
Travel Agencies

Cosmopolitan Travel, L. Alem 986, 7th floor, Buenos Aires, Argentina, tel: 311-6684/6695/2081/2474. Telex: 9199 CASSA AR. 24 hour service available and many languages spoken.

Flyer Travel, Reconquista 621, 8th floor, Buenos Aires, Argentina, tel: 313-8165/8201/8224.

STO Travel, Hipolito Yrigoyen 850, Buenos Aires, Argentina, tel: 34-0789/5913/7336. Telex: 22784 SHABA.

Sol Jet Travel, Florida 118, Buenos Aires, Argentina, tel: 40-8361/3939/7030. Telex 17188 SOLIT AR.

Foreign Representatives

Australia, Santa Fé 846, 8th floor, tel: 312-6841.

Bolivia, 25 de Mayo 611, 2nd floor, tel: 311-7365.

Brazil, C. Pellegrini 1363, 5th floor.

Canada, Suipacha 1111, 25th floor, tel: 312-9081.

Chile, Sn. Martin 439, 9th floor, tel: 394-6582.

Colombia, Florida 939, 4th floor, tel: 311-7399.

Costa Rica, Esmeralda 135, 6th floor, tel: 45-8427.

Cuba, V. del Pino 1810, tel: 783-2213.

Dom. Republic, Sta. Fe 1206, 2nd floor, tel: 41-4669.

Ecuador, Quintana 585, 10th floor, tel: 804-6408.

Jamaica, Corrientes 127, 4th floor, tel: 311-4872.

Mexico, Larea 1230, tel: 824-7061.

Panama, Esmeralda 1066, tel: 311-7661.

Paraguay, Maipu 464, 3rd floor, tel: 392-6536.

Peru, Tucumán 637, 9th floor, tel: 392-1344.

South Africa, M.T. Alvear 590, 7th floor, tel: 311-8991.

Switzerland (British interests), Luis Agote 2412, tel: 803-7070.

United States, Colombia 4300, tel: 774-7611.

Uruguay, Las Heras 1907, tel: 803-6032.

Venezuela, Esmeralda 909, 4th floor, tel: 311-8337.

Airline Companies

Aeroflot, tel: 312-5573.

Aereolineas Argentinas, tel: 393-1562.

Aero Mexico, tel: 392-4821.

Aeroperu, tel: 311-4115.

Air France, tel: 313-9091.

Alitalia, tel: 312-8421.

Austral, tel: 49-9011.

Avianca, tel: 312-3693.

British Airways, tel: 392-3489.

Canadian Airlines, tel: 392-3765.

China Airlines, tel: 312-0664.

Cruzeiro-Varig, tel: 35-3014.

Ecuatoriana, tel: 311-1117.

El Al, tel: 392-8840.
Flying Tigers, tel: 311-9252.
Iberia, tel: 35-5081.
Japan Airlines, tel: 392-2005.
KLM, tel: 311-9522.
Korean Air, tel: 311-2937.
Lade, tel: 361-0853.
Lan Chile, tel: 311-5336.
LAPA, tel: 311-2492.
Lloyd Aereo Boliviano, tel: 35-3505.
Lufthansa, tel: 313-4431.
Pluna, tel: 394-5356.
Qantas Airway, tel: 312-9701.
Sabena, tel: 394-7400.
Singapore Airlines, tel: 33-3402.
South African Airways, tel: 311-5825.
SAS, tel: 312-8161.
Swissair, tel: 312-0669.
Thai International, tel: 312-8161.
United Airlines, tel: 312-0664.
Viasa, tel: 311-5298.

Practical Tips

Emergencies
Security and Crime

The crime rate in Buenos Aires is low compared to other cities of its size, but economic hardship has made theft more common, and some poorer parts of the city dangerous. The best advice is to use common sense: lock valuables in the hotel safe, don't leave luggage unattended, watch your handbag or wallet in crowds, don't walk through deserted areas late at night. Violent crime is still very rare, but should you have the bad luck to be held up, don't resist.

Medical Services

The health care in this country is good, especially in the private hospitals and clinics. Hospitals have trained personnel, who have studied here and abroad. There are specialists in most of the medical fields, who make it a point to attend international medical congresses, to inform themselves on the recent advances in medical science and to bring these to Argentina. The biggest obstacle is lack of funding.

The cost of medical care of course will depend on the type of attention needed and the individual clinic or hospital visited. But count on at least $50 for a medical consultation.

For emergencies in the Buenos Aires area:

Burn Wounds Hospital:	923-4082
Emergency Medical:	
Assistance:	107
Fire Department:	100
Poison Unit:	962-2247
Police:	101

HOSPITALS

Hospital Británico, Perdriel 74, tel: 304-1081.
Hospital de Niños Pedro de Elizalde, Avenida Montes de Oca 40, tel: 307-4788.
Hospital Francés, La Rioja 951, tel: 866-2546.
Hospital Alemán, Avenida Pueyrredón 1640, tel: 821-1700.
Hospital Israelí, Terrada 1164, tel: 581-0070.
Hospital Italiano, Gascón 450, tel: 981-5010.
Hospital Municipal Fernández, Cervifío 3356, tel: 801-5555.

If you need medicine outside of business hours, at least one pharmacy in each neighborhood is open 24 hours. Check the signs located in all pharmacies' windows that say *farmacia de turno*, which lists the days of the week and the corresponding pharmacy with address.

Business Hours

Monday through Friday, business hours are from 9am–6pm, and banking hours are from 10am–3pm. Stores open at 9am and close between 7–8pm. In residential neighborhoods, some stores close for siesta from 1–4pm. On Sunday almost everything (except some museums, entertainment venues, cafes, and restaurants) is closed.

Media
Newspapers

There are two major dailies, *Clarín*, the most widely read, which follows a popular line, is run as big business, stressing business and middle-of-the-road political and social views, reducing editorial involvement to a mini-

mum, with juicy police stories, tales of misery and deprivation, etc.

On the other end of the rainbow stands *La Nación*, geared for middle to upper-middle class readers with a refined taste for news and editorials. No controversial issues published here either.

Another traditional Buenos Aires daily is *La Prensa*.

Businessmen feed avidly on *Ambito Financiero*, a weekday business paper known for its scoops and controversial shop gossip. *Financiero* is also a booming business organization.

The *Buenos Aires Herald* is the only English-language newspaper in BA, and in Argentina, for that matter. Founded in 1876 originally as a maritime paper, it is an uncompromising daily whose loud and clear message has transcended the country's boundaries on such thorny issues as human rights, the evils of dictatorship, oppression, the Malvinas war and the "disappeared" Argentines.

Magazines

A foreign observer once said newsstands on Buenos Aires streets were the best-stocked in the world. He was possibly very close to the truth. You can bet you will find your favorite magazine on any display of the downtown Florida newsstands. But if you do not, just ask the newsvendor for it. He will surely be able to give you the address of the local distributor. You may also wish to go to one of the major bookstores on the same street or to one just around the corner.

Radio

There are two radio stations which offer music non-stop, allowing only for a couple of minutes interruption per hour for newscasts and commercials. Pop on Radio Laser 102, classical on Radio Clásica.

Talk radio is popular in chatty BA, and there are several interesting programs. The BBC is on from 5pm to about 12:30am. Musical offerings include international pop hits, tango, and classical music.

Television

There are four metropolitan TV stations, three private (Channels 9, 11 and 13) and one state-run, ATC or Channel 7. Channel 2, broadcast in the capital of the province of Buenos Aires, La Plata, is also viewed in the city of Buenos Aires, although reception is not always good.

Most of the programs are bought in from the US, and some from Europe. Local productions include drama series and afternoon soap operas.

Postal Services

Varyingly unreliable. The best bet for sending important letters out of the country is to send them registered. Never enclose money or valuables. Even checks have been known to disappear.

The main post office is located on Sarmiento 151, and operates Monday to Saturday from 8am–8pm. Also there are over 60 branches scattered throughout the city, open Monday to Friday 10am–6pm and Saturday 10am–1pm. Some of the downtown branches are located at 757 Avenida de Mayo – three blocks from the Plaza de Mayo, 543 Avenida Córdoba – near the intersection with Florida, 1539 Tucumán – two blocks from both the Teatro Colón and Avenida Corrientes, and one inside the Retiro train station.

If you need to send something quickly, Federal Express, UPS and DHL all have offices downtown.

Telecoms

Argentina's notoriously inefficient state-run telephone company has recently been privatized, which has improved service considerably, but not solved all of the problems. The phone service remains a sore subject with Argentines – it is outrageously expensive, and a lack of lines in Buenos Aires can making calling a challenge. The two private companies that now service the entire country are Telecom (French) and Telefónica (Spanish), although there is no freedom of choice yet, businesses and residences are assigned to one or the other depending on neighborhood, city, and province.

The easiest way to make international or regular phone calls in Buenos Aires is to go to a *locutorio*, where upon entering you are assigned to a private phone booth, make your phone call, and pay upon exiting. Almost all of them feature international service and

fax. You can dial direct internationally by marking 00 + country code + number, or 000 for the international operator. To place a collect call mark 000 and request *cobro revertido*, but you will of course be charged the outrageous Argentine rates. The largest *locutorio* downtown is located on the corner of Corrientes and Maipú, but there are literally hundreds all over the city with about the same service.

Most large hotels have international phone and fax service, although beware of stiff surcharges added on to the actual call. The most economical option is to bring along a calling card from your home carrier and their Argentine access number.

There are numerous public payphones on the street which run on *fichas* or *cospeles* (tokens), good for one 2 minute local phone call, and *tarjetas* (calling cards) which cost around $6 and are good until the value runs out. Both of these may be purchased in *kioscos* or *locutorios*.

Tourist Offices

There are two main sources for tourist information in Buenos Aires, the municipal tourism bureau and the national tourism board. The city office, located inside the San Martìn Cultural Center, is very helpful and has lots of material (a good bit in English) including a wonderful city map, tourist magazines and newspapers, and information on hotels, restaurants, entertainment, and tourism agencies. They also offer free, guided city tours, both on foot and in bus. This office sponsors the tourist kiosks on Florida Street, and in the Recoleta.

The national tourism board has some information on Buenos Aires but is most helpful regarding traveling around the country. If you are planning a trip to a specific part or province of Argentina, they can provide you with information and also refer you to that particular province's tourism office in Buenos Aires.

A brief list of office addresses, telephone numbers and opening hours follows:

Secretaría de Turismo Nacional, Avenida Santa Fe 883, tel: 312-5550; fax: 313-6834. Hours Monday–Friday 9am–5pm.

Dirección General de Turismo de Bue-

nos Aires, Sarmiento 1551, 5th Floor, tel: 476-3612; fax: 374-7533. Hours Monday–Friday 9am–5pm.

Tourist Kiosk, Florida Street, Diagonal Roque S. Peña and Florida. Hours Monday–Friday 9am–5pm.

Tourist Kiosk, Galerías Pacífico, Florida and Córdoba, inside the mall, 2nd Floor. Hours Monday–Friday 9am–5pm.

Tourist Kiosk, Recoleta, Cultural Center Recoleta, lobby. Hours Tuesday–Friday 6–8pm and Saturday–Sunday 2–7pm.

Travel Agencies

City Service, Florida 890, tel: 313-6849; fax: 313-7490.
Eurotur, Viamonte 486, tel: 312-6070; fax: 311-9010.
Flyer Travel, Reconquista 621, 8th Floor, tel: 313-8224; fax: 312-1330. (Highly recommended)
Furlong, Esmeralda 1000, tel: 318-3200; fax: 318-3244.
Viajes Verger, Reconquista 585, 6th Floor, tel: 311-6581; fax: 311-2308. (Highly recommended)

Foreign Representatives

Australia, Villanueva 1400, tel: 777-6580.
Canada, Tagle 2828, tel: 805-3032.
Great Britain, Dr Luis Agote 2412, tel: 803-7070.
Ireland, Suipacha 1380, 2nd Floor, tel: 325-8588.
South Africa, M.T. Alvear 590, 7th Floor, tel: 311-8991.
United States, Avenida Colombia 4300, tel: 777-4533.

Airline Companies

Aeroflot, tel: 312-5573.
Aerolìneas Argentinas, tel: 362-6008.
Aeroméxico, tel: 322-4821.
Aeroperú, tel: 311-4158.
Air Canada, tel: 312-0664.
Air France, tel: 327-0202.
Air New Zealand, tel: 312-0664.
Alitalia, tel: 312-8421.
Austral, tel: 778-4000.
Avianca, tel: 322-2731.
British Airways, tel: 325-1009.
Canadian Airlines, tel: 322-3632.
China Airlines, tel: 312-0664.
Cubana, tel: 326-5292.
Ecuatoriana, tel: 311-1117.
El Al, tel: 322-6937.
Iberia Viasa, tel: 326-5075.
KLM, tel: 480-9470.

Ladeco, tel: 361-7071.
Lan Chile, tel: 311-5334.
LAPA, tel: 812-3322.
Lloyd Aereo Boliviano, tel: 327-1961.
Lufthansa, tel: 319-0600.
Malaysia Airlines, tel: 313-4981.
Pluna, tel: 342-4420.
South African Airways, tel: 311-5825.
Swissair, tel: 319-0000.
United Airlines, tel: 326-9111.
Varig, tel: 329-9211.
Vasp, tel: 312-8520.

Getting Around

Public Transport

Buses

There are over 100 city bus lines within the city limits, which can take you literally from one end of Buenos Aires to the other, and almost anywhere in between. The problem is knowing the numbers and routes. The *colectivos* are identified by a number as well as the major destinations above the windshield. But you will most likely have to inquire at a kiosk or a newspaper stand, a very common practice even among *porteños*. You board at the front door, where you will notice a large automatic coin machine, which after depositing the fare will print your ticket (the drivers don't collect fares). The buses stop every three or four blocks, so just before you want to get off, push the buzzer near the back door and the driver will stop at the next bustop. Be warned, the *colectivos* can get rather crowded, especially around late afternoon rush hour, with people packed together in the center aisle.

Long distance travel on buses is also available. A very large and modern bus terminal is located in Retiro, where you can find buses going to almost anywhere in the country. Information on their destinations and prices can be obtained at the terminal from the different companies.

Trains

The Argentine train system used to crisscross the entire country but service has been drastically reduced due to lack of funding. But you can still take the trains to the suburbs, or for daytrips outside of the city to Tigre, La Plata, or Luján. The three main train stations are Retiro, Constitución, and Once. Most of the train lines are in the process of privatization, so there is no central information office – you must go to each station separately or inquire at the tourism bureaus.

Subway

The subway system, better known as the *Subte*, is the fastest and most economical way to get around town. It's also the oldest subway system in Latin America. Trains pass through the various stations every 3–5 minutes and the rides are quick, taking no more than 20 minutes. There are five subway lines, four that begin downtown near Plaza de Mayo and spoke out into the rest of the city, and one that crosses the other lines east/west from Retiro to Constitución. Maps of the city almost always indicate the subway system. The art work in some of the stations is quite unique and has an interesting background. Many of these painted tiles were baked by artisans in Spain and France at the beginning of the century and around the 1930s.

Taxis

These are easily recognized, black with a yellow roof, and readily available 24 hours a day. Fares are reasonable, the meter starting at just over a dollar, and an average trip within the downtown area costing between $3 and $5. A bit of advice: be careful when paying and make sure the correct bill is given. Quick exchanges of bills have been known to take place, especially with the tourist who doesn't know the language or the currency. If you don't have small change, inquire before getting in if the driver can break larger bills. Tipping is not a custom, although leftover small change is appreciated.

Ferries

Going to Uruguay on the ferry is a pleasant trip, fairly inexpensive and entertaining. Buquebus, located at

Avenida Córdoba 867 (Tel: 313-4444), has ferries that go to both Montevideo and Colonia, and Ferry Lìneas Argentinas, on the corner of Córdoba and Maipú (Tel: 300-1348), has ferries to Colonia, for just a little less than Buquebus. If you want to enjoy a stroll on the deck and the fresh air, you'll want to opt for the older, slower ferries – the new hydrofoils are completely enclosed.

Private Transport

Remises

Remises are private automobiles available for hire (with driver) by the hour, excursion, day or any other time period. They don't make much sense for short trips within the city, but on longer trips they are less expensive than taxis. Remises are listed as such in the telephone directory, and hotels will have their own recommendations.

Car rental

Renting a car in Argentina is not only expensive, but also a harrowing experience if not accustomed to the local, insane driving tactics. For getting around the city it is totally unnecessary and parking quite a hindrance. But if you want to hit the open road and explore (be careful out there) the following are some of the better known agencies.

ABC Rent A Car, Cerrito 1060, tel: 811-1565.
Al Rent A Car, M.T. Alvear 678, tel: 313-1515.
Avis, Cerrito 1257, tel: 326-5542.
Budget, Av. Santa Fe 869, tel: 311-9870.
Dollar, M.T. Alvear 523, tel: 315-8800.
Hertz, Dr Ricardo Rojas 451, tel: 312-1317.
Rent a Car, M.T. Alvear 866, tel: 315-8105.
Serra Lima, Av. Córdoba 3100, tel: 961-3065.

Where to Stay

5-Star ($200 and up)

Alvear Palace Hotel, Avenida Alvear 1891, tel: 804-4031; fax: 804-9246. Buenos Aires' most elegant hotel in the city's chic-est neighborhood. French decor, excellent restaurant and tearoom, boutiques, health club, business center.

Caesar Park, Posadas 1232, tel: 814-5150; fax: 814-5148. Modern, large luxury hotel in the Recoleta. Lobby piano bar, three restaurants including elegant buffet, health club with pool, business center. Popular with business set.

Claridge Hotel, Tucumán 535, tel: 314-7700; fax: 314-8022. Very British, old-fashioned, centrally located. Health club with pool, penthouse suites with gardens, pleasant bar.

Crowne Plaza Panamericano, Carlos Pellegrini 525, tel: 348-5000; fax: 348-5250. Located on 9 de Julio in the shadow of the Obelisco, renovated modern 18 floor tower, health club with pool, popular with conventions/conferences, excellent restaurant Tomo 1.

Hotel Inter-Continental, Moreno 809, tel: 340-7100; fax: 340-7199. Four blocks from Plaza de Mayo in Monserrat, modern 19-story hotel, popular with business people, restaurant/bar, health club and indoor pool.

Libertador Kempinsky, Avenida Córdoba 690, tel: 322-2095; fax: 322-9703. Located in the heart of the microcenter, tall modern hotel with bar and pool on the top floor, restaurant, popular with European business set and tourists.

Marriot Plaza Hotel, Florida 1005, tel: 318-3000; fax: 318-3008. Newly renovated, elegant hotel on Plaza San Martín, favorite with visiting heads of state and royalty. English/French decor, famous restaurant Plaza Grill, health club, outdoor pool.

Park Hyatt, Posadas 1082, tel: 326-1234; fax: 326-3736. Near the French Embassy and the Recoleta, fairly new, large modern hotel in French style, two restaurants, lounge, health club and outdoor pool, popular with business set and visiting rock stars.

Sheraton Buenos Aires, San Martín 1225, tel: 318-9000; fax: 318-9353. Located in Retiro, enormous highrise towers commanding magnificent view of the river and port area. 24 stories, rooftop bar, international restaurants, tennis courts and pool, favorite with business set.

4-Star ($100–$200)

Carsson Hotel, Viamonte 650. Tel/Fax: 393-0029. One block from Florida, faded elegance but charming, quiet, English style bar, most affordable of this group.

Gran Hotel Colón, Carlos Pellegrini 507, tel: 325-0717; fax: 325-4567. Across from Teatro Colón on 9 de Julio, modern but cozy, luxury suites available with patio, rooftop outdoor pool, restaurant, popular with tourists.

Gran Hotel Dorá, Maipú 963. Tel/Fax: 312-7391. Where Argentine author Borges took his afternoon tea, around the corner from Plaza San Martín, antique inside and out but tasteful, good service.

Hotel Bisonte/Hotel Bisonte Palace, Paraguay 1207, tel: 816-3941; fax: 816-5775. M.T. Alvear 902, tel: 328-4751; fax: 328-6476. Two branches with same ownership, highly recommended, pleasant, modern, conference rooms available, bar.

Hotel Continental, Diagonal R. Sáenz Peña 725, tel: 326-1700; fax: 322-1421. Managed by the Marriot chain, located between Plaza de Mayo and the Obelisco, classic French-style building, cafe 24 hours.

Hotel Crillon, Santa Fe 796, tel: 312-8181; fax: 312-9955. French-style antique building refurbished, very modern inside, many services for the business traveler, 24 hour room service, located on Plaza San Martìn.

Hotel Park Plaza, Parera 183, tel: 815-5028; fax: 815-4522. Located on quiet side street in the Recoleta, elegant classic European style, 8 floors – each one dedicated to different famous painter.

Hotel Plaza Francia, E. Schiaffino 2189. Tel/Fax: 804-9631. Classic brick colored building, located in the Recoleta near the Fine Arts Museum, quiet, good breakfast served in rooms, highly recommended.

Hotel Recoleta Plaza, Posadas 1557, tel: 804-3471; fax: 804-3476. Attractive, small French-style hotel in Recoleta, with restaurant and room service.

Lafayette Hotel, Reconquista 546. Tel/Fax: 393-9081. Conveniently located in microcentro, recently remodeled English-style decor, restaurant and room service.

Lancaster Hotel, Córdoba 405, tel: 312-4016; fax: 311-3021. Very European, fancy lobby, pretty sunlit rooms, nice bar/tearoom.

3-Star ($100 and under)

Gran Hotel Hispano, Avenida de Mayo 861, tel: 345-2020. One block from Plaza de Mayo and close to San Telmo, renovated antique building, popular with European budget travelers.

Gran Hotel Orly, Paraguay 474. Tel/Fax: 312-5344. Basic, inexpensive accommodations, good location.

Hotel Diplomat, San Martín 918, tel: 312-6124; fax: 311-2708. Around the corner from the Plaza Hotel and Plaza San Martín, 70s style decor, good service.

Hotel Embajador, Carlos Pellegrini 1185. Tel/Fax: 326-5306. Good location at 9 de Julio and Santa Fe, modern, large rooms, cafe.

Hotel Impala, Libertad 1215. Tel/Fax: 812-5696. Two blocks from shopping street Santa Fe and very near to Recoleta, modern, basic accommodation, cafe.

Hotel Phoenix, San Martín 780, tel: 312-4323; fax: 311-2845. Best of the group with 4 star service, old world charm, beautiful turn of the century building with antique iron elevator and glass cupolas, next door to Galerías Pacífico.

Hotel Promenade, M.T. Alvear 444, tel: 312-5681; fax: 311-5761. Clean, 70s modernish decor, basic accommodations, dark rooms.

Hotel San Antonio, Paraguay 372, tel: 312-5381. Charming, small, with air of old-fashioned European pension, good value.

Hotel Waldorf, Paraguay 450, tel: 312-2071; fax: 312-2079. Close to Florida and Santa Fe shopping streets, modern, comfortable, bar, larger rooms and suites.

For longer visits, a good alternative is an aparthotel or suite hotel which give you the services of a hotel with the convenience of a furnished apartment, including kitchenette. Per-night prices range from $100 for a studio to $333 for a 3-room apartment. Corporate and longer stay discounts are offered.

Feir's Park All-Suites Hotel, Esmeralda 1366, tel: 327-1900; fax: 327-1935. One block from Libertador in elegant neighborhood, room service, pool, healthclub, business center, option of connecting suites.

Suipacha y Arroyo Apart Hotel, Suipacha 1359, tel: 325-8200; fax: 325-1886. In same upscale neighborhood near Libertador and 9 de Julio, good service, healthclub and outdoor pool, patio and garden, parking garage.

Torre Cristóforo Colombo Suites, Oro 2747, tel: 777-9622; fax: 775-9911. In Palermo two blocks from US embassy, tall modern tower, excellent service, rooftop bar, restaurant, healthclub, outdoor pool.

Plaza San Martín Suites, Suipacha 1092, tel: 328-4740; fax: 328-9385. Between Plaza San Martín and 9 de Julio, newly built and modern, health club, room service.

Ulises Recoleta, Ayacucho 2016, tel: 804-4571; fax: 806-0838. Across from the Alvear Palace in the Recoleta, European style, classic building with only 25 apartments, antique furnishings, warm atmosphere.

Eating Out

Dining out is a favorite pastime of *porteños*, but the menu is not the only attraction. Restaurants are a place to socialize, to see and be seen, and share a bottle of wine until the wee hours. Nevertheless, *porteños* take eating seriously, and we've compiled this list of eateries conscious of the weight of our decisions. But don't be afraid to try any clean, well-lighted place that strikes your fancy. There are hundreds of good restaurants in the city, where the food is almost universally fresh and well-prepared in a simple Southern European style.

Restaurants in Buenos Aires open for lunch at noon, and for dinner around 8pm. But no one dines out in the evening before 9pm, with restaurants really coming alive between 10 and 11pm. Weekends, restaurants stay busy much after midnight. Price categories are for two people, with house wine:

Inexpensive	$40 or less
Moderate	$40 – $80
Expensive	$80 or more

Beef

El Mirasol, Davila 202, tel: 315-6277. Upscale *parrilla* in posh Puerto Madero, elegant atmosphere, reservations. Expensive.

La Cátedra, Cerviño 4699, tel: 777-4601. In the heart of the pleasant Palermo district, nice atmosphere, grilled beef but also interesting international cuisine and fresh salads. Moderate.

La Estancia, Lavalle 941, tel: 326-0330. Grilled beef in the traditional gaucho tradition in the center of the cinema district. Moderate.

La Veda, Florida 1, tel: 331-6442. Basement floor, dark wood panelling, excellent steak poivre, tango dinner show most evenings. Reservations. Expensive.

Los Años Locos, Av. Costanera R. Obligado, tel: 783-5126. The most popular of the riverfront *parrillas*. Moderate.

Río Alba, Cerviño 4499, tel: 773-5748. Also in Palermo, popular restaurant famous for brochettes and enormous filet mignon steaks. Moderate.

Italian and Mediterranean

Bice, Davila 192, tel: 315-6216. The original is in Milan, with over ten around the world, the BA version in Puerto Madero, a very new and very posh Northern Italian eatery, with modern twists on traditional pasta. Expensive.

Fellini, Paraná 1209, tel: 811-2222. Trendy and lively restaurant overlooking beautiful plaza, interesting fresh and imported Italian pastas, gourmet pizzas, and specialty salads. Moderate.

Filo, San Martín 975, tel: 311-0312. Eclectic, arty decor, bar in front and upbeat music, serves unusual pizzas, fresh pastas and salads. Inexpensive.

Piola, Libertad 1078, tel: 812-0690. Just off Santa Fe, similar in style, atmosphere, and menu to Filo, but smaller and cozier. Inexpensive.

Restaurant Como, Juncal 2019, tel: 806-9664. Stylish and colorful Barrio Norte favorite, Mediterranean menu including innovative chicken and fish, and grilled beef. Moderate.

Teatriz, Riobamba 1220, tel: 811-1915. Casual, warm atmosphere with a touch of elegance, also in Barrio Norte, Mediterranean menu with interesting pasta, chicken and fish, and wonderful desserts. Moderate.

International and French

Au Bec Fin, Vicente Lopez 1825, tel: 801-6894. Classic French cooking in a splendid restored mansion, a Buenos Aires institution, dinner only. Reservations. Expensive.

Catalinas, Reconquista 875, tel: 313-0182. Country French decor and innovative menu (rabbit with figs, fish with hazelnuts, grilled baby eels), including lots of seafood choices. Reservations. Expensive.

Cholila, Davila 102, tel: 315-6200. New restaurant run by Argentina's hottest chef, Frances Mallman, in BAs' most happening spot, Puerto Madero. A truly international and innovative menu, including wonderful dishes from all over the world but distinctly Argentine. Great portside patio. Moderate.

El Gato Dumas, Junin 1745, tel: 804-5828. Offerings from the idiosyncratic master chef Gato Dumas include such dishes as "ecstatic double chicken breasts" and "perfumes of crayfish and chicken." Reservations. Expensive.

Le Trianon, Avenida Del Libertador 1902, tel: 806-6058. A charming, intimate restaurant located in the palace garden of the Ornamental Art Museum, featuring a truly gourmet French menu and a simple, elegant atmosphere. Reservations. Expensive.

Lola, Ortìz 1805, tel: 802-3023. Nouvelle and original cuisine, including rabbit, lamb, and duck dishes, in attractive atmosphere. Reservations. Expensive.

Mora X., Vicente Lopez 2152, tel: 803-0261. Menu created by the same culinary director of Au Bec Fin, with a loft/gallery atmosphere heightened by mural size paintings and tall ceilings, features informal French cooking and grilled meats. Moderate.

Spanish

El Globo, H. Yrigoyen 1199, tel: 381-3926. One block from Avenida de Mayo, near Congreso, try their *paella* or *puchero* (seafood stew). Moderate.
Pedemonte, Avenida de Mayo 676, tel: 331-7179. A favorite with BA politicians, turn-of-the-century decor, featuring Spanish cuisine, pastas and grilled beef. Reservations. Expensive.
Plaza Mayor, Venezuela 1389, tel: 383-0788. Spanish seafood dishes are the house specialty, situated amongst the mini independent-theater district, popular with younger crowd and open late-night. Moderate.
Tasca Tancat, Paraguay 645, tel: 312-5442. Squeeze in at the long, antique wooden bar and enjoy Spanish-style squid, delicious potato omelettes, grilled mushrooms, and creamy custard for dessert, all to soft jazz and warm lights. Closed weekends. Inexpensive.

Pizza

Los Inmortales, Corrientes 1369, Lavalle 746, Callao 1165. Small chain of legendary BA pizzerias where the decor is dedicated to the life and times of tango stars and the pizza is consistently good. Try the classic *napolitana*, covered with tomatoes and garlic. Inexpensive.
Pizzería Guerrín, Corrientes 1372. Typical *porteña* pizzeria in the heart of the Corrientes theater district, with a mind-boggling selection of toppings. Inexpensive.
El Cuartito, 937 Talcahuano at Paraguay. The closest BA comes to a sports bar, with clippings and photos covering the walls, soccer on the television, delicious pizzas and cold beer. Inexpensive.

Regional Argentine

El Ceíbal, Güemes 3402, tel: 823-5807; Cabildo 1421, tel: 784-2444. Great place to try specialties from Northern Argentina, including *locro* (corn chowder), *humitas* (tamales) and *empanadas*. Inexpensive.

Popular Eateries

Barbaro, Tres Sargentos 415, tel: 311-6856. A BA landmark, an old world version of the hole-in-the-wall bar, a great place for a simple midday meal or music, beer and bar food in the evening. Inexpensive.
Chiquilín, Sarmiento 1599, tel: 373-5163. One block from Corrientes, with the quintessential BA-restaurant atmosphere, serving very reasonable pasta and beef specialties. Fills up quickly on weekends. Inexpensive.
El Trapiche, Paraguay 5099, tel: 772-7343. Typical neighborhood restaurant in Palermo, with cured hams, tins of olive oil and bottles of wine decking the walls and ceiling. Great grilled beef, homemade pastas and seafood. Inexpensive.
La Casa de Esteban de Luca, Defensa and Carlos Calvo. In the heart of San Telmo, restored colonial-era home of the Argentine "poet of the revolution", popular Sunday lunch after the San Telmo fair. Inexpensive.
Pippo, Montevideo 345. No frills but great atmosphere and unbeatable prices. Try a *bife de chorizo* (T-bone steak), or a bowl of *vermicelli mixto* (pasta noodles with pesto and bolognaise sauce), washed down with the house red and seltzer. Inexpensive.
Restaurant Dora, L.N. Alem 1016, tel: 311-2891. An upscale version of a popular eatery with rave reviews on the enormous steaks and simple seafood dishes, a downtown "don't miss". Moderate.
Rodi Bar, Vicente Lopez 1900, tel: 801-5230. Cozy, neighborhood restaurant nestled amongst the famous gourmets of the Recoleta, featuring simple homemade food. Inexpensive.

Vegetarian

Yin Yang, Paraguay 858, tel: 311-7798, Echeverría 2444, tel: 788-4368. A delicious respite from Argentine beef, featuring fresh salads, soups, homemade wheat bread, brown rice and stirfried veggies, and various other meatless treats. Inexpensive.

Cafes and Confiterías

Café Tortoni, Avenida de Mayo 829.
Confitería del Molino, Rivadavia 1801.
Confitería Ideal, Suipacha 384.
El Taller, Serrano and Honduras.
Florida Garden, Florida and Paraguay.
La Biela, Quintana 600.
La Esquina de Trollo, Paraguay and Paraná.
La Giralda, 1449 Corrientes.
Las Violetas, Rivadavia 1801.
Le Trianon, Avenida del Libertador 1902.
Plaza Dorrego Bar, Defensa and Humberto 1°.
Richmond, Florida 468.

Attractions

Cultural

The Argentina people are culture-orientated. Thus, a wide range of activities are available. Museums, galleries, theaters, bookstores and several libraries are all worth a visit. Be sure not to miss any of the ones listed below while in Buenos Aires.

Museums

Museo de Arte Hispanoamericano "Isaac Fernández Blanco", Suipacha 1422. Open: Tuesday–Sunday 2–7pm. Spanish-American Art Museum, with the largest collection of colonial silverwork in South America, including works commissioned by the church and state. Located inside the famous neocolonial Palace Noel.
Museo de Arte Moderno, Avenida Corrientes 1530, 9th Floor. Open: Tuesday–Sunday noon–8pm. Modern Art Museum, with a wonderful collection of works by Matisse, Utrillo, Dalí, Picasso, as well as Argentine contemporary artists.
Museo de la Ciudad de Buenos Aires, Alsina 412. Open: Monday–Friday 11am–7pm; Sunday 3–7pm. City Museum, housed in a turn-of-the-century residence in the heart of Monserrat, their quirky exhibits give a glimpse into the city's fascinating past.
Museo del Cabildo, Bolívar 65. Open: Tuesday–Friday 12.30–7pm; Sunday 3–7pm. Cabildo Historical Museum, whose collection includes artifacts dating from the country's founding in the late 1500s to the May Revolution in 1810.
Museo de Motivos Argentinos "José Hernández", Avenida Del Libertador 2373. Open: Wednesday–Friday 1–

7pm; Saturday–Sunday 3–7pm. Argentine Motifs Museum, features the most complete collection of folkloric art in the country. Many gaucho artifacts, earthenware, silverware, musical instruments, etc.

Museo Nacional de Arte Decorativo, Avenida Del Libertador 1902. Open: Wednesday–Monday 3–7pm. Ornamental Art Museum, displays works, including furniture, porcelain, crystal, and tapestries, from the XV to the XIX century, housed in a beautiful baroque style palace.

Museo Nacional de Bellas Artes, Avenida Del Libertador 1473. Open: Tuesday–Sunday 12.30–7.30pm; Saturday 9.30am–7.30pm. National Fine Arts Museum, whose collection includes the usual assortment of European masters, but on the second floor is the more interesting and most complete collection of Argentine art.

Museo Nacional del Grabado, Defensa 372. Open: Sunday–Friday 2–6pm. Printmaking and Etching Museum, featuring interesting exhibits of contemporary artists from around the world.

Theater

The theater season in Buenos Aires usually opens in March, with a large number of varied plays to please everyone. The Argentina like to go to see a good play and are highly critical. There is always something worthwhile seeing. Check the local paper or with the hotel for the current and best ones available. Recitals and concerts are promoted by the Secretary of Culture in an effort to bring culture to the people. The public responds enthusiastically by attending all events. Open-air concerts are very popular on hot summer evenings and are held in any one of the numerous parks in the city.

Teatro Colón: Most of the renowned performers of the world are well acquainted with this magnificent theater. The building is in the Italian Renaissance style with some French and Greek influence. It has a capacity for 3,500 people, with about 1,000 standing. The acoustics is considered to be nearly perfect. Opera is one of the favorite programs for the season. In 1987, Luciano Pavarotti performed *La Bohème* here and tickets were sold out well in advance. Ballets are another favorite, performed by greats

such as Nureyev, Godunov and the Bolshoi Ballet.

The local company is very good and many of its members go on to become international figures. The Colón also has a magnificent museum, where all of the theater's history and its mementos are stored. It is an enlightening experience to have a guided tour of the theater and the museum. This can be arranged by calling 355-114 or 335-116 for an appointment. Tickets can be purchased at the box office located on Libertad Street.

San Martín Theatre: Offers a variety of plays and musicals. Check the local paper for performances.

"On-Corrientes" Popular Productions

Fundación Banco Patricios, Callao 312, tel:373-0656.
La Plaza, Corrientes 1660, tel:373-8781.

(plus the multitude of other Corrientes Theaters, easily identifiable by their enormous marquees and bright lights)

Small, Independent Productions

Babilonia, Guardia Vieja 3360, tel:862-0683.
Foro Gandhi, Corrientes 1551, tel:374-7501.
Liberarte, Corrientes 1555, tel:375-2341.
La Carbonera, Balcarce 998, tel:362-2651.
Payro, San Martín 766, tel:312-5922.
Teatro Del Sur, Venezuela 1286, tel:383-5702.
Teatro IFT, Boulogne Sur Mer 549, tel:962-9420.

State Sponsored

Teatro Colón, Libertad 621, tel:382-5414. (Box office - Tucum·n 1111)
Teatro Municipal General San Martín, Corrientes 1530, tel:374-8611.
Teatro Nacional Cervantes, Libertad 815, tel:816-4224.

Cultural Centers

Centro Cultural Borges, Viamonte and San Martín, tel: 319-5450.
Centro Cultural Recoleta, Junín 1930, tel: 803-1040.
Centro Cultural Ricardo Rojas,

Corrientes 2038, tel: 953-0390.
Centro Cultural San Martín, Sarmiento 1551, tel: 374-1251.

Cinema

Going to the movies is another popular form of entertainment. And cinemas stay open past 11pm. Recent national and international films are shown, and the price of a ticket is less than in most countries. Regular listings appear in the local papers.

Cine Avenida, Avenida de Mayo 675, tel.331-6626.
Cine Club TEA, Scalabrini Ortiz 532, tel.854-6671.
Leopoldo Lugones, Corrientes 1530, tel.374-8611.
Lorange, Corrientes 1372, tel.373-2411.
Lorca, Corrientes 1428, tel.371-5017.
Losuar, Corrientes 1743, tel.371-6100.

Tours

Estancia Getaway: Visitors to Buenos Aires have the chance to get away from the buzz of the city, in the small town of San Antonio de Areco, about 110 km (70 miles) away. In this peaceful location, with beautiful scenery, the Aldao family has converted the Estancia La Bamba into a country inn, with all the facilities to make a stay both comfortable and memorable. For more information, contact 392-0394 or 392-9707.

Amusement Parks

Ital Park: Libertador and Callao, only a few blocks from Retiro station. Open: every day, weekdays 2pm; weekends 10am. Rides, games, shows for the youngest. Refreshments, tel: 41-6405.
Parque de la Ciuded: Cruz and Escalada. Open: weekends (Saturday 1pm, Sunday 11am), tel: 601-3332.

Rides

Treat yourself to a Bing Crosby-Grace Kelly style coach ride through the shady greenery and wide promenades of the Palermo parks. You can hire coach services at the entrance of the Zoological Gardens, Plaza Italia. Take your camera along. Another 19th-century treasure is pedal-boat rides on the

Palermo lakes. Very romantic in the spring and autumn, a bit breezy and wet in winter, but still a challenge for those jet-lagged legs of the long-distance traveler.

Zoos

Buildings in an elaborate turn-of-the century style. The variety of animals is considerable, but their living conditions are appalling, by 20th-century standards.

Tango Shows

A good tango show can be found almost everywhere, but the best shows are in Buenos Aires. Reservations are suggested for the following where such shows are staged:
Taconeando, Balcarce 725, tel: 362-9596 or 362-9599.
Casa Rosada, Chile 318, tel: 361-8222.
El Viejo Almacen, Av. Independence corner Balcarce, tel: 362-4626.
Il Castello, Pedro de Mendoza 1455, tel: 285-270.
Michelango, Balcarce 4332, tel: 306-542.

Dinner shows

Cantina Feli Cudi, Suarez at Hernandarias (La Boca).
La Querandí, Perú 302, tel: 345-1770.
La Veda, Florida 1, tel: 331-6442.
Tango Mío, Ituzaingó 1200, tel: 307-6044.

Cocktail shows

Bar Sur, Estados Unidos 299, tel: 362-6086.
Cafe Homero, Cabrera 4946, tel: 773-1979.
Casablanca, Balcarce 668, tel: 334-5010.

Cafe concerts

Cafè Tortoni, Avenida de Mayo 829, tel: 342-4328.
Clasica y Moderna, Callao 892, tel: 812-8707.
Club del Vino, Cabrera 4737, tel: 833-0050.
La Cumparsita, Chile at Balcarce, tel: 302-3387.

Dance halls

Club Almagro, Medrano 522.
Club Sin Rumbo, Tamborini 6157.
La Argentina, Rodriguez Peña at Corrientes.

La Trastienda, Balcarce 460, tel: 342-7650.
Salon Canning, Scalabrini Ortiz 1331.

The nightlife in Buenos Aires is quite a bit more active than in most major cities of the world. Argentineans enjoy staying up late. People walk carefree in the late hours of the night. Crime, although on the rise, is still not major concern. The center part of town, on Calle Florida and Lavalle, at midnight might appear to most as midday.

The big cities of the interior, like Córdoba, Mendoza, Bariloche, Salta, etc., that attract many tourists, have a considerable nightlife. The theater shows are not as varied as in Buenos Aires, but a little bit of everything is available.

Discos, nightclubs, cabarets and bars can be found in most of the city. Hear the latest hits from around the world and dance into the morning at, for example, Cemento, located on Estador Unidos 1238, or for a more formal crowd, dance at Le Club, on Quintana 111, or at Hippopotamus, Junin 1787. Other possibilities are:
Africa, Av. Alvear 1885.
Contramano, Rodriguez Pena 1082.
Man Man, Arroyo 866.
New York City, Av. Alvear Thomas 1391.
Puerto Pirata, Liberated 1163.
Snob, Ayachcho 2038.
Club 100, Florida 165.

Shopping

San Telmo has rows of little dusty shops as well as palace-like emporiums of works of art and antiques from all over the world, by the best artists

and artisans living and dead. On Sunday a stupendous antique fair assembles at the San telmo plaza. You will not want to miss it, even if you don't do any actual buying. Take your camera and comfortable shoes. You will probably hear a number of street musicians, including a peppy Brazilian *ecola da samba* (they'll have the entire market swing in a few minutes). You'll also see artisans at work, poets reading their works, young groups doing theater, pantomime, and impromptu tango. A few names and addresses to remember in the antique market are:
Antique Casa Pardo, Defensa 1170, tel: 361-0583.
Bontempo, Callao 1711, tel: 41-8265.
Galleria Studio, Libertad 1271, tel: 41-1616.
Gallery Space, Carlos Pellegrini 985, tel: 312-1342. Marcelo Torcuato de Alvear 628, tel: 4236.
Naón y Cia, Guido 1785, tel: 41-1685.
Roldán y Cia, Rodriguez Peña 1673, tel: 22-4714; Defensa 1084; tel: 361-4399; Florida 141, tel: 30-3733 (auctions) Santarelli; Florida 688, tel: 393-8152.
Saudades, Libertad 1278, tel: 42-1374.
Vetmas, Libertad 1286, tel: 44-2348.
Zurbarán, Cerrito 1522, tel: 22-7703 (also art gallery).

Furriers

Carles Calfun, Florida 918, tel: 311-1147.
Maximilian, Marcelo T. de Alvear 684, tel: 312-0623.
Pieles Libero, Guido 1890, tel: 44-5501.
Berthe, Santa Fé 1227, tel: 41-2284.
Ana-Ra, Cerrito 1020, tel: 393-6441.

Jewelers

Santarelli, Florida 688, tel: 393-8152
Ricciardi, Florida 1001 (Plaza Hotel), tel: 312-3082.
H. Stern, At the Plaza Hotel, Sheraton and Ezeiza Airport.
Belgiorno, Santa Fé 1349, tel: 41-1117. Best silver designer jewelry.
Antoniazzi-Chiappe, Av. Alvear 1895, tel: 41-6137. Santa Fé 896, tel: 311-4697.
Guthman, Viamonte 597, tel: 312-2471
Jean Pierre, Alvear 1892, tel: 42-8303.
Ricardo Saúl, Quintana 450, tel: 41-1876.

Leather

Chiche Farrace, Florida 940. Ciudad del.

Cuero Shopping Mall, number 43, tel: 311-4721.

Echeverria 2252 "23", Belgrano, tel: 781-2885. Libertador 16465. San Isidro, tel: 747-8881.

López, Marcelo T. de Alvear 640, tel: 311-3044.

Sagazola, Libertador 7112, tel: 70-3988 (Nuñez). Guido 1686, tel: 42-5428.

Jota U Cueros, Tres Sargentos (behind Harrod's) 439.

Lederland, Talcahuano 862, tel: 41-6693.

Rossi y Carusso, Santa Fé 1601, tel: 41-1538.

López, Marcelo T. de Alvear 640, tel: 311-3044.

Pullman, Esmeralda 321, tel: 45-5959. Florida 985, Πhone 311-0799.

Sagazola, Libertador 7112, Nuñz, tel: 70-3988. Agué. Cerrito 1128, tel: 393-3066.

Hersé, Florida 961, tel: 311-1842.

Riding gear

López Taibo, Corrientes 350, tel: 311-2132.

Rossi y Carusso, Santa Fé 16011, tel: 41-1538.

H. Merlo S. y Cáa, Juncal 743, tel: 22-6116.

H. Melos y Cia, Julio A Roca 1217, Hurlingham, tel: 665-4859.

Ladie's shoes

Norberto, Florida 817, tel: 311-1488.
Peruggia, Alvear 1866, tel: 42-6340.
Avella, Quintana 309, tel: 41-5198.
Boniface, Florida 891. parera 145. Santa Fé 1781.
Botticelli, Florida 891. Quintana 488 Tel: 44-3906.
Lonté, Rodriguez Peña 1221.
McShoes, Florida 849, tel: 312-4781.
Raffi-Lu, Alvear 1824, tel: 44-2398. Libertad 1157, tel: 44-5695.

Men's shoes

Boniface, Florida 598. Parera 145. Santa Fé 1781.
Delgado, Corrientes 161, tel: 331-0173.
Grimoldi, Florida 251, tel: 394-2405.
Guante, Florida 271, tel: 394-7127.
Guido, Quintana 333, tel: 41-4567, Rodriguez.

Peña 1290, Tel: 42-9095. Florida 704, tel: 392-7548.
López Taibo, Corrientes 350, tel: 311-2132.
Los Angelitos, Florida 529, tel: 393-4477.
McShoes, Florida 849, tel: 312-4781.
Callao 1714, tel: 44-6535.

Pret-a-Porter

Christian Dior, Quinta 545. Florida Corner of Viamonte.
Elsa Serrano, Mansilla 3045, tel: 824-9571.
Graciela Montefiore, Alvear 1889.
L'Interdit, Uruguay 1196, tel: 42-5602.

Designer

Gino Bogani, Rodriguez Peña 1044, tel: 44-0862.
Best Seller, Alvear 1883.
Nina Ricci, Alvear 1539, tel: 22-8283.

Argentine Regional Gifts

Martin Fierro, Santa Fé 904, tel: 392-6440.

Artesanian Argentinas, Montevideo 1386, tel: 44-2650. Non-profit organization which promotes the work or Indian artisans living in the north and northwest of Argentina.

El Altillo de Susana, Marcelo T. de Alvear 515, tel: 311-1138.

Rancho Grande, Leandro N. Alem 564, Tel: 311-7603.

Matra, Defensa 372. A state-run cooperative for local craftsmen.

Kelly's, Paraguay 3431 Sweaters, ponchos and scarves of llama wool.

Bookstores

Foreign books are quite difficult to obtain in Argentina as import duties are high and there is much red tape involved in bringing in foreign publications. There is only a precious trickle of them coming in each month. The bookstores may nevertheless prove quite helpful in putting you on the right track to your sought-after volume. Give them a call. **Ateneo**, on Florida (block between Corrientes and sarmiento) is a three-story-high haven of the written word. Fiction and otherwise. In the basement you will find a moderate-size selection of English and American books (plus French and Italian). A run-of-the mill sprinkle of classics and current best-sellers, tel: 325-6801

The **ABC**, on Córdoba and Maipú is

better stocked, and it adds to its displays luxury editions, as well as records and an array of art book. The bookstore is German-owned and run. Tops, tel: 322-7887

Another German-oriented bookstore is **Goethe**, on Corrientes 200, right across the avenue from the Goethe German Institute, of learning and culture promotion. Periodic sales and discounts make the Goethe bookstore an interesting place to visit while in BA.

Specializing in textbooks, dictionaries and business books is the **Rodrigues** bookstore, on Florida, in front of Ateneo. It is run like a college bookstore, not a very romantic place for a book lover since there is not enough room to browse around and attendants are over-zealous.

Other bookstores are:

Librería del Turista, Florida 937, tel: 312-2226
Hachette, Córdoba 936, tel: 392-6497.
Rivadavia 739, tel: 34-8481 (French books and magazines).
Kier, Av. Santa Fé 1260, tel: 41-0507. (Art and philosophy books).

Libraries are few and far between in BA. But for the avid English/American reader, there is a golden corner of silence with records, tapes, magazines and newspapers from the United States, at the Lincoln Center, on Florida 935, a few steps from the San Martin park, the Plaza and the Sheraton. It is open from 9.30am–6.30pm. Don't forget to take along your passport, which will be checked (and you frisked) at the downstairs entrance.

Sports

Participant Sports

Ice Skating

This has become the latest form of entertainment for young and old. You'll be able to find ice skating rinks all over Buenos Aires and in most of the major cities of the provinces.

Boating & Sailing

There is boating in the **Tigre** (River Plate delta) some 45 minutes north of the city. From Retiro station, the train ride to Tigre is both fast and interesting. The train crosses through old stately suburbs as well as populous neighborhoods such as Belgrano. Tours of Tigre are also available through T-bar SA, on Libertador 14434, tel: 798-9969/9043. There you will find sail ships, sailboats, motors, kayaks and windsurf boards. There you can also contract cruises to Uruguay's main tourist and nautical resort, Punta del Este, as well as to Brazil.

Golf

Municipal Golf Course, Tornquist and olleros, palermo woods, tel: 772-7576.

Argentine Golf Association, Corrientes 538, tel: 394-3743/29972.

Jockey Club and Blue Course, **Links Golf Club**, **Club Náutico San Isidro**, are other possibilities, although not so readily available, since they are strictly private clubs. Another possibility is afforded by a stretch of good golfing grounds on the Costanera. It is on Costanera Norte and Salguero. It is run by the local golf association and you can rent your clubs there.

Squash

Posadas Squash Club. Posadas 1265, 7th floor, Tel: 22-0548. Two courts, plus sauna, whirlpool, closed-circuit TV, bar and restaurant.

Olimpia Cancilleria. Esmeralda 1042, Tel:s 311-8687. Five courts. One racquetball court. Plus gym, sauna, bar.

Tennis

Almost everywhere in the city and suburbs are municipal courts, well lighted and with round-the-clock security. With instructors, if desired. Your best bet is inquiring about the nearest one at the hotel where you are staying. Some private courts that may be worth your looking into are:

Baakerloo: Pampa 1235, Belgrano neighborhood. Three clay courts.

Break Point: Yatay 943, Caballito neighborhood. Two courts.

Bustamante Tennis Bar: Sanchez de Bustamante 1256, tel: 88-6277.

Caballito Tennis Club: José María Moreno 953, Cabollito. Three clay courts.

Daria Kopsic: Hernandarias 2050, La Boca neighborhood. Eight clay courts (two indoors), tel: 28-3276

Parque Norte: Cantilo and Guiraldes (Costanera Norete) Tel: 784-9653.

Solís Tennis Courts: Solís 1252. Seven clay courts.

Tatum Tennis Club: Yerbal 845. Caballito. Five clay courts

Tennis Colonial: Donato Alvarez 224. Two courts.

Municiapal Courts: Parque Sarmiento. Av. del Tejar 4300, Saavedra. Fourteen hard courts. Tel: 541-3511 Parque José Hernández. Hernández 1302. Parque de Palermo. Hard and clay courts. Tel: 782-2619.

Water Sports

Water Skiing: There is a water skiing school in Tigre at the Jorge Renosto establishment. Tel: 875-0128-783-5181. Renosto is a former South American Ski Champion. Equipment provided.

Windsurfing: Parque Norte, Cantilo and Guiraldes, (Constanera Norte). El Molino. Elcano and Perú, Acassuso. Hoopika. Italia and river, Vicente López.

Boxing & Wrestling

At the downtown **Luna Park**, **Corrientes** and **Madero**, right on the waterfront. The Luna Park also brings to Buenos Aires top shows from around the world, such as top-level circuses, ballets, singers and other performers.

Pato

It is a combination of polo and basketball on horseback. Very exclusive clubs.

The game is played almost year round in the provinces, but teams come to the Buenos Aires area in October and November for weekend tournaments at the Campo de Mayo, located on a military compound in the western region of Greater Buenos Aires (reachable by train from the Retiro Station). The event of the year is the Argentine Open, played in December at the Polo Fields in Palermo. For more detailed information call the Argentine Pato Association at 331-0222.

Polo

Clubs in the neighborhood of Palermo, and in the suburbs of Hurlingham, San Isidro and Tortugas.

Most matches are played in springtime, October and November, the finals sometimes being pushed into December due to rain. The Hurlingham Open is held at a traditional riding club in the suburb of the same name. The biggest tournament, the Argentine Open, is played at the Campo Argentino de Polo in Palermo, at Libertador and Dorrego. For more detailed information call the Argentine Polo Association at 343-0972.

Language

The Spanish spoken in Argentina is to the Castilian Spanish of Spain what American English is to BBC English: it stands on its own; proudly, enriched and developed by local custom and refreshingly unperturbed by "how it should be said." The most vivid grammatical contrast is between the Spanish *tu* form (second person singular, informal), and the Argentine *vos* form. Example: Instead of the Spanish *Tu vienes*? (Are you coming?) the Argentine will ask, *Vos venis*? The concept of vos has ancient roots in the Castilian vosotros (second person plural). Speakers of Castilian will observe that the verbs corresponding to vos are conjugated similarly to the Castilian vosotros verbs, with some variations. The subject is thorny even for advanced students of Argentine Spanish, but fortunately Argentines are all familiar with the standard *tu* form. As in the rest of Latin America, "you" plural is expressed by third person plural with the pronoun *ustedes*. To use the same example, *Ustedes vienen*? (Are you all coming?)

Slang: Slang is an equivocal business, as most visitors know from using it in their own languages. It's an undercurrent of language with precise meanings, and unless it's used impeccably, can make the speaker sound foolish or even rude. Thus the following is a descriptive, rather than proscriptive, list of some commonly used *porteño* slang words. Note: Spanish translation in bold and *porteño* translation in italics).

Woman/**Mujer**/*Mina*
Man/**Hombre**/*Tipo, Flaco*
Child/**Niño**/*Pibe, Purrete, Pebete*
To look/**Mirar**/*Junar*
To eat/**Comer**/*Mangiar*
To sleep/**Dormir**/*Apolillar, Torrar*
To chat/**Charlar**/*Chamullar*

The best expression of slang is in the heartfelt tango. When foreigners get to the point of understanding the lyrics of old-time tango, the will have gained a certain insight into the world of slang, and will be better able to understand the thoughts, actions and emotions of a *porteño*.

Further Reading

General

The Afro-Argentines of Buenos Aires: 1800-1900 by George Reid Andrews. Madison: Univ. of Wisconsin Press, 1980.

The Disappeared: Voices From a Secret War by Jana Bennett and John Simpson. (London, Robson Books, 1985).

The Uttermost Part of the Earth by E. Lucas Bridges. New York: Dutton, 1949.

In Patagonia by Bruce Chatwin. New York: Summit Books. 1977.

The Buenos Aires Affair and *Betrayed by Rita Hayworth* by Julio Cortázar.

The Voyage of the Beagle by Charles Darwin. USA: Bantam Books, 1972.

The Whispering Land and *The Drunken Forest* by Gerald Durrell.

Los Paragues Nacionales de la Argentina by F. Erize. Buenos Aires: Incafo, Reprint of 1935 edition.

Currents in the Contemporary Argentine Novel by David Foster. Univ. of Missouri Press, 1975.

Tierra del Fuego by R. Natalie P.

Goodall. Buenos Aires: Edicions Shanamaiim, 1979.

The Battle for the Falklands by Max Hastings and Simon Jenkins. New York: W.W. Norton and Co., 1983.

Far Away and Long Ago; Birds of La Plata; *Idle Days in Patagonia* by W.H. Hudson. London: Everyman's Library, 1984.

Tales of the Pampas by W.H. Hudson. Berkeley: Creative Arts Book Co., 1979.

Twenty-Four Years in the Argentine Republic by Anthony King. Reprint of 1846 edition.

Two Thousand Miles' Ride Through the Argentine Provinces by William Mac Canna. Reprint of 1853 edition.

The Cloud Forest by Peter Matthiessen. New York: Viking, 1961.

Life Among the Patagonian Indians by George Musters.

Perón: A Biography by Joseph Page. New York: Random House, 1983.

The Little School: Tales of Disappearance and Survival in Argentina by Alicia Partnoy. New York: Cleis Press, 1986.

Argentina 1516–1987: from Spanish Colonization to the Falklands War and Alfonsín by David Rock. (University of Calif. Press, 1987).

La Colonizacion Galesa en el Valle del Chubut by B.M. Ruiz. Buenos Aires: Ed Galerna, 1977.

On Heroes and Tombs, and *The Tunnel* by Ernesto Sábato.

A Funny, Dirty, Little War by Osvaldo Soriano.

And for something really special... Argentina goes on-line. There is now a web site on the Internet run by a group of Argentine independent journalists and political activists...it's called *The First Page For Argentina*, and has information on current news and events, human rights, politics, and environmental issues.

Other Insight Guides

Among the 190 *Insight Guides*, other titles which highlight destinations in this region include a general 400-page guide to *South America*, plus individual guides to *Argentina, Chile, Ecuador, Peru* and *Venezuela*.

From the highest peaks of the Andes to Tierra del Fuego, from the Pampas to Patagonia, *Insight Guide: Argentina* takes travelers on a journey through one of the largest countries in the world.

Insight Guide: Peru contains detailed text and dazzling photography, which reveal the vibrant culture and beautiful scenery of this country at the very heart of South America.

Index

A
B
C
D
E
F
H
I
J
a
b
c
e
f
g
h
i
j
k
l